Critical Approaches to Children's Literature

Series Editors: **Kerry Mallan** and **Clare Bradford**
Critical Approaches to Children's Literature is an innovative series concerned with the best contemporary scholarship and criticism on children's and young adult literature, film and media texts. The series addresses new and developing areas of children's literature research as well as bringing contemporary perspectives to historical texts. The series has a distinctive take on scholarship, delivering quality works of criticism written in an accessible style for a range of readers, both academic and professional. The series is invaluable for undergraduate students in children's literature as well as advanced students and established scholars.

Published titles include:

Cherie Allan
PLAYING WITH PICTUREBOOKS
Postmodernism and the Postmodernesque

Clare Bradford, Kerry Mallan, John Stephens & Robyn McCallum
NEW WORLD ORDERS IN CONTEMPORARY CHILDREN'S LITERATURE
Utopian Transformations

Alice Curry
ENVIRONMENTAL CRISIS IN YOUNG ADULT FICTION
A Poetics of Earth

Helen A. Fairlie
REVALUING BRITISH BOYS' STORY PAPERS, 1918–1939

Margaret Mackey
NARRATIVE PLEASURES IN YOUNG ADULT NOVELS, FILMS AND VIDEO GAMES
Critical Approaches to Children's Literature

Kerry Mallan
SECRETS, LIES AND CHILDREN'S FICTION

Andrew O'Malley
CHILDREN'S LITERATURE, POPULAR CULTURE AND *ROBINSON CRUSOE*

Christopher Parkes
CHILDREN'S LITERATURE AND CAPITALISM
Fictions of Social Mobility in Britain, 1850–1914

Michelle Smith
EMPIRE IN BRITISH GIRLS' LITERATURE AND CULTURE
Imperial Girls, 1880–1915

Forthcoming titles:

Elizabeth Bullen
CLASS IN CONTEMPORARY CHILDREN'S LITERATURE

Pamela Knights
READING BALLET AND PERFORMANCE NARRATIVES FOR CHILDREN

Susan Napier
MIYAZAKI HAYO AND THE USES OF ENCHANTMENT

Critical Approaches to Children's Literature
Series Standing Order ISBN 978–0–230–22786–6 (hardback)
978–0–230–22787–3 (paperback)
(*outside North America only*)

You can receive future titles in this series as they are published by placing a standing order. Please contact your bookseller or, in case of difficulty, write to us at the address below with your name and address, the title of the series and the ISBN quoted above.

Customer Services Department, Macmillan Distribution Ltd, Houndmills, Basingstoke, Hampshire RG21 6XS, England

Revaluing British Boys' Story Papers, 1918–1939

Helen A. Fairlie

© Helen A. Fairlie 2014

All rights reserved. No reproduction, copy or transmission of this publication may be made without written permission.

No portion of this publication may be reproduced, copied or transmitted save with written permission or in accordance with the provisions of the Copyright, Designs and Patents Act 1988, or under the terms of any licence permitting limited copying issued by the Copyright Licensing Agency, Saffron House, 6–10 Kirby Street, London EC1N 8TS.

Any person who does any unauthorized act in relation to this publication may be liable to criminal prosecution and civil claims for damages.

The author has asserted her right to be identified as the author of this work in accordance with the Copyright, Designs and Patents Act 1988.

First published 2014 by
PALGRAVE MACMILLAN

Palgrave Macmillan in the UK is an imprint of Macmillan Publishers Limited, registered in England, company number 785998, of Houndmills, Basingstoke, Hampshire RG21 6XS.

Palgrave Macmillan in the US is a division of St Martin's Press LLC, 175 Fifth Avenue, New York, NY 10010.

Palgrave Macmillan is the global academic imprint of the above companies and has companies and representatives throughout the world.

Palgrave® and Macmillan® are registered trademarks in the United States, the United Kingdom, Europe and other countries.

ISBN 978–1–137–29305–3

This book is printed on paper suitable for recycling and made from fully managed and sustained forest sources. Logging, pulping and manufacturing processes are expected to conform to the environmental regulations of the country of origin.

A catalogue record for this book is available from the British Library.

A catalog record for this book is available from the Library of Congress.

Typeset by MPS Limited, Chennai, India.

For dad, with love
In memory of Brian A. Fairlie, 1932–2012

Contents

List of Illustrations	viii
Series Preface	ix
Acknowledgements	x
Introduction	1
1 Setting the Scene: Critical Perspectives, Producers and Consumers	18
2 The Moral Code of Inter-War Story Papers	42
3 Understanding School Worlds	67
4 The Imperial Hero: Story Paper Hero-Figures	92
5 Inter-War Story Papers and the Rise of Children's Cinema	116
6 Story Papers as Cultural Artefacts: Contexts and Content	146
Conclusion	181
Appendix: Boys' and Girls' Story Paper Reading	189
Bibliography	195
Index	206

List of Illustrations

0.1	Example of an advertisements page from *The Magnet*, 18 October 1924, p. 28. IPC Media Syndication	12
2.1	Opening illustration from Red Circle story, *The Hotspur*, 11 April 1936, p. 36. D. C. Thomson & Co., Ltd	61
5.1	Film/reality continuum	129
5.2	Story paper/reality continuum	129
6.1	Internal advertisement, *The Magnet*, 2 June 1934, p. 20. IPC Media Syndication	160
6.2	Internal advertisement, *The Hotspur*, 26 August 1939, p. 3. D. C. Thomson & Co., Ltd	161
6.3	Internal advertisement, *The Hotspur*, 30 September 1933, p. 94. D. C. Thomson & Co., Ltd	162
6.4	Quaker Oats advertisement, *The Hotspur*, 13 July 1935, p. 51. D. C. Thomson & Co., Ltd	164
6.5	Fry's advertisement, *The Magnet*, 5 May 1934, p. 21. IPC Media Syndication	166
6.6	Wrigley's advertisement, *The Hotspur*, 8 April 1939, p. 9. D. C. Thomson & Co., Ltd	167
6.7	Extract from editor's column, *The Magnet*, 28 November 1936, p. 27. IPC Media Syndication	169
6.8	Editor's column, *The Hotspur*, 23 March 1935, p. 1. D. C. Thomson & Co., Ltd	170
6.9	Front cover of *The Hotspur*, 4 April 1939. D. C. Thomson & Co., Ltd	174
6.10	'When the Fifth Form Went Crazy', *The Magnet*, 4 April 1936, p. 7. IPC Media Syndication	175
6.11	Mr Smugg and the wrestler, *The Hotspur*, 6 April 1936, p. 8. D. C. Thomson & Co., Ltd	176
6.12	Front cover, *The Magnet*, 9 June 1934. IPC Media Syndication	178

Series Preface

The *Critical Approaches to Children's Literature* series was initiated in 2008 by Kerry Mallan and Clare Bradford. The aim of the series is to identify and publish the best contemporary scholarship and criticism on children's and young adult literature, film and media texts. The series is open to theoretically informed scholarship covering a wide range of critical perspectives on historical and contemporary texts from diverse national and cultural settings. Critical Approaches aims to make a significant contribution to the expanding field of children's literature research by publishing quality books that promote informed discussion and debate about the production and reception of children's literature and its criticism.

Kerry Mallan and Clare Bradford

Acknowledgements

Thanks are due to the staff of the following institutions, who were unfailingly helpful in the course of my research: The British Library; The British Film Institute Library and Film Archive; The Trustees of the Mass-Observation Archive, University of Sussex; and The University of Warwick Library.

Special thanks are also due to: Dr Christine Wilkie-Stibbs, for her support, advice and understanding during the research process of my PhD; to my internal and external examiners, Dr Hilary Minns and Professor Jean Webb; to the series editors Professor Kerry Mallan and Professor Clare Bradford, and the publisher's anonymous reviewer, for their detailed and insightful comments on the draft script; to Ian Rudge, for having the (mis)fortune to be working on a thesis at the same time as me; and to Mark, for everything.

Thanks to IPC Media Syndication and D. C. Thomson and Co. Ltd for permission to reproduce illustrations from the story papers; to Paula Kennedy and Peter Cary of Palgrave Macmillan for their help and advice as the project developed; and to Monica Kendall for her exceptional efficiency in steering the manuscript through the production process.

Introduction

Historians of children's literature in Britain, and of publishing for children in general, are broadly agreed that the late Victorian years, leading up more or less to the outbreak of the First World War, were a golden age. These were the years of Kipling and Carroll, Nesbit, Grahame, Potter and Barrie – the definitive classics of children's literature, which were by any standards a hard act to follow. Historians of children's literature are also broadly agreed that what came after, in the years between the wars, significantly failed to live up to the promise of that golden age. They are, almost without exception, dismissive of the period in their haste to speed past these seemingly barren years towards the 1950s, the next acknowledged great age of publishing for children. John Rowe Townsend covers everything he finds worthy of note in the inter-war years in a scant 27 pages (Townsend, 1990); Robert Leeson dubs it the 'age of brass' (Leeson, 1985: 110); Peter Hunt borrows his title for the chapter covering this period from Robert Graves's and Alan Hodge's social history of the time, *The Long Weekend*, which manages to imply a sense of frivolous time off from the real work of 'serious' publishing (Hunt, 1999).

Their various condemnations are remarkably similar, though the strength of opinion varies. Marcus Crouch sees the period as characterised by 'a vast output of characterless conventional writing, of some experiment and some achievement' (Crouch, 1962: 39). Townsend refers to 'a great expansion in quantity [after the war], but a sad lack of quality' (Townsend, 1990: 128). Hunt quotes Geoffrey Trease:

> A new story in 1920 or 1930 tended to be a fossil in which one could trace the essential characteristics of one written in 1880 or 1890 ... serious reviewing hardly existed. (Hunt, 1999: 106)

Frank Eyre goes even further – for him the trend towards 'Bumper' books in the early 1920s led to 'a flood of the worst and most tasteless children's picture books ever produced' (Eyre, 1971: 22). John Feather, in a survey of the publishing world in general, comments rather sadly that between the wars 'the fact is that very little was happening that was either new or exciting' (Feather, 1988: 203). Even contemporary commentators could find little worth valuing. Both Hunt and Leeson quote the *Library Association Review* from 1932:

> a few admirable books, submerged in an ocean of terrible trash ... unreal school stories, impossible adventure, half-witted fairy tales ... in every respect disgraceful. (Hunt, 1999: 106; Leeson, 1985: 110)

My starting point for this book is to question this fundamental dismissiveness, and to look in more detail at the values which underpin these opinions. It seems to me that these retrospective valuations have failed to take account of the lives and experiences of the children of the time, dismissing contemporary readers and the use-values they assigned to their reading. For these critics and historians, readers and their reading lives do not have a place in a system of valuing which privileges texts themselves above the relationships between texts and readers. The cultural role of reading practices, the status of child readers as consumers and the effects of relations of power on the author–text–reader dynamic have seemingly been overlooked by these critical commentators whose focus is primarily the immanent factors of literary 'quality'. Following the lines of argument of the critics and historians referenced above, the story paper genre has been undervalued on three interconnecting levels: in terms of its perceived lack of literary quality; in terms of its status as 'popular' literature, through which it has been accorded a minimum of critical attention; and in terms of its ephemeral physical nature, which compounds to restrict its selection for archiving and historical preservation. This system undervalues text–reader interactions on each level. This book explores the detailed functioning of patterns of valuing, aiming to redress the balance through focusing on readers and their lived experiences. By raising key questions about reading lives it offers a different kind of perspective on the story paper genre. In doing so, the book focuses on children's own reading choices – what were children *actually* reading and enjoying at the time? How far is it possible to explore what they thought of the books, magazines and comics that they bought, borrowed or exchanged with friends? And on a wider perspective, what social, economic, political and historical factors led to the apparent drastic decline in the quality of children's publishing? Was it, in fact, a lowering of standards, and if so, in whose terms? How far did it matter to contemporary children that there was a dearth of so-called quality publishing at the time? What uses did these children make of, and what meanings did they take from, their growing consumption of popular literature? What, in effect, made popular literature so popular?

In exploring some possible answers to these questions, the book offers a revaluation of inter-war boys' story papers which situates them as a cultural phenomenon worthy of more detailed critical attention than they have hitherto received in the literature. Although more recent years have seen the beginnings of a cultural renaissance of interest – see, for example, the work of Nelson (1997), Boyd (2003) and Ferrall and Jackson (2010) – the story paper remains a relatively neglected format, and the inter-war period relatively under-researched in the field of children's literature. (There has, however, been an expansion of interest in inter-war youth (as distinct from children and adults), both male and female, in terms of a historiography of young people's lives, work and leisure – see, for example, Bingham (2004), Todd (2006), Fowler (2008).)

Three main strands of investigation are woven through the thematic chapters presented here, which both frame and construct the field under discussion: a social-cultural strand, focusing on relations of power between producers and consumers; a literary critical strand offering analysis of story paper content, with a particular emphasis on author–text–reader interactions; and an historical strand, exploring contextual issues of publishing economics and social trends. These strands are interconnecting rather than discrete, forming a network of relationships on which the discussion stands. In working to connect these strands, I take up a critical position similar to that of Kirsten Drotner, who argues for a perspective on literature which combines 'text-extrinsic' and 'text-intrinsic' theories (Drotner, 1988: 8).

Each strand is informed by a research methodology which incorporates both theoretical analysis and historical investigation. My critical and theoretical approaches are centred on a broadly new historicist/cultural materialist perspective which draws on the work of Raymond Williams (1961, 1977, 1988), Stephen Greenblatt (Gallagher and Greenblatt, 2000) and others (see, for example, Dollimore and Sinfield, 1994). Situating this alongside discussion of mass culture theory, the predominant critical approach of the time, serves both to highlight the tensions between the two perspectives, and to frame an assessment of the reasons for the long-standing critical invisibility of the story papers.

Although new historicist approaches have been seen as problematic by some literary theorists (a point which I explore further in Chapter 1), it is a useful background to the explorations of this book in that it focuses on power relations (in this case, between producers and consumers), and also works to integrate text and context. Reader response theory also offers a valuable theoretical underpinning to my investigation of the text–reader dynamic in story paper reading (see, for example, Holub, 1984; Iser, 2000). The later chapters of the book draw on theories of cultural production (see, for example, Bourdieu, 1977, 1986, 1993 and 1995), ideology (see, for example, Althusser, 1971; Eagleton, 1976; Williams, 1977, 1988), film theory and narrative poetics (see, for example, Barthes, 1966; Metz, 1974; Todorov, 1977; Silverman, 1983; Mulvey, 1989), and texts and paratexts (Genette, 1997), all of which serve to illuminate my analysis of the texts.

The texts themselves and their readers are at the very centre of this book, and my historical investigations have focused on accessing original copies of the story papers, mainly in the collections of the British Library, and on reviewing archive material relating to the lives and experiences of children of the inter-war period. The painstakingly preserved survey materials in the Mass-Observation Archive are particularly useful in this respect: housed at the University of Sussex, this archive specialises in preserving material about everyday life in Britain, and contains papers generated by the original Mass-Observation social research organisation (1937 to early 1950s), and newer material collected continuously since 1981. The early methodology of Mass Observation and the paid staff who were sent out to observe public life has been the object of some criticism, in particular concerning the status of the observers, who were 'neither anthropologists nor their informants but somewhere in between, not quite the subjects of study nor those who carried it out' (Purbrick, 2007: 168). The criticism levelled at the collection is one of subjectivity, in that those collecting the information necessarily have an interpretative role, particularly in the case of interviews with children. While the later, post-1981 methods work towards overcoming these difficulties, with the inter-war materials we must be aware of the provenance of the data, and of their inherent biases (Sheridan, 2000 [online]), as well as their 'subjective, impressionistic ... [and] idiosyncratic' character (Pollen, 2013: 214). Nevertheless, as Pollen points out, while subjectivity can be seen as a source of bias and error, researchers using new approaches to the interpretation of qualitative social and historical data can also value the 'emotional richness' of the Mass-Observation data (Pollen, 2013: 217).

Information from records in the library of the British Film Institute helps to form the background to Chapter 5. I also draw on a range of autobiographical texts, which document the reading lives of children of the era, albeit with the hindsight of adulthood (see, for example, Beer, 1968; Roberts, 1973; Rose, 2001; Scannell, 1971; West, 1963). Clearly it is not possible to recreate entirely the effects of reading on the original audiences, but the examination of published materials, both contemporary surveys and later autobiographical accounts mainly published between the 1950s and 1970s, is an attempt to reconstruct what Raymond Williams calls 'the lived experience' of the time, approaching as closely as possible to the lives and opinions of child readers in their own contexts. It is important to note, however, that these accounts have their own 'inherent distortions and biases' (Rose, 2001: 2) and in the case of the historical record in relation to children, the evidence, as Drotner points out, 'contains either a class, an age, or a gender bias, or various mixtures of them all' (Drotner, 1988: 12). Although Rose's work has shown that published memoirs can be as illuminating of working-class life as of other classes, there has until relatively recently been a tendency for the business of publishing to privilege the educated, middle- or upper-class male writer. Any attempt at reconstruction, then, is inescapably selective.

In taking this approach I have chosen not to pursue a more ethnographic oral-history-based method, which, in my view, would have produced a differently mediated view of the past. In Annette Kuhn's view, 'the past is ... mediated, indeed produced, in the activity of remembering' (Kuhn, 2002: 9), and such work is as much about memory as it is about the specific object of the research (in Kuhn's example, the activity of cinema-going). This is particularly the case in memory work relating to adults' recollections of their own experiences as children, in that such memories are both mediated by adult sensibilities towards past selves, and shaped by the solipsism of childhood. As Alan Bryman points out, 'oral history may well emphasize "the past", but the experience of the present in forming accounts cannot be ignored' (Bryman, 2002: 22). Although autobiographical accounts are subject to similar concerns in that they represent assessments of individuals' lives at a particular time (Bryman, 2002: 60) they stand as a version of 'truth' which can be used to approach a view of a particular historical period. Interview data collected some 70 years on would provide fascinating insights, but would essentially be addressing a rather different set of questions.

From the vast output of story papers from the 1920s and 1930s it has been necessary to select two in particular on which to focus. I have chosen *The Magnet* and *The Hotspur*, as representative of the output of the two main publishers of the genre in the inter-war period, Amalgamated Press (producers of *The Magnet*) and D. C. Thomson (publishers of *The Hotspur*). They are also among the top five popular story papers for boys aged 12–15 years, as registered in a survey of children's reading habits conducted in 1938 (Jenkinson, 1940: 68–9). Most interestingly, both *The Hotspur* and *The Magnet* also feature on the list of most popular story papers amongst girls aged 12–15 years in Jenkinson's survey. Although specifically aimed at a male readership, the appeal of the stories to girls was such that boys' story papers made up around a quarter of their story paper reading (see Tables A.7 and A.8 in the Appendix). The gender and class base of the story papers' audience is discussed in more detail in Chapter 1. As Melanie Tebbutt points out, more recent studies of youth culture in the inter-war years have challenged the notion of homogeneity by highlighting the significance of class, gender, poverty and locality in the formation of youth identities (Tebbutt, 2012: 19), and I have tried to reflect this in the chapters that follow.

The selection of two representative story papers allows for detailed comparison of the approaches to publishing of the two producers, as well as for analysis of contrasting narrative styles and characterisations. Contingent on the selection is accessibility, and in both cases complete runs of the story paper series are held in the British Library. Facsimile editions of *The Magnet*, published by Howard Baker Press in the 1970s, are also available in compendium volumes. In recent years the internet has become an excellent source for otherwise difficult-to-source materials, and the efforts of dedicated individuals now mean that the complete run of issues of *The Magnet* is available online at www.friardale.co.uk. Whilst other major libraries do hold limited stock of other story paper titles, I was unable to locate complete runs of any other series, and so far only small numbers of issues of other series are available online. This seeming lack of interest in the preservation of the story paper genre is due partly to the ephemeral nature of their construction, and the difficulties of physically conserving the paper bindings, and partly to the fact that the genre was held in such low regard by contemporary authority figures, including acquisitions librarians. The individual stories referenced in the Bibliography are those which are directly referred to in the text; these are paradigm texts representative of the narratives presented in the story papers and are selected from the many hundreds of stories read during the course of my research.

The following section of this introduction presents an overview of the two selected story paper series, describing key characters, settings and narrative structures. Chapter 1 then acts as a part two of the introduction, exploring in more detail the critical/theoretical and historical perspectives which underpin the main arguments, offering an overview of the history of publishing set in the economic context of the inter-war period. Chapter 1 also discusses gender and class in relation to story paper readership. The main body of the book is arranged in thematic chapters, each of which builds on the multi-stranded approach outlined above. Chapter 2 focuses on the ideological functioning of the moral code of story paper worlds. Chapter 3 sets in context the school story genre as represented in the selected story papers, exploring the ways in which the stories both develop and subvert the genre, and underlining the tensions for readers between fictional and real school worlds. Chapter 4 analyses the construction of hero-figures in story paper narratives, showing how the texts' versions of masculinity are influenced by changing imperialist ideologies which impinge on children's cultural lives as well as their reading matter. Chapter 5 makes direct connections between the rise of the story paper genre and the popularity of the cinema in the inter-war years. Comparing narrative styles and the nature of 'reader–text' interaction between the two media, it shows how story paper producers were able to develop the genre by drawing on specific features of cinematic storytelling. Chapter 6 explores the story paper as artefact, situating it in cultural context as one of the first commodities designed for children to buy for themselves, and analysing in detail the functioning of and interrelationships between texts and paratexts in the story papers.

An introduction to *The Magnet*

The Magnet was launched in 1908, as a sister paper to *The Gem*, launched in 1907. Both papers were produced by Amalgamated Press, a large London publishing house owned by Alfred Harmsworth. Like its sister paper, *The Magnet* was a 28-page story paper for boys, published weekly and sold through newsagents priced at 1d. (later 2d.). Each issue of *The Magnet* featured a long (20,000-word) story, plus one or more smaller feature stories, most of which were written by Charles Hamilton, under the pseudonym Frank Richards. These long stories built up the fictional world of Greyfriars School, its pupils and staff. (*The Gem* had a very similar structure, featuring St Jim's School stories, also written by Charles Hamilton under the pseudonym Martin Clifford.) Over the years of *The Magnet*'s publication, Greyfriars and its key characters remain surprisingly constant – the settings and characters stay the same, and only incidents and plotlines change. (*The Magnet* ceased publication in 1940, ostensibly because of wartime paper shortages. Characters and settings will be explored in some detail in the following sections.)

By 1908, the school story genre was well established – in fact, it has been noted that 'the unending stream of fiction describing, analysing, criticising and defending the public schools' only began to slacken in the 1930s (Musgrave, 1985: 202). Frank Richards was able to draw on a well-developed tradition in depicting Greyfriars as a minor public school, run on 'traditional' lines that would have been familiar to any reader of school stories from *Tom Brown's Schooldays* to Talbot Baines Reed's stories in *The Boy's Own Paper*. As McAleer points out, however, there are a few deviations from the tradition here: at Greyfriars there are no compulsory games, no chapel, no cadet corps and no houses (McAleer, 1992: 277). Frank Richards's apparent reason for these innovations was that he did not want to complicate the narrative. Richards did not himself attend public school, so it may be that he simply felt more comfortable inventing his own rules for his fictional worlds. A more likely reason is that Richards and his publisher were trying to appeal to a mass general audience, and realised that, to their readers, the excitement of events in the storylines was more important than whether or not the picture of public school life they painted was true. Further evidence of this, according to McAleer, is that at Greyfriars the boys play football, not rugby:

> This clearly points to the intended audience of non-public school boys, for whom soccer was the chief sport, an assumption reinforced by the presence in *The Magnet* of a regular soccer column. (McAleer, 1992: 277)

Frank Richards's achievement was to take the 'traditional' public school and make it real for those boys who could never hope actually to attend one. By focusing on strong plotlines and key themes (friendship, loyalty, team spirit, the moral code), Richards could build a fictional world which not only enthralled readers but which seemed to have meaning for them in their own lives. In the following sections we will explore in more detail both how this was done and how readers responded to it.

Greyfriars is largely peopled by solid middle- and upper-middle-class characters. Parents are rarely referred to, and most of the boys seem well supplied with money to meet their needs. All of the boys are boarders, a fact which sets clear boundaries between school and home. The school therefore functions as a closed world in which boys must live on their own wits, adapt to the hierarchies and find support from their friends in order to survive. In effect the school is both home and family in surrogate form. The key characters who remain central to the Greyfriars stories throughout the life of *The Magnet* are collectively known as Harry Wharton and Co., also referred to as the Famous Five of the Remove. Harry is Captain of the Remove, and is portrayed as a natural leader (and, naturally, is given Study No. 1, on the Remove corridor). His 'chums' are Bob Cherry, Johnny Bull, Frank Nugent and Hurree Jamset Ram Singh. It is possible to chart the popularity of these characters from readers' letters to *The Magnet*, as reported on the editor's page, many of which ask for more details of their favourites' lives. George Samways, a long-standing editor at Amalgamated Press, notes that it was Bob Cherry who emerged as the readers' real favourite:

> Bob had all the qualities which endeared him to youthful hearts – his sunny disposition, his gay courage, his sportsmanship, his irrepressible high spirits and his ready championship of the underdog, all combined to make him not merely well liked but universally beloved. (Samways, 1984: 182)

By contrast, Harry Wharton 'was inclined to be too heavy-handed at times, and there was a touch of arrogance about him which caused him to be less liked' by readers (Samways, 1984: 182). In the stories, Harry's leadership is largely unquestioned, and there is a definite sense that, even if that leadership had not been officially sanctioned in his status as Captain, he would nevertheless have been a key focus for the respect of his peers. Harry does, however, have an impetuous streak of rebelliousness, a character trait which is used with judicious regularity by Richards in order to build a sense of vulnerability in Harry. Storylines which highlight this aspect of Harry's character are in the main built on incidents of mistaken identity or misunderstandings, which leaves the way clear for a resolution which restores Harry's status. In the story series which begins with 'The Complete Outsider', in *The Magnet*, 5 March 1932, and continues over a number of weeks, Harry is mistakenly led to believe that his uncle, and benefactor, thinks that he is 'thoughtless, selfish and utterly ungrateful' (*The Magnet*, 5 March 1932: 24). His distress at this apparent betrayal leads to outbursts of anger which almost cause his expulsion from the school. His eventual discovery of the error is an important moment of self-discovery, although his obstinacy and sulkiness towards his chums is forgotten very quickly indeed.

Richards faced certain difficulties in the development of his characters. Each story had to function effectively as a stand-alone piece, given that his readers could not be guaranteed to have read all – or any – of the preceding episodes. Keeping basic characters and settings the same gave him a solid basis to build on, but even so it would have been impossible to introduce details of home life or other background motivations that would have helped him to explain a character's actions or behaviour without having to repeat them in more or less every story for the benefit of new readers. In this artificially closed world, Richards built believable characters by giving them detailed emotional lives and focusing on action and reaction.

The least effectively drawn of the chums is Hurree Singh. Although he is the constant companion of Harry Wharton and Co., and is clearly meant to be interpreted as their equal, he never fully participates in the narrative action. His spoken language is bizarre to the point of unintelligibility, but this is never criticised, nor even particularly noticed by any other character, peer or teacher. For example, in 'Bunter's Body Guard', in *The Magnet*, 8 September 1928, the boys encounter an elephant escaping from a nearby circus:

> 'Sounds like thunder!'
> 'Can't be thunder,' said Nugent.
> ...
> 'My esteemed chums!' said Hurree Jamset Ram Singh. 'If we were in my own excellent and execrable country, I should say that a wild elephant was somewhere nearfully ... It is an esteemed elephant,' said the Nabob of Bhanipur with conviction. 'Perhapsfully he is taking an esteemed walk.' ('Bunter's Body Guard', *The Magnet*, 8 September 1928: 7)

And, when the elephant tramples their bikes and smashes them:

> 'The repairfulness will have to be terrific,' said Hurree Jamset Ram Singh. 'We are strandfully landed.' *(The Magnet*, 8 September 1928: 8)

In an article published in *Horizon* in 1940, George Orwell singled out Richards's portrayal of foreign characters for particular criticism:

> The assumption all along is not only that foreigners are comics who are put there for us to laugh at, but that they can be classified in much the same way as insects. (Orwell, 1962: 188)

Clearly Hurree Singh is comic, and readers are meant to laugh at him. Richards's response to Orwell's comment was, simply, that 'foreigners *are* funny' (Richards, 1968: 491). But there is something more subtle happening here. Readers may laugh at Singh's language, but Harry Wharton and Co. *do not*. He does not have to endure the same ridicule as Bunter, even though Bunter's language can be equally unintelligible at times. This could be pure 'snob-appeal', as Orwell puts it, as Singh carries the aristocratic title of the Nabob of Bhanipur. But Jeffrey Richards feels that the author had other reasons for his characterisation of Hurree Singh:

> By making an Indian boy a comrade on equal terms with English schoolboys, Frank Richards felt that he was contributing his mite towards the unity of the Commonwealth and helping to rid the youthful mind of colour prejudice. (Richards, 1988: 281)

Whilst this does, it seems to me, push the point a little too far, there is more to Hurree Singh than pure comedy. (We will explore this point in more detail in Chapter 4, which looks at aspects of imperialism and masculinity.)

Similarly, Billy Bunter, possibly Richards's most well-known and enduring creation, begins as a comic turn but grows into much more. Orwell's view of Bunter was that he was the only 'really first class character' in any of the boys' weeklies. Jeffrey Richards writes that Bunter may not have been the most popular of the characters, but he was: 'a comic figure, a catharsis for anarchic impulses, the epitome of everything one should not be' (Richards, 1988: 283).

Bunter does indeed operate outside rule systems. He is motivated above all by greed, through his endless search for food, and thinks nothing of stealing, lying and defying teachers' orders if there is food to be had. He is a figure of fun as much for his behaviour and language as he is for his size – and in fact he is one of the few characters whose physical characteristics are noted in detail. Bunter's antics attracted a great deal of attention from readers, some of whom actually sent in money to alleviate Bunter's perpetual financial difficulties – in the narratives he is consistently depicted as waiting for a postal order which never arrives, and is consequently always short of funds.

Each issue of *The Magnet* commonly contained 'a magnificent long complete story' about Greyfriars (although longer serial stories, sometimes spread over several months, were often published in the summer). Another common feature was a spoof school magazine, the Greyfriars Herald, edited by Harry Wharton, with columns and features by the rest of the chums – and, most notably, 'Billy Bunter's Footbawl Kollum'. In the 1920s the magazine also featured vignettes on key characters – a very useful reference for new readers:

> No 42: Arthur Woodhead Carne: chum of Loder, and only inferior to him as an utter rotter. Plays the gay dog. Also plays cricket and footer with ability, but very much over-values himself. Was once a prefect, is so no longer. So far has escaped expulsion, but his turn may come. (Vignette no. 42, *The Magnet*, 7 February 1920: 9)

Also notable is the range of adverts carried by *The Magnet*, a regular feature of the back-cover page – an example of which is shown in Figure 0.1. From 'nerve strengthening treatment' to cures for blushing and patent remedies for growing several inches taller, most of these sound like blatant exploitation of the vulnerable, but it is impossible to tell at this distance whether any readers were actually moved to respond to them.

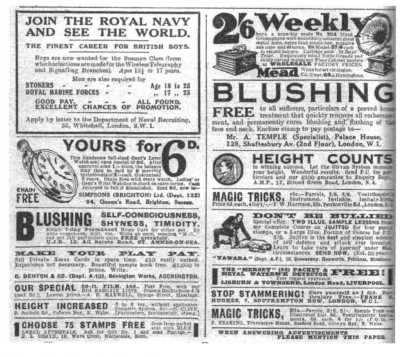

Figure 0.1   Example of an advertisements page from *The Magnet*, 18 October 1924, p. 28

An introduction to *The Hotspur*

The D. C. Thomson Company of Dundee launched a number of new story paper titles in the inter-war period, but most notable amongst these were the 'big five': *Adventure* (launched in 1921), *The Rover* and *The Wizard* (both launched 1922), *The Skipper* (launched 1930) and *The Hotspur* (launched 1933). Like the others (and like *The Magnet*), *The Hotspur* was a 28-page colour-fronted story paper aimed at a readership of boys aged 12–15.

By the time *The Hotspur* first appeared, the other four of the 'big' D. C. Thomson titles were well established, and their innovative style had proven hugely popular with readers. In McAleer's view, the D. C. Thomson secret was:

> a combination of creativity, spontaneity and imagination which took boys out of the traditional school story setting, confronting them with all sorts of adventures and inventions. (McAleer, 1992: 169)

D. C. Thomson's main innovation over the Amalgamated Press papers was to move away from the format of one long complete story to include a number of shorter pieces, some complete tales and others serialised week by week. Rather than concentrate on the setting and regular characters, the Thomson papers presented snapshot stories in a bewildering variety of locations, with narratives flashing past at breakneck speed and very little space for thought, emotion or real character development of any kind.

Issue 2 of *The Hotspur*, from 9 September 1933, presents the following stories:

'Buffalo Bill's Schooldays' ('Read about the log school in the backwoods where the Famous Western Scout was a pupil')
'The Traitor of the Team' (a clever combination of school life with amateur league football)
'Dead-Wide Dick' (a 'Red Circle School' story, featuring the 'world's champion slacker')
'Colorado Kid' ('born and bred in the wilds of Colorado', 'more used to snow shoes ... than he was to algebra and geometry')
'The Big Stiff' (tales of the schoolteacher at Pendlebury Village Old School)
'The Son of Scarface' ('the schoolboy who is a gangster against his will')
'The Swooping Vengeance' (the attacks of a giant vulture '120 feet from wingtip to wingtip') (*The Hotspur*, 9 September 1933)

Each of these is self-contained, but promises 'further adventures next week'. The other 'big five' D. C. Thomson papers followed a similar format, but, interestingly, *The Hotspur* is the only one of the five to have a school focus. As is clear from the list above, these are not traditional public school stories, but feature either 'specialist' schools in wild or unlikely places (the depths of the wild west) or 'outsider' characters brought in to more recognisably traditional settings (the 'Colorado Kid' at school in Tuppington Village).

As in *The Magnet*, *The Hotspur* featured an editor's column every week ('Sez Me!') but the editor also specifically invited readers to write in, not only with comments about their favourite characters and stories, but also with contributions for a 'Sez You!' column, which featured tricks and jokes. There was in addition a slightly more overtly educational element, albeit well sugared with a 'well fancy that!' style, in '*The Hotspur's* Trip Round the World' column (snippets of 'interesting' general knowledge) and in the regular question and answer running heads ('Why do flowers have a sweet scent? To attract the bees and insects which carry pollen' (*The Hotspur*, 9 September 1933); 'Where are the world's largest apples grown? Apples weighing 8lbs each have been grown in Japan' (*The Hotspur*, 25 April 1936)). Although the general knowledge column was in fact rather shortlived, the question and answer running heads continued throughout most of *The Hotspur*'s run.

The Hotspur's editorial column is framed in a companionable style which positions the editor as friend, as compared with the teacherly and slightly patronising style of *The Magnet*. This style may well be due to the D. C. Thomson policy of employing writers and editors straight out of college – in general they were not much older than the readers themselves. Writers and editors were also instructed to keep their ideas as contemporary and relevant as possible. McAleer quotes George Moonie, *The Rover* sub-editor from 1930 onwards, on the D. C. Thomson approach to writing:

> You don't want too foreign a background: you want a normal background, with normal people. You've got to keep up to date, have your eye on the paper and your ear to what's going on in school. Kids have got to identify: if he doesn't understand it, he's finished. (McAleer, 1992: 180)

D. C. Thomson papers were written by a team of authors, working to a strict editorial policy. These authors were never credited in the papers, which meant that D. C. Thomson papers were able to accommodate changes in tastes more easily, by using different writers. It also shows that the D. C. Thomson company valued variety and spontaneity over the cult of the author.

Writers for *The Hotspur* were also able to introduce new storylines on a regular basis. In the first six months of its life, *The Hotspur* featured at least 11 new stories, replacing existing storylines which had either declined in popularity or lost momentum. New stories appearing during this period included: 'Black Wolf' ('the Year's greatest story of mystery and terror', beginning 18 November 1933); 'The School Amid the Snows' ('where they teach the secrets of the frozen North', 9 December 1933); 'The Teacher from Dartmoor' (an escaped convict poses as a teacher, 9 December 1933); 'The Kids of Caravan College' (Buffalo Bill's school goes on a trek, 23 December 1933); '6 Yellow Knife Men' (a boy from Tibet is trailed to a British school by six Tibetan avengers, 30 December 1933); 'The Champ from the Swot Brigade' (the son of a champion boxer vows to devote himself to study, 13 January 1934); and 'Tiger Jake's Academy' (a circus school where the teacher is an animal trainer, 10 February 1934).

The one constant through all of this variety is the Red Circle School, which features in every issue. Like Greyfriars, Red Circle School is a traditional-style public school, and the authors who contributed to the long-running series clearly drew on the basics of what was by then a very well-established genre.

Given the short length of the Red Circle School stories, there is very little scope for detailed scene-setting, or complicated plot or character development. There is almost no description of the school building or its daily routines – again, as with Greyfriars, it would have been difficult for writers to include such detail given that new readers were picking up the story paper every week and would come to each story possibly with little or no prior knowledge of characters or settings. The Red Circle School stories therefore rely on strongly delineated characters with obvious skills, attributes or foibles. Pringle and Moxon, for instance, are unmitigated 'rotters', whilst Dead-Wide Dick Doyle is quickly established as a 'champion slacker' who tries to avoid physical exertion at all costs, but has a sharp brain which often puts him centre stage in resolving the main plotline. In 'Oh Mr Smugg, What a Mug!', for example, from *The Hotspur* of 25 January 1936, it is Dead-Wide Dick who solves the mystery of who booby-trapped Mr Smugg (the most hated teacher in the school) and covered him in green paint. Dick's simple detective work shows up the real culprit (Pringle), and secures the reinstatement of Sergeant Cogg, the porter, mistakenly sacked for the offence.

Each week the Red Circle School story focuses on one key group of characters, from the third, fourth or fifth form. Each form has its lead figures: Dead-Wide Dick, Pringle and Moxon are fifth-form regulars, along with Tubby Ryan (the fifth-form captain), Jim Stacey and Cyrus Judd. The fourth form has an almost identical group of 'goodies', 'rotters' and comic turns: Dave Hardy (also known as 'the Moke') and Toughy Wilson square up against Lasky and Hedges, 'the bounders', with light relief provided by Scatty Saunders, 'the fathead of the fourth'. As at Greyfriars, the school sport is football, not rugby; but unlike Greyfriars, Red Circle School has houses. The houses are in fact an interesting innovation on the tradition. At Red Circle the three houses are based geographically according to where the boys' parents live: Home House is for boys whose parents live in Britain; Trans-Atlantic House (or 'Yanks') is for US/Canadian residents, and Colonial House (or 'Conks') is for boys from the rest of the Empire. This device allows the writers to introduce all manner of foreign-sounding characters, but these rarely progress beyond offering a line or two of dialogue for comic effect. The idea of setting up houses on these lines is rather underused, and house allegiances are rarely the source of story development.

There has been much criticism of the D. C. Thomson characters, and Red Circle School characters in particular, as stereotypes. Musgrave is scathing of what he calls the 'standardisation of characters' (Musgrave, 1985: 219), and quotes C. E. Raven from 1928:

> Take a juvenile athlete as your chief ingredient, add a wit, a bully, a persecuted fag, an awkward scholar, a faithful friend, a dangerous rival and a batch of distorted pedagogues; mix these up in an atmosphere of genial romanticism; insert a smoking scandal, a fight, a cribbing scene and sundry rags, and a house match or two; bring them all to the boil when the hero scores the winning try or does the hat trick; serve the whole hot, and with a title associating the dish with an establishment which the initiated can identify; and the suburbs will raid the libraries for the result. (Musgrave, 1985: 219)

Raven is here referring to book-length school fiction in general, but his attitude was shared by many other contemporary critics of popular fiction and story papers, including George Orwell. *The Magnet* and *The Gem*, and therefore by implication *The Hotspur* too, are to Musgrave 'the worst examples of standardisation'; and to Isabel Quigly the popular school story does little more than create a 'cloud cuckoo land' (Musgrave, 1985: 277; Quigly, 1982: 250). However, as Jeffrey Richards points out, the story papers (and school stories in particular) were potent as conveyors of myth. He sees the characters in the story papers not as stereotypes but as archetypes, something very different:

> A stereotype is a carbon copy of a well-established model; an archetype is the creation of a definitive idealisation. There is irrefutable evidence in the attitude of the boy readers. The characters served as role models. (Richards, 1988: 282)

The following chapters will explore the nature of that idealisation, and look at the attitudes of the readers, the publishers, the parents and the critics.

1
Setting the Scene: Critical Perspectives, Producers and Consumers

This chapter outlines an approach to the theorisation of popular culture, drawing on the work of critical and cultural theorists, which forms a background to my arguments across the book as a whole. It also explores the nature of creators and audiences. The notion of context is important here: what do we know of the producers of the story papers and their publishing methods? Who were the consumers of the story papers and what were the contexts of their reading lives? The chapter offers an introduction to some of the key themes and perspectives that will be explored in more detail in the following chapters.

Theorising popular culture

That the Library Association could speak of children's publishing in the 1930s as 'an ocean of terrible trash' (Hunt, 1994: 106) says more about contemporary critical attitudes than it does about the books. The prevailing critical attitude was one of barely controlled horror at the apparent rise of the 'low brow', the mass-produced fictional experience, at the expense of quality literature. Retrospectively known as mass culture theory, this view was articulated most influentially by Matthew Arnold, who defined culture as 'the best that has been thought and said in the world' (Arnold, 1960: 6). This view was enormously significant from the 1870s through to the 1950s – it became the tradition to see culture in this way, and likewise to view popular culture as 'anarchy'.

Maintaining a controlling hold on 'high' culture is thus the only way to counter the perceived threat of the increasing power of the working class, the rising influence of the mass of the population. This is culture as a form of control – the 'best' people controlling the subordinate anarchic mass of 'others'. Without culture there can be nothing but anarchy;

for Arnold this unquestioned binary polarity allows for no shades of opinion or cultural practices in between.

By the 1920s and 1930s the Arnoldian 'culture and civilisation' tradition was clearly dominant as a theory which could apparently both account for the great increase in 'terrible trash' and offer some hope for countering its influence. Chief amongst its exponents was F. R. Leavis, who was in turn to dominate critical methods and the study of culture for the next 30 years.

F. R. Leavis's interpretation of the Arnoldian tradition centred on the importance of education. In order to preserve the best that has been written and said, students must be taught to appreciate, to value the best according to prescribed criteria. Schools and colleges, he wrote, should try to 'preserve and develop a continuity of consciousness and a mature directing sense of value – a sense of value informed by a traditional wisdom' (Leavis, 1979: 15).

This need for preservation and continuity underpins much of Leavis's work. Like Arnold he wanted to protect a 'traditional' value system which he saw as fundamentally threatened. For Leavis, however, the threat did not come from the masses as such, but rather from the more insidious influence of industrialisation and urbanisation. The coming of industrialisation has destroyed the old, and by implication better, ways of life, and left in their place something shabby and worthless – the standardised, homogenised and mass-produced taste. These old ways of life are characterised in Leavis's view of a traditional organic society, as one in which labour meant the pursuit of traditional manual skills, and which was united by shared moral and aesthetic values. In such a society, it was the task of the educated minority to safeguard authority and continuity, to uphold tradition and heritage. His argument is a moral rather than political one, arguing not on class-based lines but against what he sees as threats to the very essence of life for all citizens. The mass market, mass production and standardisation, for Leavis, inevitably lead to 'standardisation of persons' (Mulhern, 1981: 9). The nature of modern work, tending to the repetitive and ceaseless machines, as he sees it, leads to what amounts to a kind of brainwashing: the masses are so debilitated by soulless work that they are incapable of any form of critical judgement, and so are condemned to be exploited by the producers of mass culture.

It is now fairly widely agreed amongst cultural critics that there are a number of problems with mass culture theory (see, for example, Strinati (1995) and Storey (1993)). Failure to take account of power relations is one key problem, in particular with respect to children's literature and popular culture. By focusing purely on the value of high culture, or the quality end of the publishing spectrum, mass culture theory would deny any kind of learning experience for children from any other published material or cultural practice. It also fails to explore the nature of the relationships between writer, publisher and reader, beyond that of basic economics. A theory of popular culture, as Strinati points out, needs to look further than this, to explore consumption ('how and why goods make a profit by finding large enough markets') as well as production ('how and why goods are produced') (Strinati, 1995: 259). An exploration of consumption would point up a further problem with mass culture theory, in that it has an 'inadequate understanding of the role of the audience in popular culture' (Strinati, 1995: 46). Mass culture theory denies the audience any agency; it defines the audience as a passive, homogenised and submissive body, manipulated and exploited by the mass media, incapable of any individual thought, creative, critical or otherwise. That this view is fundamentally patronising, as well as being elitist and selective, is now widely recognised in critical theory. In choosing to dismiss the range and diversity of popular culture, mass culture theory also sets the critic in a position which both vilifies and excludes a mass audience. In effect, mass culture theory sees mass culture as *harmful* to its audience. Finally, and most damningly for the purposes of this book, mass culture theory is unable to account for social and cultural change. In its idealisation of an essentially mythical golden age, it is by definition backward-looking; its keywords, unity and continuity, imply closed conservatism.

If mass culture does not quite work as a mode of analysis from a twenty-first-century perspective, we need to seek out other ways of looking at culture. Raymond Williams offers three categories in the definition of culture:

- the 'ideal', in which culture is a state or process of human perfection, in terms of certain absolute or universal values ...
- the 'documentary', in which culture is the body of intellectual and imaginative work, in which, in a detailed way, human thought and experience are variously recorded ...
- the 'social' ... in which culture is a description of a particular way of life, which expresses certain meanings and values not only in art and learning, but also in institutions and ordinary behaviour. (Williams, 1961: 41)

The three categories operate in a kind of continuum, from the Leavisian 'ideal', through the activity of criticism implied by definition two, which, as Williams says, could either take a view very similar to the 'ideal' analysis in concentrating on high culture, or consist of a process of 'historical criticism which, after analysis of particular works, seeks to relate them to the particular traditions and societies in which they appeared' (Williams, 1961: 42). Definition three, the 'social' end of the continuum, includes historical analysis, but also analyses alternative structures:

> elements in the way of life that to followers of the other definitions are not 'culture' at all; the organisation of production, the structure of the family, the structure of institutions which express or govern social relationships, the characteristic forms through which members of society communicate. (Williams, 1961: 42)

The 'social' definition includes elements of the other two, aiming to study not just ways of life, but the ways in which life changes and develops. Williams sees value in all three definitions, and certainly an awareness of all three gives critical depth to any analysis of cultural artefacts. But it seems to me that the social definition has most to offer to an exploration of publishing for children, and in particular to an exploration of a specific historical period. Here is a way to answer some of the problems and difficulties of mass culture theory, by taking an inclusive view which focuses on lived experiences, meanings and values. For Williams, the theory of culture is 'the study of *relations between* elements in a whole way of life'; the analysis of culture is then 'the attempt to discover the nature of the organisation which is the complex of these relationships' (Williams, 1961: 46). What we will see in the later analysis in this book are the ways in which in the 1920s and 1930s specific patterns of relationships develop: relationships between children (as readers/consumers of popular literature), their families and educational institutions (as guides to/selectors of reading experiences), and publishers (as producers).

There are problems with this approach to the study of culture, too, and in particular with the notion of using the social definition to analyse a historical period. Williams is clear on this point, that it is only really possible to know in detail our own time and place. 'We can learn a great deal of the life of other places and times, but certain elements ... will always be irrecoverable' (Williams, 1961: 47). Without having shared in the lived experience of a time, we can never really appreciate 'the felt sense of the quality of life' of that time, or fully understand contemporary ways of thinking. Williams's answer to this is to suggest the existence of a kind of essence of life, which he calls the 'structure of feeling' (Williams, 1961: 48), as a way in to understanding the culture of a period. Storey explains this as 'the shared values of a particular group, class or society ... something that is a cross between a collective cultural unconscious and an ideology' (Storey, 1993: 53). The place to find these structures of feeling, these shared values, is in the arts, 'the only example of recorded communication that outlives its bearers' (Williams, 1961: 48). Yet even here we can only *approach* an understanding of a past culture, because, crucially, the documentary record, in the examples of art which are studied, is selective.

No history or cultural study can be anything other than selective. A study of a past society is reliant on the documentary sources which remain, and on the various interpretations of those sources. The selective process begins in the period itself, and remains continually active as successive generations inherit, reorder and reinterpret traditions. The obvious corollary to this is a process of exclusion – what is not selected is simply discarded. Any cultural analysis which attempts to explore the social must thus also attempt to look beyond the received record in order to give space to the neglected and excluded. Mass culture theory, by comparison, attempts to exclude the popular, and for some considerable time was successful in its selectivity.

The selective tradition is clearly a powerful force by which the dominant group reinforces its value system, but it is also inherently vulnerable, in that at any time that which has been excluded can effectively be recovered and reincorporated (Williams, 1977: 116). Because this reinterpreting and reincorporating process is itself continuous it is impossible to foresee 'the relevance of past work in any future situation' (Williams, 1961: 52). In other words, as well as looking at the process of selection and exclusion in the historical period itself, it is important to be aware of the whole subsequent evolution of selection up to and including our own contemporary values and interests. I make my own selection by choosing to focus on popular literature, and I do so from a particular theoretical standpoint which chooses to privilege certain interpretations above others. That this is precisely what historians of children's literature have also done is clear from the quotations at the beginning of the Introduction to this book. Each presents a selective view of the culture of the period – whether knowingly or otherwise. Inevitably, as Williams writes, 'we see past work through our own experience', and few of us 'make the effort to see it in something like its original terms' (Williams, 1961: 53). Analysis in Williams's terms attempts to make the personal interpretation explicit by 'returning a work to its [historical] period, [showing] historical alternatives and [relating] the interpretation to the particular contemporary values on which it rests' (Williams, 1961: 53).

Raymond Williams's work has also been used as the basis of critical historical approaches to literature which have been described as new historicism and cultural materialism. These critical methods were first discussed in the 1970s and 1980s, growing out of the work of Stephen Greenblatt and others, as a reaction against the 'traditional' conception of history as unproblematic, dealing in facts and truths, set out as a straightforward sequence of key events. New historicism and cultural materialism lead out from Williams's concept of selectivity and interpretation, both trying to return works to their historical periods, to look at 'literature *in* history, not literature *and* history' (Brannigan, 1998: 4). Such methods are also about setting writers in context, noting that they 'must draw upon a whole life-world, and that this life-world has undoubtedly left other traces of itself' (Gallagher and Greenblatt, 2000: 43). As Brannigan explains,

> both new historicist and critical materialist critics tend to read literary texts as material products of specific historical conditions ... [both view] texts of all kinds [as] the vehicles of politics insofar as texts mediate the fabric of social, political and cultural formations ... [both] see literature as a constitutive and inseparatable part of history in the making, and therefore rife with the creative forces, disruptions and contradictions of history. (Brannigan, 1998: 3–4)

This process is much more than simply seeing history as 'background' against which texts can be set, and moves decisively away from the notion of a single, unquestionable history towards an idea of multiple interpretations and multiple 'histories'.

Both approaches are also concerned to explore the nature of power, power relations, and how these are manifested in literature. New historicists borrow the concept directly from Foucault – power as seen through the forces of ideology, the self-perpetuating and inescapable determining force of society. In Foucault's terms, this is a way forward that 'consists in taking the forms of resistance against different forms of power as a starting point ... [and] in using this resistance as a chemical catalyst so as to bring to light power relations, locate their position, find out their point of application and the methods used' (Foucault, 2001: 329). A new historicist perspective attempts to reveal how power operates in literature, and to tie that interpretation to a specific historical period, identifying how power relations develop over time. A cultural materialist view takes the interpretation one stage further, by insisting on situating texts within contemporary power relations. While both of these methods would argue the importance of the notion that we can only make sense of history through an understanding of our own present position, it is cultural materialism which makes this understanding overtly political. There are also differences in the ways in which followers of each approach select texts on which to focus their explorations. For new historicists, the key is to draw on diverse texts, giving equal status to a range of primary sources which can include diaries, travel narratives, popular literature, newspapers and advertising as well as the canonical. The cultural materialist agenda by comparison is to reinterpret those texts which have been privileged as canonical and to offer new readings:

> [texts are] reconstructed, reappraised and reassigned all the time through diverse institutions in specific contexts. What [texts] signify, how they signify, depends on the cultural field in which they are situated. (Dollimore and Sinfield, 1994: viii)

Mitzi Myers has shown how both cultural materialism and new historicism could be applied very usefully to children's literature:

> A new historicism of children's literature would *integrate* text and socio-historic context, demonstrating on the one hand how extra-literary cultural formations shape literary discourse and on the other hand how literary practices are actions that make things happen – by shaping the psychic and moral consciousness of young readers, but also by performing many more diverse kinds of cultural work. (Myers, 1988: 42)

In her view, the usefulness of a new historicist approach is in exploring how and why a tale or poem came to say what it does, what were the circumstances of its production, and what uses it served for its author, its child and adult readers, and its culture. Her inclusive perspective carries both awareness of and openness to meanings and meaning-making which offer a way towards understanding the structures of feeling of a particular period. But as with other critical approaches, new historicism and cultural materialism have been popular almost to the extent of becoming *the* dominant form of critical theory. As might be expected, critics have begun to question the arguments. Brannigan in particular has a problem with the way new historicists view history: if the only focus of attention is on the way in which texts are vehicles of power relations and ideological manipulation, surely that prevents the critic from seeing through texts to the lived experience beneath? Power is everywhere, he writes, 'because power is the only thing that new historicists are looking for' (Brannigan, 1998: 77). Lynne Vallone makes a more specific criticism of new historicism in relation to the study of children's literature. A focus on power relations might have been expected at some point to lead to an analysis of the unique position of adults in relation to children. 'Such an unequal distribution of power, though a function of age, *should* have been of interest to new historicist critics' (Vallone, 1996: 102). That this has only now become a focus of critical interest is a symptom of how low a status children's literature and culture has hitherto held amongst mainstream academics. Later chapters of this book begin to address this lack by looking at points of connection between producers and consumers, and the ways in which child readers made and took meanings from their reading.

Another critical method which has direct relevance to the themes we will discuss in the following chapters is reader response theory, or reception theory. Formulated in the 1970s by Wolfgang Iser and Hans Robert Jauss, reader response theory reacts further against the arguments of the mass culture theorists by 'privileging the experience of reading [literary] texts as a uniquely valuable consciousness-raising activity' (Lodge and Wood, 2000: 188). Iser argues that, rather than seeing text as having an intrinsic meaning which is drawn out by the practice of criticism, reader and text must interact in order to create meaning. It is the act of reading, the 'convergence between text and reader', which brings the work into existence. Most importantly, Iser argues that readers create meaning for themselves by filling in the gaps and unwritten aspects of any narrative. Meaning-making is a dynamic process through which the text and the readers' imagination work together. The meanings thus made are, quite logically therefore, unique to each individual reader, as each brings his or her own background, disposition and cultural baggage into the relationship. In Jauss's terms, an act of reading (and therefore, of meaning-making) takes place within the reader's 'horizon of expectations', that is, 'the mindset that a hypothetical individual might bring to any text' (Holub, 1984: 59). Combining to create this mindset are not only social, cultural and educational influences, but also the reader's own previous experience of the genre. In school story papers in particular, authors often had to take for granted a fairly high level of familiarity with the genre, given the lack of space in the story papers for background description.

This theory not only helps to explain why different readers can interpret the same text in very different ways (and indeed the fact that the same reader can find different meanings in one text on re-reading it), but also goes some way towards an understanding of the process by which a reader can be drawn in to a text and feel personally involved in events which seem real to him or her, even when that reality is very different from his or her own. As Iser argues, the process depends on the level of effort put in by the reader:

> The impact this reality makes on [the reader] will depend largely on the extent to which he himself actively provides the unwritten part of the text, and yet in supplying all the missing links, he must think in terms of experiences different from his own; indeed, it is only by leaving behind the familiar world of his own experience that the reader can truly participate in the adventure the literary text offers him. (Iser, in Lodge and Wood, 2000: 194–5)

What this implies is that there are levels of understanding in this relationship – different horizons of expectation. Some readers will bring to their reading a range of experience and a practised imagination. These readers will supply the missing links and create a reading on a different level from those who have a more limited range of experience, and who will experience the text in a different way.

There are problems and contradictions here, however, in applying reader response theory to children's literature, and in applying it to an analysis of children's story papers. The reading process is not a standardised procedure of extracting specifically defined meanings from a text, so we also need to account for the multiplicity of meanings readers bring and also their differing mindsets. Children's literature – and story papers in particular – do not function in a straightforward author/text/reader dynamic. Readers make their meanings in the context of parental influence, where the choice of reading matter is not necessarily primarily the reader's own, and where family background and social context play a major part. The author stands outside the reader/parent relationship, but must take account of this relationship in creating the implied author. In children's story papers the implied author is both the editor figure and the author of the stories – so here readers also have to engage with multiple authors. Overseeing the whole process from author to reader is the publisher, who has ultimate control over the content of the text. As the publisher controls production, his (and they were, almost without exception, male) editorial and commercial decision-making encompasses meaning-making at all levels.

For the most part, reader response theory has been developed as an approach to literary fiction, and it has been applied less commonly to children's fiction, or to story papers for children (with some notable recent exceptions – see, for example, the work of Morag Styles and Evelyn Arizpe (Styles and Arizpe, 2001; Arizpe and Styles, 2003) and Ingrid Johnston (Johnston et al., 2007); reader response theory also features as a recommended approach in Grenby and Reynolds's recent research handbook for students of children's literature (Ross Johnston, 2011, pp. 133–41). Although there are specific problems with this kind of application, some interesting points do emerge. Story papers must be seen as a continuous series of texts, read and re-read, shared and discussed. Children typically did not read just one story paper in isolation, but kept on reading, following narratives and characters week after week. It follows in this case that the horizon of expectations – the mindset readers bring to their reading – cannot be seen as a static concept, but changes according to how many story papers in the series a reader has read, as well as to the particular individual background of that reader. In order to make sense of a story paper series, readers must not only maintain their reading of it for a number of weeks, as characters and events unfold, but also must carry with them the knowledge about those characters and events from week to week. This gives an intriguing new dimension to Iser's notion of missing links – in what ways did readers fill the gaps between those weekly issues? There is evidence to suggest that the story paper worlds were real enough for some readers to believe in them totally. As George Samways, a sub-editor on *The Magnet*, recalls:

> One young reader, feeling compassion for Billy Bunter, who was always expecting a postal order from one of his titled relations, actually enclosed a remittance for Billy. This was duly acknowledged, as from Bunter himself, and the money given to charity. This happened more than once during the period of my sub-editorship. (Samways, 1984: 94)

Samways is convinced that, to many of the story paper readers, the characters were not just fictional creations, but 'living, vital beings, leading a real existence in a real school' (Samways, 1984: 182); the willingness of *The Magnet* staff to maintain the illusion would have helped to reinforce readers' sense of connection with it.

The thematic chapters of this book will also make use of some concepts formulated by Pierre Bourdieu, notably the notions of *habitus* and *field*, which seem to offer useful correlations to the theories of reader response discussed above. Bourdieu's interpretation of the concept of habitus is defined as 'a set of dispositions which generates practices and perceptions', the result of a long process of 'inculcation' beginning in early childhood (Johnson, 1993: 5). Eventually (and inevitably), these dispositions become habitual – a kind of mindset which is so much part of an individual as to be largely unquestioned. Habitus is an acquired, socially constructed state formed through the interconnecting influences of family, education, social context and environment: 'habitus, as systems of dispositions, are effectively realized only in relation to a determinate structure of positions socially marked by the social properties of their occupants, through which they manifext themselves' (Bourdieu, 1993: 71). Although Bourdieu describes this process as inculcation (which implies both deliberateness and force), there must also be an element of the unconscious here too, in that dispositions can be absorbed from social contexts, or passed from parent to child, without conscious thought just as much as they can be deliberately taught. Bourdieu writes that the dispositions represented by the habitus are 'structured structures', in that they incorporate the objective social conditions that surround them. This accounts for 'the similarity in the habitus of agents from the same social class and authorises speaking of a class habitus' (Johnson, 1993: 5). It also implies a combination of the active and the passive – active in terms of being able to incorporate ideas, but passive in terms of mostly doing so in an unreflective mode, which leads to the homogeneity of a class habitus. These structured structures are self-perpetuating ('durable' in Bourdieu's terms), and function as a framework for class relations.

Following this formulation, habitus will have an influence on the ways in which readers interact with texts, and the meanings they take from them – and indeed on the nature of the producer/consumer dynamic. The related concept of field was developed by Bourdieu to describe the concrete social situations in which agents act, and this again is useful in an analysis of the production and consumption of cultural artefacts. Any social formation is structured by way of a hierarchically organised series of fields (the economic field, the educational field, the political field, the cultural field, etc.) each defined as 'a separate social universe having its own laws of functioning independent of those of politics and the economy' (Bourdieu, 1993: 162).

Fields are both discrete, with their own rules and structures, and interconnecting. As Grenfell and James point out, all fields exist in structural relation to each other in some way – that is, their interconnectedness is a necessary part of their structure (Grenfell and James,

1998: 16). The educational field, for example, is a highly structured space with its own subfields (nursery, primary, secondary, tertiary), but it also operates in structural relationship with the economic field (the funding of education systems, the economic benefit of educated citizens in society), the political field (schools as institutional state apparatuses, embedded ideologies in school curricula) and the cultural field (through explicit study of cultural artefacts as well as teaching about cultural value) amongst others. Although education is a field in its own right, it is not possible to map its structure fully except in relation to connected fields. The opposite also applies – so that writing about children's culture necessarily involves explorations of economics, politics and education, and other related fields. As Grenfell and James write, the relations between fields 'determine and reproduce social activity in all its multifarious forms' (Grenfell and James, 1998: 16).

Bourdieu's theories can be connected with both Williams's work (in the exploration of social relations and cultural practices) and with that of the reader response theorists (in the analysis of social and cultural influences on readers and their contingent effects on meaning-making). Chapter 6 explores these connections in detail, linking the concepts of habitus and field with Bourdieu's explorations of symbolic capital, making particular reference to the story papers and their readers.

So far, this chapter has outlined some key theories and definitions, and shown how these will be useful in the chapters which follow. In the following section we will take a brief look at some of the social and cultural developments of the 1920s and 1930s, with a particular emphasis on the business of publishing at the time, through which the texts are to be interpreted, and also look in turn at issues affecting producers and consumers.

Historical perspectives

Producers

To return to the historians of children's literature quoted at the beginning of the Introduction, the dominant view of children's literature of the 1920s and 1930s is one of sad decline in both physical and literary quality. By concentrating on a direct comparison of 'high' and 'low' culture, the 'classic' against the 'popular', it is quite tempting to agree with this view. But looking beyond these easy distinctions, it is clear that there were more complex developments in the contemporary publishing world which need to be taken into account.

John Feather writes that 'for much of the inter-war period, British publishing was as similar as it could be to the pre-war years' (Feather, 1988: 196). There may have been little in the way of purely technical innovation in publishing at this time, but there was a steady and continual process of change in the economic aspects of the trade and in the social and cultural position of books, and reading, in public life.

In economic terms, the post-war world was a difficult place in which to keep a publishing business viable. Kingsford reports a 200 per cent increase in printing charges on pre-war figures, as well as wildly fluctuating paper costs – he notes that paper costs dropped from 9d. per pound in January 1920 to 3¾d. in May 1921, only to rise again dramatically later that year (Kingsford, 1970: 87). The huge increase in production of so-called 'Bumper' books, so roundly decried by Eyre, can be seen in part as a direct reaction to these economic conditions. But what seems to have worked well for the publishers worked less well for others. The use of artificially bulked-out paper, making books significantly fatter, may have helped publishers' profits by allowing them to charge more for each title, but there were widespread complaints from wholesalers and booksellers about increases in carriage costs and the fact that the books took up so much room on the shelves (Kingsford, 1970: 98).

The increased trade in 'Bumper' books is a key indication of change in publishers' perceptions of, and attitudes to, their market. From the 1850s onwards, books were being seen less as luxury items and more as 'almost a necessary of life' (Barnes, n.d.: 210). By the 1920s this sense of the place of the book in cultural life had developed to the extent that publishers were confident enough to economise on quality, to use and re-use illustrations and storylines, to bulk out paper and raise prices without fear of jeopardising sales. It is interesting to note, too, that this compromise on quality happened particularly with children's books – making it hard to resist the thought that publishers assumed that children were either not going to notice, or that children were insufficiently important as consumers for their attitudes towards books really to matter. Even so, this is not just a case of pure publishing exploitation, as the 'Bumper' years were short-lived. By the 1930s, whether because of pressure from wholesalers, or changes in the paper supply, or simply because illustrations and storylines could only be reworked so many times, they had all but disappeared.

Other markets were opening up, however, and publishers were quick to spot them. Beaven notes that the number of books published rose from 8666 in 1914 to 14,904 in 1939, while book sales rose from 7.2 million in 1928 to 26.8 million in 1939 (Beaven, 2005: 181). The inter-war period saw dramatic growth in both the public library and the educational markets. By the 1930s borrowing figures had risen dramatically, following the introduction of the Public Libraries Act (1919) which allowed local authorities to spend more on stock (Dewey, 1997: 192). (Dewey quotes the following borrowing figures: 1913–14: 54 million lends; 1934–35: 116 million.) This growth affected children's books especially, leading to the setting up of specialist bodies such as a new division of the Publishers' Association, and the appointment of professional editors for children's books in the major publishing houses.

Similarly, legislative developments in education gave publishers access to many more children through growth in school attendance. The 1918 Education Act raised the compulsory school attendance age to 14, increasing the elementary school population by a quarter of a million over the next few years. By 1920–21 there were 5,816,000 children in elementary school, with a further 618,000 in grant-aided or secondary or independent schools (Norrington, 1983: 67; the upper years of elementary schooling (11–14-year-olds) were referred to as senior school; those passing the 11-plus exam attended secondary or grammar schools). This represented a huge expansion in the schoolbook market, and there was a consequent rush to fill the gap. Not all publishers, however, looked beyond turning a fast profit. Norrington quotes Basil Blackwell's impressions of the quality of the general output:

> I visited an educational supplier and spent £1 on an armful of [school books] for examination. It was a shocking experience. The dominant consideration was cheapness, and to this were sacrificed the contents, physical and intellectual. The ruling impression was of hack work shoddily produced. (Norrington, 1983: 67)

Blackwell's response was to publish for schools himself. His *Histories* series, written by Marten and Carter, with four titles published between 1925 and 1927, was 'so unusually good as to out-distance all else of the kind' (Norrington, 1983: 84), and sold over 1000 copies a week. Although the Board of Education did not prescribe textbooks – leaving the curriculum and choice of books to local authorities and headteachers – the market was seen as a growing and lucrative one, and new textbooks for the elementary market followed Marten and Carter. Cannadine et al. call these 'a new generation' of textbook authors, who treated history in particular more imaginatively and appealingly, including Eileen and Rhoda Power (*Boys and Girls of History*, 1929), and C. B. Firth's *History Series*, beginning in 1931 with *Children of Athens, London and Rome*.

While sales to libraries and schools may have been booming in the inter-war years, the general book trade was not. Alongside the relatively successful 'Bumper' and reward books, booksellers mostly sold reprints of older titles, with fewer new ones appearing (Feather, 1988: 200). There are a number of key reasons for this. Most importantly, as Feather points out:

> For the first time, the printed word was no longer the only means of mass communication or mass entertainment. The cinema had been increasingly familiar in Britain since before the turn of the century, but its real popularity is a phenomenon of the 1920s. (Feather, 1988: 196)

Cinema alone represented a huge threat to the monopoly of the book as an affordable means of entertainment – but cinema combined with radio, and later television, offered entertainment and educational value that threatened to wipe out the book trade completely. Feather notes that in 1926 (when the BBC was first established), 2 million radio licences were issued; this had increased to over 9 million by 1939 (Feather, 1988: 196); McKibbin points out (1998: 456) that this meant around two-thirds of working-class households had a licence. Dewey notes that cinema attendances grew from 400 million seats filled per year in 1913, to 987 million by 1938 (with 23 million attendances per week) (Dewey, 1997: 184).

Cinema and radio were, undeniably, phenomenally popular. But the printed word survived too, perhaps principally because of the relatively stable economic climate. McKibbin quotes a survey of adolescents which found that 'listening in' to the radio was in fact one of the *least* favourite ways of spending an evening, with only 5.5 per cent saying that was how they had spent the previous evening (unfortunately it is not recorded how many said they had spent the evening reading) (McKibbin, 1998: 457).

With rising standards of living and increasing leisure time, more activities were available to more people – more people had money to spend on books as well as other forms of entertainment. (In 1925, 1.5 million manual workers had paid holidays; by 1937 this had risen to 4 million (Dewey, 1997: 195–6).) This huge increase in the market works reciprocally with the development of alternative forms of leisure activity: as more consumers began to spend, so producers (film-makers, cinema owners, the BBC, publishers) had more to invest in producing more for them to consume. In purely economic terms this period saw the emergence of a new mass market, which was served by various forms of mass production – forms of entertainment designed to appeal to the mass of the population. Books still had a place in this new market, but it was no longer a dominant place, as they shared space with other emergent forms of entertainment.

In the 1920s and 1930s, newspapers, magazines and comics, rather than books, were the main source of reading matter and popular fiction for the majority of the population. According to Dewey, by 1939, 69 per cent of the population over 16 read a daily national newspaper, whilst 82 per cent claimed to read a Sunday paper (Dewey, 1997: 190). The under-16s were also well served by this form of mass-market publishing. Alfred Harmsworth's Amalgamated Press had begun to exploit the emergent children's market at the turn of the century, having noted that halfpenny papers ostensibly aimed at adults actually had a large following among children. Beginning with weekly companion papers, like *Halfpenny Marvel* (launched in 1893) and *Boys' Friend* (1895), which were 'allegedly invented in an idealistic attempt to debunk and destroy the morally vile and pernicious penny dreadfuls' (Drotner, 1988: 126), Harmsworth built a fictional world for his readers in which imperialist values were paramount, and strongly British heroes always won out over faintly ridiculous foreign foes. His papers for girls, *Girls' Friend* (1899), *Girls' Home* (1910) and *Girls' Reader* (1908), followed similarly closely structured moral patterns. From the success of the companion papers, Harmsworth was able to develop the single-genre story paper, focusing on detective stories and school stories, the most popular of which were *The Gem* (1907) and *The Magnet* (1908).

After the war, the Amalgamated Press extended its monopoly of the children's periodical market by producing a further range of school story papers for girls (*School Friend* (1919), *Schoolgirls' Own* (1921) and *Schoolgirls' Weekly* (1922) – all of which proved very popular with girls, as shown in Tables A.7 and A.8 in the Appendix). The entry of the D. C. Thomson company into what had hitherto been a stable story paper market, however, represented a major restructuring of the field. Not only did Thomson destroy the Harmsworth monopoly, but his innovations reshaped the way story papers were written and produced. As Joseph McAleer points out, two schools of thought influenced the expanding market for popular fiction – the 'improving', optimistic school, which grew out of Victorian liberalism, and the commercial, entrepreneurial school, which sought to exploit a major new sales opportunity (McAleer, 1992: 12). Both Harmsworth and Thomson operated a combination of the two, but Thomson's approach, favouring the more solidly commercial, proved more successful.

This commercial, potentially exploitative style worried contemporary commentators. Kathleen Box conducted a survey of children's reading habits in Fulham in 1940 and comments that 'the weekly papers must have an enormous influence in forming opinion and determining the shape(s) of wish-pictures and symbols in people's minds' (McAleer, 1992: 7). This is echoed by George Orwell, who saw the magazines as a 'form of social control' (McAleer, 1992: 4), presenting an unquestioned middle-class right-wing world-view. A key question here is how far it is possible to tell the real motivations of the magazine publishers – was pure commercialism more important than the paternalistic, 'moral guardian' role which the magazines assumed for themselves? Alfred Harmsworth's editorial directives in particular show how seriously he took the role of developing children's moral attitudes, aiming for

> the cultivation of physical fitness in the young, the encouragement of adventure abroad and enterprise at home. In all [the stories] the bugle call of patriotism was loudly sounded, pride in Great Britain and the empire. (McAleer, 1992: 37)

It seems reasonable to infer from this that for Harmsworth the patriarchal role was at least as important as commercial considerations – that he was concerned rather more with attempting to inculcate particular attitudes than with the meanings that children *actually* took from their reading. The 'editor's chat' page, a Harmsworth innovation, is another example of this. As Carpenter points out, the editor has a crucial function as a mediator between reader and publisher: as the reader's friend, the editor can act as both paternal adviser and publisher's mouthpiece. Moral guidance is thus combined with adverts for other Harmsworth publications, and 'repeated exhortations to readers to win new converts' (Carpenter, 1983: 52).

Whilst it is easy to see that D. C. Thomson magazines carried similar sets of values, it is also clear that the company was more driven by straightforward commercial interests. Thomson himself seems to have been much more concerned about the opinions of his readers. His overtly market-orientated approach is described by McAleer as 'a reciprocal one governed by commercial considerations; the changing tastes of the reader were carefully monitored and accommodated within certain moral boundaries' (McAleer, 1992: 245). Interestingly, too, Thomson sent out representatives to canvass readers' opinions directly – largely by waiting at school gates to question children as they came out. The representatives' monthly reports were fed back to editors and writers, who were able to keep storylines as up-to-the-minute as possible. Commentators have noted that this reciprocal process means that we can, to a certain extent, see the story papers as 'a useful barometer of the tastes, ideals and aspirations of [their] readers' (McAleer, 1992: 9). However, these are tastes, ideals and aspirations heavily influenced by editorial style. While key influences in this reciprocal argument can be picked out, it is not possible to say for sure that the magazines were the main source for children of information about the ways of the world, or vice versa. Moreover, it is not simply a two-way relationship in this case. In order for the magazines to reach their intended audience, they had first to be acceptable to parents. In McAleer's view, the magazines cannot be a wholly accurate reflection of children's taste, 'because of the degree of parental supervision in the choice of reading matter' (McAleer, 1992: 252). Undoubtedly, some parents will have taken more of a role in influencing children's choice than others, but from the publishers' point of view the parents' opinions must have been an important consideration. With this in mind, D. C. Thomson 'carefully screened all contents of its papers for boys, for fear that a parent might object and ban them from the house' (McAleer, 1992: 145).

This research work points to a shrewd commercialism on the part of the publishers, but publishing ventures are only successful so long as they do not lose sight of their readers. Evidence suggests that the Thomson style was a genuine attempt to be reciprocal, and the company sales figures confirm the status of Thomson story papers as bestsellers in the inter-war years. In 1924, the total sales of Amalgamated Press's *Union Jack* series (including *Union Jack, Marvel, The Magnet* and *The Gem*) were 354,694 copies; D. C. Thomson managed to achieve sales of 380,000 copies on the launch issue of *Rover* in 1922, and 560,000 on the first issue of *Wizard*, also launched that same year. Thomson's determination to commercialise magazine production clearly has something to do with his success, but, in McAleer's view, his success lay in his break with tradition:

> [D. C. Thomson's] secret involved a combination of creativity, spontaneity and imagination which took boys out of the traditional school-story setting, confronting them with all sorts of adventures and inventions ... The Big 5 papers offered young readers a whole new kind of weekly magazine: bright, varied and personal. (McAleer, 1992: 167, 245)

What is interesting here is that this was a huge publishing risk. The Amalgamated Press story papers had been enormously influential, and Thomson could have reasoned that more of the same would be a prudent strategy, with every chance of success. That he chose to risk launching a completely new kind of magazine shows that the company had not only invested in effective market research, but that the writers had a well-developed understanding of the lives of their readers, and were able to draw on current themes and influences – the cinema, the radio, the general topics of conversation amongst children at home and at school.

This change in content is crucial to the growth and popularity of the story paper genre, and in the chapters which follow we will look in more detail at how this affected readers and their meaning-making. Did readers simply reject other forms and styles of storytelling in favour of the innovative and up-to-date? What really informed their choices of reading matter?

Consumers

The scale of production of story papers and magazines for boys and girls shows that there was a large and ready market for this kind of publication, and we have already seen that the massive expansion of popular literature offended many. George Orwell criticised the popularity of boys' weeklies in particular, disturbed by the 'unbelievable' quantity and variety of magazines, and their 'unrealistic, over-optimistic world view' (Orwell, 1962: 175). From the publishers' point of view, in sales terms, the genre was an overwhelming success. But did children actually *read* them? What was it they enjoyed about reading magazines? Were they enjoying magazines more than books? And how can we really know what meanings and values they were taking from their reading? Finding answers to questions about children's lives is not easy, as evidence is sparse. There is, however, some statistical evidence on children's reading preferences at the time. A survey of children's leisure activities in St Pancras, published in 1933, showed that

> half of all pupils between the ages of 11 and 15 read upwards of 3 comics or storypapers per week, while a third of these children managed 6 or more issues during that time. (Drotner, 1998: 190)

Jenkinson's 1938 survey of children's out-of-school reading habits confirmed these findings, underlining the fact that story papers and comics were the most popular form of reading matter, that boys read more weeklies than girls, and that at the age of 12, on average, boys would read 3.7–4.2 comics or magazines per month, and girls 2.0–2.7 (Jenkinson, 1940: 64, 211). In Jenkinson's survey, boys preferred D. C. Thomson magazines – *Rover, Hotspur* and *Wizard* – whilst girls preferred *Schoolgirls' Own, Schoolgirls' Weekly* and *Girls' Crystal*. *The Hotspur* in particular is popular, coming second only to its sister paper *The Wizard* in most groups (see Appendix). Amongst the secondary school boys questioned, both *The Hotspur* and *The Magnet* were popular with 12-year-olds, with 47 per cent having read *The Hotspur*. In the senior schools, over 50 per cent of boys said they had read *The Hotspur* during the period under study, in all three of the year groups. *The Magnet* features in the list for all age groups, but is consistently placed lower in popularity than each of the 'big five', with the exception of 15-year-old secondary school boys. As Jenkinson himself says, these figures are in a way slightly misleading, as they only record the different titles mentioned, not the number of those titles read (so although a boy might have read five issues of *The Hotspur* in the period, it would still only count as one in the table). There is nevertheless a notable difference in reading rates between secondary and senior school boys, with a distinct downturn in numbers of papers read by secondary school boys at age 15; while the monthly reading rate for senior school boys remains fairly steady at four story papers read, by age 15 secondary school boys record only 0.8 copies per month. Jenkinson attributes this to the fact that boys at this age have correspondingly less leisure time due to the pressures of school examinations.

Although publishers at the time tended to divide their audience – and their output – along clearly demarcated lines according to gender, readers themselves were not so prepared to fit into neatly defined categories. Jenkinson's survey shows the popularity of boys' story papers amongst girl readers at all ages. At age 14+ two boys' story papers (*The Wizard* and *The Rover*, two of the D. C. Thomson 'big five') are read by more than one girl in five (see Appendix), and *The Hotspur* and *The Magnet* also feature in the girls' lists. This act of 'cross-gendering' is not reciprocated, however, with boys very rarely recording that they had read girls' story papers. Jenkinson points out that the boys' papers make no attempt to appeal directly to girls, and wonders if the underlying reason for girls' choice of boys' stories might be 'a strong, if subsidiary, desire to be boys' (Jenkinson, 1940: 217). The real reason might be somewhat more straightforward: as Dorothy Burnham notes, she never read girls' stories, as she 'found them insipid and meaningless', preferring to identify instead with more subversive characters from *The Magnet*, such as Vernon Smith, 'who smoked, gambled and even split an infinitive or two' (Burnham, quoted by Rose, 2001: 379). The perceived lack of inspiring role models in the girls' papers might also stem from the fact that they were almost exclusively written by men, under female pseudonyms.

Sarah Mahurter's survey of adults' memories of their childhood reading focuses mainly on books, but her respondents do recall reading and enjoying a range of comics including *Girl's Own Paper*, *School Friend* and *School Girl* (Mahurter, 1999). McAleer also notes that each magazine was commonly shared between groups of friends, estimating that Thomson story papers were each read by between 60,000 and 1,500,000 children in the inter-war years. Jenkinson's survey also highlights the scale of this practice, although he notes it was much more widespread amongst boys than girls: 'The girls who answered this questionnaire did not once mention hand-to-hand trading of "bloods" amongst themselves, whereas the boys frequently mentioned it' (Jenkinson, 1940: 213). Anecdotal evidence of this comes from published autobiographies. Drotner quotes Jim Wolveridge, who describes growing up in Stepney in the 1930s:

> I would buy a copy of *Bullseye*, and when I'd finished reading it I would swap with Abie Roberts for a copy of the *Wizard*, and after finishing that I would swap it with Robbie Hope for a copy of the *Magnet*. In this way I could read at least 50 books. (Drotner, 1988: 189)

Similarly, Paul West was a fan of the 'big five', and 'took *The Wizard* and *The Hotspur*, swapping with friends to get the others' (West, 1963: 79). Robert Roberts describes how he and his friends were 'addicted' to Frank Richards's school stories:

> I knew boys so avid for current numbers of the *Magnet* and *Gem* that they would trek on a weekday to the city railway station to catch the bulk arrival from London and buy first copies from the bookstall. (Roberts, 1973: 160)

As Drotner points out, there is in fact a distinct lack of recorded social and cultural detail of children's lives from the inter-war period, as from other periods:

> Not only are juveniles in our society without any direct economic, social or political significance, making them poor objects of serious

analysis or academically influential investigation, but they have also left few permanent traces of their lives and thoughts. Children and adolescents have been either illiterate and too busy working for sheer survival to care about posterity, or if they have not been labourers, they have lived individual existences in economic dependence and social subjugation to their parents and to society in general. (Drotner, 1988: 11)

Moreover, those accounts we do have are in the main only from children at the upper end of the social scale, or are actually written by adults, mostly men, as is the case with the accounts quoted above. Equally, the survey material that exists must be seen in context – how were the children who took part selected? Did the style of interview affect the responses that they gave? A Mass-Observation survey of 13–16-year-olds in Middlesbrough in 1937 asked children to write an essay entitled 'Why I read books'. In this case it is difficult to believe that they would all have given honest and spontaneous opinions; it seems likely that at least some would have been tempted to write what they thought was expected of them. Their answers read as a mixture of wanting to tell the truth and wanting to say the right thing (and it is interesting to note how many of the respondents interpreted the word 'books' as meaning story papers):

The books about adventure have more grip than books about love, but I read them to increase my vocabulary and for the spelling of the words.

I get much pleasure in reading books better known as twopenny bloods. I also read books in order to gain knowledge.

Most boys enjoy reading twopenny books because of the exciting tales. Of course I am one of these kind. (Mass-Observation Archive, TC Reading Habits 1937–47, 20/1/B: 'Why I read books', children aged 13–16 in Middlesbrough area, September 1937; quotations from A. Hoyland, Malcolm Race and John Barker respectively)

This survey does not record the class status of its child respondents, though from the mention of school forms 'upper 4A' and 'lower 4B' we can infer that at least some of them were secondary school pupils. Jenkinson's data cover both secondary and senior school children, and can therefore be seen as representing a sample of lower-middle- and working-class readers. That the story papers were in the main aimed at such a wide audience is not in doubt – as Richards himself said, 'every paper desiring a wide circulation must circulate, for the greater part, among the working classes, for the simple reason that they form nine-tenths of the population' (Richards, 1968 [online]). The data, however, show that amongst both boys and girls the story paper reading habit transcended both class and educational ability lines, being as prevalent in senior schools as in secondary schools, especially at age 12+.

The chapters which follow focus on themes and styles in the story papers, and show how they change and develop in the inter-war years. By focusing on editorial input in the story papers, story content, and children's reactions wherever possible – through children's own letters to the story papers as well as through other published accounts – the aim is to approach a sense of children's experience of reading, the lived reality of the time, and the ways in which ideologies were developed and sustained.

Summary and conclusions

This chapter has outlined a range of critical, theoretical and historical perspectives which will be used in the later chapters of this book as a background for the explorations of the story papers, their contexts and content. The interlinked nature of all of the theoretical approaches outlined above seems to lead eventually back to Williams and the notion of selectivity. Selectivity is inescapable, but what is important is to be aware of the process and its effects. For the purposes of this book, there are elements of all of the theories outlined above which will be useful: mass culture theory, as representing the dominant cultural theory of the period; Williams's explanations of selectivity and structures of feeling in approaching an interpretation of the cultural experience of the time; the new historicists' insistence on drawing from a broad range of sources to illustrate power relations, and cultural materialism's linking of historical study with contemporary values in underlining that our own present cultural baggage inevitably influences our views of historical periods. I make no apology for the selectivity of my approach, nor for the exclusion of other possible interpretations and meanings – as Williams points out, the selective process is 'evident in every field of activity' (Williams, 1961: 50). What this book will try to do, then, is to make a range of inferences from the available evidence, which is understandably limited in terms of the written record left to us by the children of the period (as children, and later, as adults). It will use the selected theories in order to construct an interpretation and revaluation of a selected historical culture, focusing on a range of selected key texts (and not forgetting that the whole is situated in contemporary, left-leaning, middle-class academic values).

2
The Moral Code of Inter-War Story Papers

Story paper worlds may have their fair share of crime, dishonesty, bad behaviour and violence, but ultimately the characters in them only find success through conforming to profoundly moral standards. But what does that moral code look like in the story papers? How do its various strands function in the stories, and how did publishers and authors seek to frame moral meanings in the narratives? Most importantly, how did child readers interpret these moral framings? Are readers simply 'absorbing a set of beliefs' (Orwell, 1962: 200), or is there any space for subversion? By exploring the perspectives of consumers and producers, this chapter analyses the patterns of relationship which develop, and looks in more detail at the ideologies embedded in the story narratives.

Theorising moral codes

Alfred Harmsworth's publicly stated aim for his story papers for children was to counter the 'vile' effects of the penny dreadful. As Cadogan and Craig write,

> Always imbued with a crusading sense of responsibility for the moral social values of his readers, Northcliffe realised the efficacy of fiction as a means of influencing young minds. (Cadogan and Craig, 1976: 127)

This apparently very worthy motivation conceals a number of assumptions. The first is an unquestioned certainty that children's reading matter has a direct effect on their character and behaviour; that this influence can be detrimental is as confidently asserted as the notion that a different, or 'better', selection of reading matter would have an 'improving' effect. Secondly, there is a corresponding assumption that it is the publisher's role to take responsibility for children's moral development. Clearly these attitudes are rooted in the Victorian emphasis on didacticism in children's literature, the notion of stories for instruction rather than entertainment. Harmsworth's moral 'crusade' grows directly from this assumption, and from the conviction that if children enjoyed and were entertained by their reading, its moral influence could be even stronger. This is mass culture theory with a twist – while it is unlikely that Harmsworth would have argued that his story papers represented the best writing for children, he clearly signalled their worth above the 'blood and thunder' penny magazines by virtue of their higher moral status.

The third assumption implicit in Cadogan and Craig's description of Harmsworth's method is that this sense of moral responsibility outranks all other considerations, including economics. Focusing on content (and in particular on the content of story papers for girls), Cadogan and Craig make no mention of Harmsworth's role as a producer of commodities for children. That Harmsworth was a shrewd businessman with a sound knowledge of his market is obvious from his success in developing a new kind of journalism for adults in the *Daily Mail* (launched 1896) and the *Daily Mirror* (launched 1903). These publications made no attempt at moral crusade, rather they were the result of the relentless pursuit of mass circulation and huge daily sales figures. It is important not to lose sight of this: Harmsworth may well have had genuinely moral intentions, but these must always be seen in their commercial context. Harmsworth wanted to maximise his circulation figures – in any case, had the story papers not found a market, they could hardly have exercised any moral influence. As Claudia Nelson points out, children's story papers, and the Harmsworth papers in particular, 'are simultaneously "moral" and commercial, mingling the impulse to improve with the impulse to profit' (Nelson, 1997: 15). It could be argued that the moral background of the story papers was simply another way of securing circulation – Harmsworth could have assumed that to establish clear moral values was an important way of securing parental support, a crucial element in the successful management of producer/consumer relationships in publishing for children. This combination of morality and commercialism, the balancing of impulses between education and entertainment, grows out of both a shrewd business sense and deeply felt personal values on Harmsworth's part.

The general response to story papers in the 1920s and 1930s, as we have seen in the Introduction, was largely critical – at least amongst the adult population. Mass culture theorists declined the apportioning of any value to published writing other than the 'classic', and Harmsworth himself seems to have approached the story paper genre mainly in reaction to his distaste for the 'penny dreadful'. Orwell's stance is rather different, in that his criticism is not directed against the genre per se, nor in particular at the quality of the writing. On the one hand, he acknowledges the story papers' moral foundations: 'It ought to be emphasized that on its level the moral code of the English boys' papers is a decent one' (Orwell, 1962: 194). On the other, he is deeply critical of what he sees as the outmoded ideology of the stories. In his view, the key problem is the failure of the story papers to take account of contemporary politics – fossilised in the imperial ethos of the turn of the century, the moral code can only be partially successful in that it fails to present a realistic and balanced world-view: 'the clock has stopped at 1910, Britannia rules the waves, and no-one has heard of slumps, booms, unemployment, dictatorships, purges or concentration camps' (Orwell, 1962: 197).

As with the Cadogan and Craig quotation above, there are a number of assumptions here. Orwell is similarly unquestioning of the role of the author/publisher as moral guardian. He has also assumed a homogeneous child audience which mutely receives meaning from stories as intended by the authors and publishers. There is no space in Orwell's critical model for child readers to make and take meanings from stories for themselves. Nor is there any sense that children's understanding of the world might be constructed from a range of sources, including their reading – again, the assumption is that ideologies embodied within the story papers were simply swallowed whole. Written in 1940, this essay shows evidence of the dominant critical approaches of the time, which assumed the existence of relatively simplistic relations between producers and consumers. With the benefit of the later work of the reader response theorists, it is possible to question these assumptions, using a critical approach which posits meaning-making as an interaction between text and reader (see Iser, in Lodge and Wood, 2000; Holub, 1984). Orwell's interaction with story paper narratives does not necessarily produce the same meanings as a child-story interaction might, and authors' intended meanings can be interpreted in a multiplicity of ways by individual readers.

Orwell also seems to imply an assumption that story papers were consumed by their readers to the exclusion of all other reading matter. Jenkinson's 1938 survey would seem to prove exactly the opposite, offering evidence that boys (and girls) in the 11–15 age-group read widely, including classics as well as popular fiction in their choices (see Chapter 3 for further discussion of this point; Jenkinson's data on reading choices are reproduced in the Appendix). Jonathan Rose has also argued that reading habits amongst certain sections of the working classes in the 1920s and 1930s were eclectic and limited only by access to libraries rather than personal choice. (It should be noted here that Rose's study is based on autobiographical material, a large proportion of which was produced by skilled workers – it should therefore not be assumed that his conclusions will necessarily apply across the working class as a whole.) Rose argues that readers' responses should not be inferred by studying only the texts themselves:

> Can we understand the impact of a particular work or genre in isolation without considering all the intertextual influences at play? If not, then we must make some attempt to reconstruct the entire literary diet of the audience. (Rose, 2001: 367)

Each reader has his/her own literary background, informed by social, familial and educational influences. Following this formulation, meanings are constructed in context, and one text can be the source of many meanings. Rose uses Erving Goffman's concept of the 'frame' to explore this process – that is, 'the basic frameworks of understanding available in our society for making sense out of events' (2001: 6). In Rose's view, readers generally follow certain rules of interpretation, which vary from reader to reader and from situation to situation:

> Readers can adopt any frame they choose, provided it produces some kind of meaningful reading, and provided the readers have learned the rules laid down by the frame. (Rose, 2001: 7)

The basis of this argument is very similar to Bourdieu's concepts of habitus and field (see Bourdieu, 1993; Grenfell and James, 1998; see also Chapter 6 for more detailed analysis of Bourdieu's concepts, and their relation to the story paper context). Both concepts allow readers their own space for meaning-making, giving them a sense of agency in the author–text–reader interaction. Here readers choose to adopt a frame/ enter a field, and the ways in which they interact within that space are shaped by both habitus and the rules of the frame/game. The concept of the frame, or field, also accounts for readers' ability to contextualise texts in different ways. As Rose writes:

> whether a text is 'conservative' or 'subversive' depends on the context in which it is read and the larger literary diet of the reader. The

same reader can enjoy Karl Marx and Frank Richards in separate compartments, bringing a different frame to each ... It is equally possible for the same reader to adopt different frames for the same story, relishing it on one level while seeing through the claptrap on another. (Rose, 2001: 332)

Applying this to the context of the inter-war story papers, the reader/text interaction appears to be far more complex than Orwell and the story paper producers assumed. Orwell's criticisms of the 'fossilised' ideologies of the stories may well have some truth, but direct transmission of ideology to readers cannot be straightforwardly demonstrated.

Hollindale posits ideology as a fluid construct with three operational levels:

- 'explicit': a conscious and deliberate level of 'intended surface ideology';
- 'unexamined or passive': a level at which values are unconsciously taken for granted by the writer; and
- 'the world an author lives in': the codes and rule-systems which represent the 'commonalities of an age'. (Hollindale, 1988: 12–15)

These are not intended as discrete levels of a taxonomy, but rather as interconnecting circles of influence where the explicit ideology of level one is informed by and grows out of the second and third levels. Explicit ideologies are an integral part of children's literature, which for the most part has an intended didactic function. This 'impulse to improve' is very evident in the stories in both *The Magnet* and *The Hotspur*, as the examples analysed later in this chapter will show. However, in order to demonstrate the omnipresence of ideologies at all three levels, and the integrated functioning of conscious/unconscious ideological influences, it is necessary also to analyse the author–text–reader relationship, investigating the ways in which the reading subject interacts with the text, and subject positionings in relation to that text. John Stephens links Hollindale's second level of ideology to Iser's concept of the implied reader, arguing that the notion of the implied reader distracts attention from the operations of ideology within texts (Stephens, 1992: 10). Stephens argues that a text creates a subject position for the reader, opening a space in which the reader interacts with the text's ideological messages, both explicit and implicit. This is a much more fluid and open-ended relationship than the more fixed implied author/implied reader construct which tends to function mainly at the explicit and conscious level. In Stephens's model,

> a key part of the outworking of ideology is ... the situating of readers, who, in taking up a position from which the text is most readily intelligible, are apt to be situated within the frame of the text's ideology; that is, they are subjected to and by that ideology. (Stephens, 1992: 67)

This subject-positioning process is effected by inviting readers to identify with key focalising characters. Readers who take up positions of more total identification with characters are at a greater level of openness to ideological manipulation; at the other end of the scale, however, critical positionings are possible within this formulation. Stephens posits distancing strategies either within the text or brought to the text by the reader – and these would include features and strategies such as intertextuality, multi-stranded narration and shifts in focaliser:

> Distancing strategies ... encourage the constitution of a reading self in relation to the other constituted in and by the text. This alternative process does not guarantee freedom from conditioning, since a position separate from the focaliser may well merely represent the ideological position of the narrator. (Stephens, 1992: 69)

The process of subject positioning can itself operate at conscious and unconscious levels, and this in turn has an effect on the reader's openness to and interaction with the ideological functioning of the text. Distancing strategies may encourage consciously critical interactions, but these exchanges, as Stephens points out above, are largely at the level of explicit ideologies. Decoding the 'unexamined' or 'passive' ideological framings infused through the text demands critical skills which child readers do not often possess. It is at this level that texts can be most ideologically manipulative.

Hollindale's third level of ideology focuses on the position of the writer in relation to 'the commonalities of an age' (Hollindale, 1988: 15). This connects directly with what Williams calls 'the dominant social character' (Williams, 1961: 126), and is a concept worth exploring in more detail in the context of the story papers. As we have seen in the Introduction, the dominant view of publishing for children in the 1920s and 1930s was firmly on the side of the mass culture theorists – very much in favour of stemming the flood of 'terrible trash' and of giving children the 'better' literature they deserved. Behind Harmsworth's attempts to provide something 'better' is perhaps something more fundamental than merely following the dominant moral ideology. The dominant social character is more than just a common ideological world-view, it is the result of a hegemonic process through which the dominant ideologies become accepted as 'natural' or 'commonsense'. As Williams puts it:

> [Hegemony] sees the relations of domination and subordination, in their forms as practical consciousness, as in effect a saturation of the whole process of living – not only of political and economic activity ... but of the whole substance of lived identities and relationships, to such a depth that the pressures and limits of what can ultimately be seen as a specific economic, political and cultural system seem to most of us the pressures and limits of simple experience and common sense. (Williams, 1977: 110)

Following this formulation it becomes possible to argue that Harmsworth's publications, and the other popular magazines of the period, carried a strict moral code because the pressures and limits of the dominant social character made it impossible to conceptualise an alternative mode of presentation. The power of the 'common sense' view had taken over. In William's concept, hegemony constitutes 'a sense of reality for most people in society ... beyond which it is very difficult for most members of the society to move' (Williams, 1977: 110). Even if it were possible for publishers to stand outside the hegemonic process, their publishing decisions would still necessarily be influenced by it, in that they publish for a mass audience who are still very much on the inside.

This argument can also offer an explanation for the seemingly infinite recyclability of the stories in the popular story papers. Whilst key characters and settings remain unchanged – the boys and girls never grow older – plots and storylines recur and are reworked from every conceivable angle. Accepting the notion of lived hegemony as a process which is constantly being 'renewed, recreated, defended and modified' (Williams, 1977: 112), it then becomes possible to apply this to the world of the story papers. As one generation of readers grows up, and grows out of this level of reading matter, so another grows *into* story paper reading. The re-used storylines reinforce the commonsense moral message, and the cycle continues.

So how do the ideological levels of the moral code of the story papers work in practice? How do the authors use these to shape stories and characters, and to build credible fictional worlds for their readers? The following sections will explore this in more detail, using story examples from *The Magnet* from 1934 and 1936–37, and from *The Hotspur* editions of 1936 and 1939.

The moral background of Greyfriars

The 28 November 1936 issue of *The Magnet* presents the first of a series of stories featuring Valentine Compton, 'the schoolboy smuggler' – a series which was to run over eight full issues, up to 16 January 1937. Compton, a recent recruit to the school, has impressed the boys and the staff with his sporting prowess as well as his impeccable character and behaviour. Richards takes great pains to portray Compton as a thoroughly decent chap – he is described as 'athletic' and 'handsome' at every opportunity, and is by some way the most popular person in school:

> Everybody seems to like and admire that new man in the Fifth. Sixth form prefects asked him into the prefects-room; Blundell and Co. made no end of fuss of him ...; juniors looked up to him with tremendous respect; even scrubby little fags in the Third told one another what a splendid chap 'that man Compton' was! And with all of it there was no 'swank' about him. ('Contraband!', *The Magnet*, 28 November 1936: 16)

Compton's status as a paragon of virtue and central hero-figure is heavily underlined, and Richards then uses him as a pivot around which to build a number of moral dilemmas – for Compton himself and for the other characters. Richards allows his readers to witness Compton both breaking school rules (when his smuggling activities take him out of bounds), and being party to a smuggling racket, yet invites readers to see him as completely untarnished. When Herbert Vernon-Smith voices his suspicions of Compton, none of the other boys will believe him – finding it impossible to countenance the fact that a 'splendid chap' might be involved in underhand dealings. This constant reinforcement of Compton's good character serves a number of purposes – as a narrative tool, encouraging readers to speculate on the real reasons behind Compton's behaviour; as a contrast to the behaviour of Carne, the real villain of the piece; and as a means of emphasising the moral code of the school. This code values friendship above all – the breaking of school rules counts as nothing if the safety or honour of a friend is at stake, and acting selflessly in order to protect another is the purest act of friendship. Compton's selflessness is clearly drawn, in particular in his standing up for Bunter who is being bullied by Carne (a senior prefect whose authority should be unquestioned according to school rules). This is in stark contrast to the selfishness of Carne, whose every act is motivated by self-pity. Added tension is created here as it is Compton's arrival and acceptance into the First Eleven football team which has sparked Carne's anger – he has as a direct result lost his own place in the team. All of the characters conform to this moral code – when Carne locks Compton in a secret passageway intending him to be caught out of bounds, Harry Wharton unbolts the door, putting himself at risk rather than see Carne's selfish behaviour rewarded. Similarly, Vernon-Smith (also known as 'the Bounder') keeps his suspicions of Compton's smuggling activities largely to himself, reasoning that:

> outside Greyfriars he [Compton] could do as he liked, and Smithy would not care two straws. Inside Greyfriars was another matter. That was over the limit, in the Bounder's opinion, and he would put 'paid' to it if he could. ('Contraband!', *The Magnet*, 28 November 1936: 16)

The school code operates in parallel with a separate boys' code, and a strict hierarchy of values exists within each. Punishment for breaking either code also works on a hierarchical system. Breaking the school code results in a kind of 'off-stage' retribution, with the threat of lines or other sanctions which are rarely invoked in practice. A breach of the boys' code, however, leads to swift, and often violent, retribution or revenge. In this particular story sequence, the worst punishment (being shamed in front of the whole school) is reserved for Carne. His unsporting behaviour towards Compton results in his being shunned and hissed at by even the lowly second formers, and his own sense of shame is palpable:

> Carne did not speak. He could not. His feelings were too deep for words. Even when he had told himself that he had crocked his football rival, and got back the place that belonged to him, he had felt remorse and shame for what he had done. Now he learned that even that miserable satisfaction was denied him. He had lowered himself in his own eyes, exposed himself to the scorn of a fellow like Loder – and all for nothing ... He had failed – worse than failed: he had been a scoundrel for nothing – nothing at all! ('The Boy with an Enemy', *The Magnet*, 5 December 1936: 16)

Carne's cowardliness is a worse crime in this world than Compton's involvement in smuggling. Carne offends against the team spirit, against the rules of comradeship, and the boys close ranks against him. Moral ideologies are represented at a very explicit level, through the focalising characters' actions and emotions, but the setting and ethos of the story are also imbued with an unquestioning (and unquestioned) ideological world-view. The text invites a dual subject positioning, allowing readers to identify with Carne's sense of shame, and/or with the schoolboy witnesses of that shame. The portrayal of Carne's own shame is important – the depiction of Carne's remorse enables Richards both to underline the moral code (and the seriousness of adhering to it) and to set up a possible further storyline whereby Carne can work to redeem himself in the eyes of his fellow pupils. Carne can learn from his mistakes and move on, his character reinvigorated. This is renewal and recreation of the code effectively done, reinforcing messages for readers at different levels of engagement. As with most of the stories in *The Magnet*, what is interesting here is the way in which, from a twenty-first-century viewpoint, the interconnected functioning of all three of Hollindale's ideological levels can be readily discerned. From the dominant social character of the school as institution, and the nature of emergent masculinities within it, through the passive ideologies of the power of the Empire and white Western superiority, to the explicit behaviour codes of Greyfriars, the structured network of ideological meanings acts to scaffold meaning-making for readers at both conscious and unconscious levels. (See Chapter 3 for further exploration of school as institution, and Chapter 4 for a more detailed investigation of empire and the construction of masculinities.)

Compton, by contrast, escapes punishment because his crime is entirely selfless. Compton's uncle has brought him up as his own after Compton's father disappeared in the Amazon jungle. Compton therefore helps his uncle in the smuggling racket because he owes him a debt of gratitude, and feels honour-bound to stand by him. Comradeship, again, is more powerful than any sense of the legality of what they are doing – although Richards, writing at a straightforwardly didactic level, does manage to include an interesting philosophical discussion between Compton and his uncle on the nature of justice:

> 'A man ought to stand for the law!' went on the schoolboy. 'So long as human nature's imperfect, some laws will always be unjust. Do you think a farmer ought to be allowed to shoot the tithe collector, because he's convinced that the tithe laws are unjust? We've got to

take the rough with the smooth, and play up according to rules!' ... You made me think as you do; but ... you're wrong,' said Compton. 'You can call smuggling free trade if you like, but if others have to pay the tariff, and you don't, you get a mean advantage over them. That's where your profit comes in, in fact. It's rotten and mean! It's not playing the game!' ('The Way of the Transgressor!', *The Magnet*, 12 December 1936: 23)

It eventually emerges that Captain Compton is himself being blackmailed by one of his own gang, so both characters are able to retain their hero status; they may have done wrong, but betrayal by one of their own cancels out their crime. Compton's dilemma is therefore solved through an explicit plot twist, constructed by Richards in order to close off the space for doubt and minimise the risk of subversive interpretations by readers.

The character of Billy Bunter is an interesting anomaly in this world of codes and rules. Although he seemingly operates according to his own rules, in which food is the single most important motivating factor, Bunter is in fact yet another means of reinforcing the dominant code. Bunter's crimes may be petty – stealing other boys' tuck, putting glue in inkwells, telling tales – but he is *always* punished for them. Also, he is never allowed fully to be part of the social circle of his peers, but is constantly teased and ridiculed for his failure to conform both in body and in character. Beneath all of Bunter's quirks is plain selfishness, and it is only when he finally manages a selfless act (helping Compton when he is in danger of falling off a cliff) that he is allowed any real reward – again in the form of comradeship and food.

Joseph Bristow writes that much of the narrative pleasure in school stories, and in fictional narrative in general, comes from transgression, and in particular the way in which transgression and conformity are defined against each other (Bristow, 1991: 60). This is nowhere more evident than in the case of Billy Bunter, whose many and repeated transgressions function as comic counterpoint to the Famous Five, underlining their fundamentally moral behaviour. He also functions as a key narrative tool, in that his disregard of school rules often puts him in forbidden spaces (skulking in other boys' studies, for example, stealing food), where he is able to eavesdrop, or spot irregular 'goings on'. His passing on of rumour and gossip and letting slip key points of information serve to drive plotlines forward by destabilising the moral equilibrium and causing problems for other characters. Orwell describes him as a 'really first class character' (Orwell, 1962: 177), citing him as a key reason for the enormous popularity of *The Magnet*. Jeffrey Richards is also a fan:

> He is a sacred monster like Alf Garnett, a larger-than-life embodiment of human failings, weaknesses and prejudices. His regular chastisement by beating, booting, bouncing, detention, suspension and exclusion confirms the need to check these weaknesses, to mortify the flesh and purify the spirit. The fact that he survives to offend again testifies to the enduring strength of human frailty and the undying need for vigilance in the maintenance of the code as a bulwark against it. (Richards, 1988: 272)

The fact that Bunter survives to offend again in fact testifies to much more than that. Bunter represents a distancing strategy: readers are invited to identify not with Bunter himself, but with the classmates who both observe and ridicule him. His continuing survival points to the deliberate structuring of the stories to highlight moral resolutions – Bunter is shown to be punished, but only in a minimal way so that he can return to perform his anti-hero role in the next story. (Under school rules, most of his behaviour would ordinarily result in expulsion.) It also points to the fact that Richards and Harmsworth recognised Bunter's wide popularity. Bunter quite literally carries the comic weight of the stories, and it is debatable how many readers actually saw through the comedy to his moral function beneath. Cadogan quotes from Richards himself, writing in 1956:

> [Richards was] always very much aware of the necessity of putting over standards and values 'too deftly for the youthful readers to detect the pill in the jam.' (Cadogan, 1988: 147)

Through Billy Bunter, Richards's explicit ideological didacticism is mediated by humour – a deliberate distancing which highlights other characters' conformity. Here again, however, is evidence of an author assuming an uncomplicated relationship between text, reader and meaning – a sense that the 'pill' will always have the desired effect whether the reader is aware of it or not. This point is discussed in more detail later in this section.

Comic incidents involving Bunter are often used as scene-setters to open a story. In 'The Worst Master in the School' (*The Magnet*, 2 June 1934), the story centres on an important cricket match, and begins with Bunter trying to 'wangle' his way into the team. Immediately, and very obviously, Bunter transgresses the fundamental rule of the team player – that a boy wins a place on a team through talent, hard work and loyalty (of which Bunter has none). The comedy in this episode focuses on the expectation that Bunter is setting himself up for dramatic retribution, and readers are soon rewarded by Bunter's spectacular failure as a bowler. Asked to demonstrate his skill by Lascelles the games master, Bunter is allowed to bowl one ball to Wharton at the wicket. The first attempt ends in anticlimax as Bunter slips over with the ball still in his hand, allowing Richards to build suspense for the second attempt:

> Billy Bunter took another little run! Once more he revolved like a catherine wheel. This time he did not slip. He did not fall down. The ball left his hand with plenty of force. Bunter had got speed, if he had not got direction. Where the ball went was, for a second, a mystery. Certainly it did not go anywhere near the wicket – not within yards and yards of it. It flew at an angle quite unexpected by Bunter. For one second it remained a mystery where it had gone. Then a fiendish yell from Mr Smedley apprised all Greyfriars that it had gone in his direction. ('The Worst Master in the School', *The Magnet*, 2 June 1934: 4)

At one level, this is pure slapstick, but behind the humour are some more serious implications. Bunter's outsider status – socially and physically – means that he cannot be shown to be good at games, nor ever allowed a chance to be part of a team; he is ridiculed by both peers and school staff, and given no space to redeem himself. When Bunter realises that the ball has hit Smedley, his response is to run away, putting even more distance between himself and the other boys.

Although Smedley's injury is an accident, and any other boy would have realised that these circumstances did not merit punishment, Bunter's self-obsession allows him no time to think through his situation. Again, the comic effect comes from both Bunter's position as outside the moral codes of the school/story, and his inability even to recognise the existence of those codes. The fact that it is Smedley who is hit is also significant in that he too has outsider status. Smedley is not a 'real' master, but Vernon-Smith's cousin, posing as a teacher in order to try and have Vernon-Smith expelled. With the boy discredited, Smedley stands to inherit millions from Vernon-Smith's father. The backstory of Smedley's mission has been the central feature of a series of stories in the weeks preceding this particular issue. For the benefit of new readers, this is explained in a text box in the middle of page three of the story:

> Everybody in the Remove loathes Smedley, the tyrant Form-master, but that doesn't worry Smedley. He's at Greyfriars for the villainous purpose of ruining the Bounder of the Remove. Once that is accomplished, Mr Smedley, 'the worst master in the school', intends to disappear. ('The Worst Master in the School', *The Magnet*, 2 June 1934: 3)

The purposeful contrast here between the inclusive term 'everybody', which acts as a positive focaliser to invite readers to situate themselves as one of the chums of the Remove, and the distancing language used to characterise Smedley, both constructs and reinforces the boundaries of insider/outsider status.

Like Bunter, Smedley has a total self-interest which is manifested in a complete disregard for school codes. The Bunter/Smedley incident is a satellite event which serves to draw attention to the moral centre of the story, namely the team's behaviour in the run-up to the match, and on the cricket pitch. As Smedley leaves the scene in pursuit of Bunter, order is restored:

> 'I think,' said Mr Lascelles, suppressing a laugh with difficulty, 'that we are wasting time. Let us get going.' And the games master and the Remove cricketers got going, untroubled further by William George Bunter. ('The Worst Master in the School', *The Magnet*, 2 June 1934: 4)

Both Smedley and Bunter act as subversive influences on moral codings. Smedley is clearly defined as an outsider whose motivation is to destabilise the school's moral equilibrium. In this sense the deliberate portrayal of Smedley as 'other' leads readers to identify with those who resist him. The contrast between Smedley and Lascelles is stark: Lascelles has the effortless leadership style of one who knows his own status and moral authority; Smedley by comparison is powerless. Bunter's subversive role may on the surface look just as disruptive to moral codings, but this is sanctioned subversion, which even Lascelles can find laughable. The resolution of this incident is achieved through a refocusing on adult authority. Lascelles is complicit in laughing at Bunter, which confirms his status as a focalising character.

The remainder of the story centres on the cricket match, and Smedley's attempts to set a trap for Vernon-Smith, to catch him disobeying a detention order. Smedley's scheming allows Harry Wharton in particular to display strong leadership skills. Vernon-Smith functions as a dramatic counterpoint to Harry – Vernon-Smith is a boy who struggles to conform to any rules, social or institutional. He is, however, the best cricketer in the Remove, so Harry must put aside his personal feelings in favour of the team. When Smedley threatens to bar Vernon-Smith from the match, Harry's response is entirely selfless.

'May I point out, sir, that Vernon-Smith can't be spared from the Remove eleven?' he asked. 'I'd as soon stand out myself as leave Smithy out.'

'Indeed! I was not aware you were such close friends!' answered Mr Smedley sarcastically.

'We're not close friends,' said Wharton. 'I've had more rows with Smithy than with any other fellow in the Form. That's got nothing to do with cricket. Smithy's down to play because he's wanted in the team. If I loathed the sight of him I should play him all the same.'

('The Worst Master in the School', *The Magnet*, 2 June 1934: 4)

This exchange shows an interesting power relationship between the two characters. The dialogue is presented almost as an exchange between equals. Harry's direct language undermines Smedley's assumed status – this is a mode of address used for peers, not masters. Here again, Smedley makes a fundamental error in his interpretation of school codes. His assumption that friendship might play a part in the team selection process is an insult to Harry's honour and the code of fair play, which can only serve to heighten Harry's, and readers', sense of the injustice of the situation.

Harry Wharton also co-ordinates the team's concerted response to Smedley, helping to form a protective ring around Vernon-Smith in order to prevent his emotional outbursts from causing further trouble. Vernon-Smith's violent temper obstructs his judgement, but Harry and the others perform a calming function which allows him to reflect on, and modify, his behaviour. Vernon-Smith's difficulties in this story are largely not of his own making, but the result of Smedley's schemings. That he should be unable to control the situation is unusual for Vernon-Smith, and this sense of dislocation opens a space for some critical thought about his own actions. The text invites a subject positioning which allows readers to share in Vernon-Smith's mental struggles, and in the process take part in the dismantling and rebuilding of moral codings. At the explicit level, Vernon-Smith clearly does break rules, by breaking out of detention to go and play cricket, but in this case he goes unpunished because the detention itself has been imposed unfairly by Smedley. Vernon-Smith wants to play in the match partly for his own selfish pursuit of glory. He therefore has to be humbled first – by the actions of his team-mates standing up for him against Smedley – before he is allowed to take his place in the team and win the match. Through the complicated plot device of Smedley and his schemes, Vernon-Smith's rebellious attitude is for once legitimised, allowing readers to enjoy the subversive feelings of breaking rules and getting away with it. Again the author's largely unexamined ideological adherence to the value of comradeship is clear.

The examples explored here show that the Greyfriars moral code is very clearly drawn; it is also strongly maintained throughout the stories. Evidence from readers' autobiographies shows that children did draw moral meanings from the stories even if they were sometimes unaware of the process. Paul Fletcher, for example, the son of a colliery winder, grew up in Lancashire in the 1920s:

> Although I never realised it at the time, it proved to influence me more than any other book ... and that includes the Bible. After all, the Greyfriars code was as well-defined as the Scriptures [were] nebulous. (Rose, 2001: 323)

Interestingly, it is only with critical distance that Fletcher is able to discern the level of influence that *The Magnet* had on him as a child, implying that the depth of his engagement with the stories effectively prevented the development of any objective or critical positionings. For Paul Fletcher at least, Frank Richards's 'pill-in-the-jam' approach seems to have worked very efficiently, allowing Fletcher to construct a text–reader relationship which connected the story paper world directly with his own life experiences. This is, of course, the effect Richards and his publisher had aimed for: the direct transmission of values and standards.

The largely uncritical absorption of values and ideologies is also the process which so worried Orwell. However, readers' responses are not so straightforwardly homogeneous, and for every example of Paul-Fletcher-style willingness to submit to the apparent ideological brainwashing of the stories, there is another example which shows a reader with more critical self-awareness and objectivity. The essays in the Mass-Observation Archive from 1937 are illuminating on this point. Robert Hylton writes:

> The reason why I read books is that it is the only way one can reach himself. By reading books shows [*sic*] one how he should talk and

express himself. Some books I read for pleasure. (Robert Hylton, 'Why I read books', Mass-Observation Archive, TC Reading Habits 1937–47, 20/1/B)

Here, Hylton is actively discriminating on his own terms between reading for pleasure and reading for meaning in his own life. Although he does not indicate which books he reads, personal choice is implied as is the selection of particular meanings – styles of talk and self-expression. Although this shows that readers did draw on story worlds in order to construct meanings for themselves, it also underlines the fact that the process is a fundamentally selective one. Another self-aware reader, A. J. Mills, recalled that:

> his teachers made a pathetic attempt to teach an honour system, but 'the nearest any of us got to knowing about the honour system was to read *The Magnet* to find out how the other half lived'. (Rose, 2001: 324)

Here, the reader has constructed a frame for interpreting the text which allows him to see story paper characters as 'other'. This sense of separateness gives him space to judge the relevance, or lack of it, of the value system represented in the story papers to his own world. But even so, it seems that Mills believes that *The Magnet* stories show a true picture of public school life, depicting how others live, not fiction.

Rose argues that the framing process allows readers to accept selected meanings while screening out others, and that the readers his work focuses on, those whose written evidence is available for study, were particularly adept at this. Writing about the school story genre in general, he argues that readers were able to 'tune out' messages and meanings which did not appeal to them:

> To a remarkable extent these stories did transmit a public school ethos to Board school children, but they generally failed to make them idealists. Even after a half-century of unrelenting indoctrination, most working people knew little of the Empire and cared less. This case study illustrates ... that reader response depends entirely on the frame of the audience, which in turn depends entirely on their education and other reading experiences. (Rose, 2001: 322)

Although Rose's generalisations are not necessarily as widely applicable as he claims, it seems that many readers were able to distil a code of 'decent' moral behaviour from the more general imperialistic ideologies of the stories. Frames constructed from their own experiences helped readers to build meanings with logical connections to their own lives. In this sense meanings relating to personal character development and peer relationships carry far more weight, especially for child readers, than broader issues of nationalism and Empire.

Representations of moral codings in *The Hotspur*

The Red Circle School stories, of all the stories in *The Hotspur*, are closest in style and setting to Greyfriars. They also offer greater scope for comparison, given that the Red Circle series is the only story series which continues for the whole life of the story paper – hence there is a larger body of material to draw upon. Having said that, however, each of the Red Circle School stories is self-contained; there are no serial stories in which characters' behaviour and motivations can be explored in more depth.

A key innovative feature of *The Hotspur* was that it moved beyond the traditional school story setting. Even though Red Circle School is ostensibly a school in the traditional mould, the stories themselves break new ground both in the style of storytelling and in their portrayal of individual characters. The D. C. Thomson writing teams faced a considerable challenge: to present a complete story in three or four pages, focusing on the actions and emotions of key characters (but with no space for background information), in a style which would not only hold the attention of readers, but would also keep within the D. C. Thomson editorial guidelines – fast-moving, up-to-date and above all founded on a strict moral code. In the following quotation, George Moonie, a long-standing D. C. Thomson author, explains how they were instructed to write:

> You see we never stepped into politics, we avoided religion, and we never took advantage of people who were crippled or hurt in some way. We never did that. We really kept it very straight, moral. If there was anybody bad, it had to be rectified. If anybody did anything that was wrong, it had to be punished. It was editorial policy throughout all the papers to keep a very strict control over what went into publication. (McAleer, 1992: 187)

The Red Circle School writers made the most of their available space by taking the setting itself – the traditional minor public school – largely as understood. Given that the school story genre was well established by the 1930s, writers could make reasonably safe assumptions about their readers' level of familiarity with the setting. As with the Greyfriars stories, the third-person narrative style implies an omniscient narrator, which in turn implies a level of shared knowledge between narrator and narratee (Stephens, 1992: 57). This leaves textual gaps for readers, which require not so much the use of the imagination as a level of knowledge built up from reading other school stories. School rules, therefore, do not really need explanation, nor does the structure of the school day or the relationships between forms, pupils and prefects. Similarly, the code of conduct which underpins the school and the stories – loyalty, friendship, team spirit – is never made explicit. But underneath all the frantic action and slapstick humour, moral rules apply: rewards for moral behaviour, punishment or ridicule for those who transgress.

There is a rather unexpected sense of paradox in the representations of the moral code in the Red Circle School stories. The style of characterisation (the somewhat one-sided reliance on one key behaviour trait or foible to characterise individuals) could very easily have led to a straightforwardly dichotomous depiction of good versus bad. But in fact, the dilemmas of key characters often lead them to behave in ways which break the rules. Such storylines actually demand quite a high level of interaction on the part of the reader, in decoding the position of characters against the traditional moral hierarchy. By the end of each story, however, the authors consistently ensure that any ambiguities are resolved.

Dead-Wide Dick, a regular throughout the whole run of Red Circle School stories, is a good example of a character with multiple and conflicting behaviour traits. 'The champion slacker' is always too tired for anything, be it schoolwork or play with his chums. This key characteristic sets him against the moral code of the school, in that his tiredness leads him to disobey teachers and prefects in every story, and in that he seems to have no compunction at all in breaking school rules. It also sets him against the code of friendship – he would seemingly choose sleep above any sense of loyalty. In this respect he has some affinities with Billy Bunter, who would choose food above all else. But interestingly, Bunter's transgressions are always totally selfish, whereas Dick's character is redeemed by his willingness to support his friends or the school team when the situation really does demand it. Transgression, again, is a key source of narrative pleasure, but in this case transgressions are always tempered by acts of conformity.

In 'Too Tired to Work – Too Lazy to Play!' (*The Hotspur*, 25 April 1936: 87–90), for example, Dead-Wide Dick is chosen as a reserve for the First Eleven football team, when a number of regular players are taken ill. As any reader would recognise, a place for a fifth-former on the team is almost too good to be true; something that most boys, in the traditional school story world at least, could only dream about. Dick's reaction, though, is one of horror – his only thought is how he can possibly avoid having to expend the energy of actually playing in the match. Much of the story revolves around his attempts to avoid playing, but, in the end, yet another player drops out and he is forced on to the pitch. Rather than let the side down, Dick does actually play up, and scores the winning goal. The moral code is restored, and Dick can take a well-earned rest. Dick's status as a focalising character in the stories means that he must in the end be seen to be firmly on the side of the moral code. In this way, readers who identify with Dick in his transgressive mode can be brought back to positions of conformity at the resolution of the story.

In '3rd Form Brains v. 5th Form Beef', in *The Hotspur*, 11 April 1936, readers are invited to take sides: 'Would you rather be a great fighter than a great wangler? Read this story and then make up your mind' (Figure 2.1).

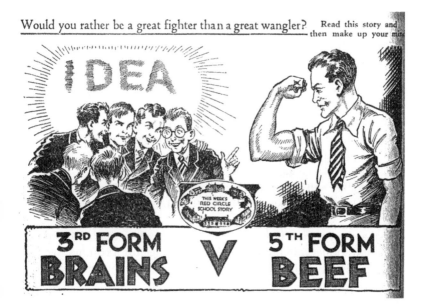

Figure 2.1 Opening illustration from Red Circle story, *The Hotspur*, 11 April 1936, p. 36

At first glance this is a straight distinction between brains and brawn, and the picture which introduces the story underlines that impression. It shows a group of very young-looking third-formers, next to a heavily muscled, much more adult-looking fifth-former. Clearly the expectation is that readers will initially side with the fifth-former – it seems obvious that the lowly third-formers will never be a match for such strength.

The picture signals the appeal of maturity, underlining the power of a physical manliness to which younger readers might be expected to aspire. But, once the story takes shape, it becomes clear that the fifth-former in question is Pringle, and the balance shifts in the third-formers' favour. Pringle is a bully, using his position of power to prey on the weaknesses of the younger boys. Far from being a straight fight, this is a battle to outwit a character who refuses to play by the rules. Significantly, Pringle is a loner – in this story even Moxon, his regular henchman, deserts him. Selfish and self-obsessed, he is unable (or unwilling) to see the extent of his predicament. The third-formers, somewhat inevitably, win the day, tricking Pringle into owing them money. Pringle's £5 IOU to a local gambler is paid off by the younger boys, who then seal the incriminating document in an envelope and deposit it with the Head:

> 'I told him it was an important document. He's keeping it in his safe for me. He'll give it me back whenever I ask for it.'
> If looks could have killed, Goggles would have died on the spot from the glare Pringle gave him.
> 'You'll get it back – at once, do you hear?' snarled the 5th-former.
> 'I don't think,' retorted Goggles. 'That bit of paper cost the Third Form five quid. We know you haven't got that much, and we aren't a lot of sharks like Joe Banks. You can pay us back at five bob a week.'
> 'You – you – you,' spluttered the baffled Pringle.
> 'And,' said Goggles severely, 'just behave yourself in future, or Dr. Walker will see what's in the envelope.' ('3rd Form Brains v. 5th Form Beef', *The Hotspur*, 11 April 1936: 42)

Just as at Greyfriars, it is the code of friendship which matters most here. The third-formers are protecting each other against a common enemy, and seem happy to break school rules and transgress other moral standards in the process. Their treatment of Pringle amounts to blackmail, but they are allowed to get away with this in the name of friendship and loyalty. Conversely, Pringle escapes with only the *threat* of punishment – the Head does not discover the truth about his gambling, and in fact

Pringle has gained a new freedom given that the gambler to whom he was in debt is no longer chasing him for repayment. Pringle and his 'beef' are the losers here, but it is the code of friendship, rather than the 'brains' per se, that proves the winner. The moral position with which readers are invited to identify constructs a masculinity which emphasises loyalty and mental agility above physical strength. (There is a more detailed exploration of this point in Chapter 4.)

Perhaps because of the relatively short length of the Red Circle School stories, which gives them less space for detail, the reinforcement of the moral code is in most cases less overt than in *The Magnet*. This is true of the majority of stories in *The Hotspur*, but the emphasis does change in 1939 in the run-up to and following the outbreak of war. The ethos of wartime prompted the D. C. Thomson writers to bring a more didactic approach to their writing. As writers work harder to ensure that their intended message is directly delivered, ironically the stories become weaker and less likely to interest their readers. From a twenty-first-century viewpoint it is possible to see this change in style as a contributory factor in the gradual decline in popularity of the story papers from 1939 onwards.

'Red Circle in Wartime' (*The Hotspur*, 21 October 1939) is a good example of such heavy-handed didacticism. Presented as 'the greatest school story ever written', it tells of the arrival of 200 evacuated boys at Red Circle School. The evacuees come from Canal Bank School in the industrial town of Ironmoor, implying from the outset that these are working-class sons of factory workers, and thus setting up the expectation of some difficult encounters to come when they meet the 'posh' boys of Red Circle School. Although this defines the Canal Bank boys as outsiders, the story's main function is to show the happy integration of the new boys into their 'place of safety'. In order to do this both groups must be seen to display selflessness and team spirit, overlooking personal differences: evacuees must be brave in facing change and grateful for their being distanced from the war; Red Circle boys must be loyal to the spirit of the school and welcoming and supportive to their visitors. The message is reinforced continually through the use of repetitive language and recurring plot devices. The mothers who are seeing their boys off on the train are, it is stressed, 'relieved' to see them go, and three times in the space of one page it is repeated that Red Circle School is a 'place of safety'. To be within school boundaries is to be separate from the outside world and immune to its dangers; similarly, the whole experience can change characters for the better. For example, Eggy Boiler, the bully of Canal Bank School, is transformed in the course of the train journey from thug to baby-sitter, taking charge of looking after small boys instead of beating them up:

> 'I don't have to worry over Eggy Boiler any more,' [Mr Tugg] told himself. 'His new responsibility has made him forget all about bullying. I think he will be a greatly changed boy from now on.' ('Red Circle in Wartime', *The Hotspur*, 21 October 1939: 79)

Both sudden and complete, the transformation is given no further explanation, the clear implication being that every boy must 'do his bit' in difficult times. Even Mr Smugg, the most hated master in the school, must be part of the new spirit of inclusiveness and comradeship in adversity. He too undergoes an unexpected transformation:

> It seemed that the new order of things was causing Smugg to display an entirely new side to his character. ('Red Circle in Wartime', *The Hotspur*, 21 October 1939: 81)

When an 'invisible wall' between the two groups of boys threatens to disrupt relationships at Red Circle, it is Smugg who suggests a football match to help the boys meet on common ground – and it is Smugg, too, the Red Circle School authority figure, who shockingly suggests that the Red Circle boys should deliberately lose the match to help restore the evacuee boys' confidence.

Unthinkable in any other context, this deliberate fixing of a sporting event is permissible for its purely moral intentions, and the old order is restored once the Canal Bank boys discover the deception. A rematch is set up, resulting in a very predictable draw. This neat and harmonious resolution is the only possible outcome for a story with such obvious intentions. With Mr Smugg transformed, there are no threats within the school/story against which characters or readers can take up resistance. Instead, as the story so clearly implies, readers should devote their energies to uniting in resistance to a much larger, real-world threat.

It is easy to see why story paper writers might feel compelled to resort to such didacticism, but without the extra layer of jam the pill is much harder to swallow. By directing readers towards intended meanings, the story patronises its readers and loses dramatic impact. The increased emphasis on explicit level ideology leaves less space for the trangressive behaviours on which much of the entertainment value of previous storylines has been based. By comparison, the moral messages of earlier stories seem much more effective, assuming a greater level of interaction from the readers and a more equal relationship between author, text and consumer.

Summary and conclusions

This chapter has explored in some detail the embedded moral ideologies of inter-war story papers for boys, examining the ways in which writers and publishers sought to represent moral standards and values in the stories, and the complex processes through which readers transferred meanings from story paper worlds to their own lives and experiences. Taking George Orwell's *Horizon* essay as a starting point, it has shown how the later work of cultural critics such as Williams and Rose, and the development of reader response theory, enables a much broader critical approach to text–reader relationships than Orwell's predominantly political stance.

Orwell's key concern that publishers were attempting to influence readers' attitudes by presenting 'proper' moral conduct is in some senses true. The 'decent' moral code embedded in stories in *The Magnet* and *The Hotspur* was certainly deliberately placed, functioning at an explicit level, and it seems the publishers and writers genuinely did seek to develop moral values and behaviours in their readers. McAleer argues that they did this by making the plots carefully 'apolitical' (McAleer, 1992: 244). It is this point which so worried Orwell.

Ideological manipulation also operates at deeper levels in the stories, in the passive assumptions made by writers and in the nature of the dominant social character of the time. The upper-middle-class worldview of the stories, particularly those in *The Magnet*, is presented as 'natural' and unquestioned – and this is the case at both explicit and 'unexamined' levels. By comparison, stories in *The Hotspur* are much less class-based, breaking away from the public school setting established in the genre and democratising the stories, though consistently retaining 'traditional' moral values. In his focus on the stories themselves and their producers, Orwell neglects the role of the reader, assuming that moral values were unproblematically transmitted to readers through the stories. That this is not the case is underlined by reader response theory as well as the testimonies of child readers and autobiographical accounts. Readers did question the story settings, identifying public school characters as 'other', and they were also able to decontextualise selected generic moral standards and practices from the stories in order to apply them to their own lives. The D. C. Thomson company's practice of systematically canvassing readers' opinions in order to suggest new storylines (see McAleer, 1992: 179) underlines the more reciprocal nature of producer–text–reader relationships, allowing the influence of readers' opinions to feed back into the development of new texts.

Raymond Williams's work has been useful here in illuminating the hegemonic practices of publishers and their relationships with both writers and consumers. Presenting what Cadogan and Craig have called 'a code for decent living', the story paper producers were both reconstructing and reinforcing the dominant social character. This reconstruction work is particularly necessary in the years following the First World War, when the process of renewing selected mythologies for the nation's youth is as important as economic regeneration. The irony of this moral work is worth pointing out, given that parents, teachers and critics were quick to condemn the story paper genre as worthless. For the most part, the moral function of the stories operates with equal weight to their entertainment function, and it is only when this balance shifts in favour of the more overtly didactic that this dual role becomes unsustainable.

3
Understanding School Worlds

In this chapter the focus turns to the ways in which the stories in *The Magnet* and *The Hotspur* make use of the institution and practices of school. Why, for example, did the story paper publishers of the 1920s and 1930s choose to concentrate their efforts on stories about school, in particular? Indeed, why were school stories so popular amongst child readers? In order to understand the significance of the school as a central theme, in this chapter we will look closely at the nature and structure of the genre, approaching it from the varying viewpoints of producer and consumer.

Interconnecting the fictional and the real

By the 1920s the school story genre was very well established, and its popularity amongst readers was second only to the adventure story (see Table A.4 in the Appendix). Generations of readers had grown up with the stories of Talbot Baines Reed and his immediate followers, absorbing whether consciously or not the imperialist philosophies and ideals of masculinity that had characterised the genre since the 1850s. (The *Boy's Own Paper*, which published many of Reed's stories, was first published in 1879 and remained in print until 1967.) As E. C. Mack writes, the *Boy's Own Paper*, and the books and magazines it inspired

> helped to an incalculable extent, through their influence on the rising generation who 'read thousands of them and whooped for their heroes', to keep alive the public school legend. (Mack, 1941: 148)

'Legend' is an apt word here. The school story genre grew steadily away from the 'realistic' portrayal of public school life, fixing on the key ideals of courage and decency and manliness, which came to represent the entire ethos of the institution. As the popularity of the genre grew, so the mythic portrayal of public schools became ever more accepted as 'real'. Readers, who for the most part were unlikely ever to set foot inside a public school, were happy to take this generalised view of school for granted, although, as we have seen in Chapter 2, readers did question the story settings. As Jeffrey Richards explains, the school stories (and Frank Richards's stories in particular) 'purveyed the essence of the public school myth to non-public-school boys, creating for them a beguilingly attractive image of an idealised world' (Richards, 1988: 277). Pure enjoyment of the stories and a sense of identification with the key characters seem to have outweighed any critical view of the way in which school life was presented.

This gulf between illusion and reality is crucial to an understanding of the ways in which the school story genre functioned in the inter-war period. It is also a key tool of control in the power relationship between producers and consumers. As we have seen in the previous chapter, Alfred Harmsworth set out with crusading zeal to produce story papers through which he could offer an intended moral education as well as entertainment, attempting to wean juvenile readers off the 'corrupting' influence of the ubiquitous 'penny dreadfuls'. Cadogan and Craig are convinced of the success of his enterprise, drawing a direct correlation between story paper reading and the behaviour of conscripts in the First World War: 'if by 1914 the boys of Britain were not raring to go and have a crack at the Kaiser, it was certainly not the fault of Lord Northcliffe or his authors' (Cadogan and Craig, 1978: 30–1).

However, the process of transfer of meanings from text to reader is not so straightforward. What Cadogan and Craig have failed to note is that the school story genre – particularly in its pre-First World War form – is a product of the dominant social character of the time, and is evidence of the hegemonic process in action. Its format is a common-sense response to the dominant world-view, which in turn is accepted as 'natural'. Publishers, parents and readers are interlinked through the operation of hegemonic apparatus and the cycle of production and consumption is continuously renewed and recreated. Drawing on Gramsci's concept of hegemony, Ashley writes:

> it is clearly appropriate to explore the possible function of fiction as a hegemonic apparatus ... If we are [to do this] then its role is in the continuous reshaping of consent rather than the crude imposition of fixed ruling class ideology. (Ashley, 1997: 113)

Ashley underlines the subtlety of this mechanism, implying that the power process is a reciprocal one. Readers (and parents too, in the case of the story papers) must allow their opinions to be reshaped in order for the apparatus to be effective. This 'reshaping' process is much more successful than 'crude imposition' of ideology because it is inclusive: all partners in the process willingly submit themselves to it.

Applying this theory to the world of the story papers, and building on the arguments presented in Chapter 2, it becomes clear that by moulding and developing the school story genre, Harmsworth and Thomson and their authors found a highly effective way of transmitting dominant ideologies. Moving away from the purely didactic mode of presentation of morals and values, which was prevalent in children's stories throughout the Victorian years, the Harmsworth and Thomson story papers underlined the moral code through characters' actions and reactions. Rather than simply instructing their readers, they offered adventure and excitement which was always set within definite – but implicit – moral parameters. In the Thomson story papers in particular, those moral messages were framed and reframed in response to feedback from readers themselves, through surveys undertaken by Thomson employees outside schools, and through readers' letters to the story paper editors. In this sense readers began to take more of a role in shaping the narrative, feeding in to the reciprocal relationship.

In Ashley's terms (and here he is drawing on Althusser's theories), the story papers are ideologically *charged* texts. In his view, such texts function in specific ways:

> [texts] so address individual readers as to invite their complicity in particular ways of viewing the world. The reader who responds to the 'hailing' accepts the text's version of reality, and is temporarily the 'subject' of the text whose ideological work is thus effectively discharged. (Ashley, 1997: 113)

This is a crucial point in working towards an understanding of readers' engagement with texts. Iser argues that readers are situated inside a literary text – as John Stephens has put it, that 'the subject (the reader) is located inside the object (the narrative) it has to apprehend' (Stephens, 1992: 4). Ashley shows that there is more to the relationship than this. By responding to the text, and temporarily locating him/herself as its subjects, the reader is effectively subjecting him/herself to its ideologies. Stephens is critical of a theoretical approach which posits that the mechanism by which the readers' subjectivity is effaced as part of the reading process, locating the reader *only* within the text, is 'a mode of reading which is disabling and leaves readers susceptible to gross forms of intellectual manipulation' (Stephens, 1992: 4). Iser's model of reader response does not allow space for the operation of the readers' own critical faculties. Ashley's 'temporary' location of the subject within the text is perhaps a better formulation of the reader–text interaction, which gives readers an active part in the 'reshaping' of ideologies and opinions. We will return to this point later in this chapter.

But what of Ashley's notion that the reader 'accepts the text's version of reality'? This is an important part of the meaning-making process and is key to Iser's theory of reader response. Iser argues that the text acts as a kind of mirror, reflecting the reader's own disposition, but also presenting a reality that is different from the reader's own. This, he writes, creates a paradoxical situation:

> the reader is forced to reveal aspects of himself in order to experience a reality which is different from his own. The impact this reality makes on him will depend largely on the extent to which he himself actively provides the unwritten part of the text, and yet in supplying all the missing links, he must think in terms of experiences different from his own; indeed, it is only by leaving behind the familiar world of his own experience that the reader can truly participate in the adventure that literary texts offer him. (Iser, 2000: 194)

As we have seen in earlier sections, the world of school as represented in the story papers was vastly different from that experienced by the majority of the papers' readers. So why, and how, were readers so readily able to identify with these texts' versions of reality? What meanings would a predominantly working-class readership take from stories depicting a world of privilege and difference? There is yet another cycle of influences at work here – the separate but interconnecting 'realities' of the school and story paper worlds. Those readers who bought the school story papers week after week, following the codes and behaviours presented therein, were switching between these realities continually. Although this might seem a simple process, it is actually a quite complex relationship which needs some further analysis. From a theoretical perspective, Jean Baudrillard's theory of simulations and simulacra is helpful. Baudrillard argues that modern societies are organised around the production and consumption of commodities, while postmodern societies are organised around simulation and the play of images and signs. Kellner explains that, for Baudrillard, 'in the society of simulation, identities are constructed by the appropriation of images, and codes and models determine how individuals perceive themselves and relate to other people' (Kellner, 1994: 8). Whilst the 1920s and 1930s are firmly part of the modern, rather than the postmodern, phase, it is possible to see Baudrillard's theories at work at a micro level, in the ways in which the story paper readers used and applied the images, codes and behaviours of the school worlds of the story papers in their own lives. These are developing readers looking for ways to make sense of their own experiences, who turn to fiction in search of something 'interesting and exciting', 'a stirring tale of adventure', or 'a good thrilling story'. (These quotations are from the Mass-Observation Archive, TC Reading Habits 1937-47, 20/1/B. Quotes from W. Jefferson, A. Hoyland and F. Marwood, respectively.) In other words, in Baudrillard's terms, they are looking for a more 'intense and involving experience than the scenes of banal everyday life ... [searching for] excursions into ideal worlds ... more real than real' (Kellner, 1994: 8). 'To dissimulate is to feign not to have what one has. To simulate is to feign to have what one hasn't. One implies a presence, the other an absence ... feigning or dissimulating leaves the reality principle intact: the difference is always clear, it is only masked; whereas simulation threatens the difference between "true" and "false", between "real" and "imaginary"' (Baudrillard, 1988: 167–8). So what begins, in a sense, as escapism, becomes an alternate reality in which the logic of codes and models predominates, as the basis for constructing identities. The simulation (story paper world) becomes more powerful as a source of learning than the reality (school world). Brian Magee (born in the 'notorious slum' of Hoxton in 1930) writes of rediscovering copies of *The Wizard* in his forties, and recalling 'a degree of detail so astounding that I began to disbelieve that I could really be remembering it as completely as it felt like'. Looking at the story papers, he finds he can remember accurately words and images he read as a child:

> It was spooky. I had never consciously learnt by heart any of the verses they contained. I had simply read the stuff in my normal way, and now I found I remembered it for life. It meant that when I read those comics for the first time I must have done so with a completeness of attention and digestion that was altogether unknown to me in adult life – yet with no awareness that I was doing so. (Magee, 2003: 230)

Perhaps for working-class readers the intensity of the reading experience was all the greater because of the depth of the gap between simulation and reality, and the effort invested in creating that alternate reality.

There remains, however, the question of why the school story genre in particular should have proved so popular and successful for the story paper publishers. If the publishers' main aim was to present ideologically charged text with implicit moral messages (and to sell their papers too), it could be argued that any other story genre would have served their purposes equally well. There are potentially a number of reasons why the school story in particular should have been selected. The obvious point to make here is that the school story has an element of familiarity which makes the process of inviting readers' complicity potentially easier than for other story genres. By the 1920s and 1930s school attendance was compulsory for the vast majority of children, so almost all story paper readers would have had real school experiences to compare with the fictional story paper worlds. That these are of course state rather than public school experiences means, as noted above, that readers have to work harder to immerse themselves in the alternate reality, but nevertheless readers' knowledge of the real school world, together with their familiarity with the already established versions of the school story genre, would have given them a framework with which to interpret the morals and messages of the school story papers. The school stories work to defamiliarise the familiar, allowing readers to move from the known to the unknown.

Secondly, the boarding school setting takes characters away from the security and familiarity of home and parents, setting them in a context which is regulated by different forces. This allows the schoolboy characters space in which to experiment with identity, learning from both peers and teachers, and to test the boundaries of their new existence within safe parameters. The school operates as surrogate parent, protecting, enclosing and instructing even if the boys do not recognise the extent of that role. Through the experience of reading, of locating themselves as subjects of these narratives, readers can find safe space, albeit ideologically charged, for their own experimentation with codes and behaviours.

Thirdly, schools are quite obviously powerful institutions, and as such have their own part to play in the hegemonic process. Williams argues that hegemony is an active process of incorporation, based on the interconnecting influences of traditions, institutions and formations (Williams, 1977: 115). In the inter-war story papers we can see these interconnecting influences at a micro level. The schools portrayed in the story papers (Greyfriars and Red Circle School in particular) are ostensibly 'traditional' public schools. In other words, the authors invite their readers to believe that the stories reflect the reality of life in public schools. As we have seen in the previous chapter, however, the stories in fact present a very selective view of these very selective institutions. The story paper authors chose to build on a selected version of the school story tradition, focusing on an outdated version of schooling in order to present selected specific meanings and values. In the story papers, producers (publishers/authors) use traditions (the school story genre) and institutions (the accepted view of public school) to build a formation (a new story paper genre) in order to influence consumers (readers and parents). Williams writes that educational institutions themselves are selective:

> Education transmits necessary knowledge and skills, but always by a particular selection from the whole available range, and with intrinsic attitudes, both to learning and social relations, which are in practice virtually indistinguishable. (Williams, 1977: 117)

Story paper readers were drawn into a sophisticated meaning-making process which set the real learning experiences of school life alongside the vivid fictional relationships in the story paper worlds. To make sense of these separate realities, readers effectively had to fill the gap between fiction and reality, transferring selected knowledge and attitudes from one world to the other.

Althusser defines the school as a key Ideological State Apparatus (ISA), alongside the church, the family, political, cultural and legal systems, trade unions, and the media. These tools of the state provide the means through which the ruling class can both impose and continually renew its ideology. Althusser argues that the school has replaced the church as the dominant ISA:

> The school has a dominant role although hardly anyone lends an ear to its music: it is so silent! [The school] takes children from every class at infant-school age, and then for years, the years in which the child is most 'vulnerable', squeezed between the family state apparatus and the educational state apparatus, it drums into them, whether it uses new or old methods, a certain amount of 'know-how', wrapped in the ruling ideology (French, arithmetic, natural history, the sciences, literature) or simply the ruling ideology in its pure state (ethics, civic instruction, philosophy). (Althusser, 1971: 146–7)

The school is dominant because it has an 'obligatory audience' – the state has made it dominant by legally requiring all children to attend school. This, Althusser argues, is how capitalist societies reproduce the relations of production, by making sure that children are subjected to the ruling ideology:

> All the agents of production, exploitation and repression, not to speak of the 'professionals of ideology' (Marx), must in one way or another be 'steeped' in this ideology in order to perform their tasks 'conscientiously' – the tasks of the exploited (the proletarians), or the exploiters (the capitalists), of the exploiters' auxiliaries (the managers), or of the high priests of the ruling ideology (its functionaries) etc. (Althusser, 1971: 128)

This whole process is 'naturally covered up and concealed' (Althusser, 1971: 128) by the ideology of the school itself. By manufacturing a view of school as a universal good, and as neutral ground, the state manages to reinforce the ruling ideology on a largely unquestioning workforce. The school is therefore, for Althusser, a uniquely powerful apparatus of control in a capitalist society. In his formulation, even teachers for the most part do not see the system and practices in which they are enmeshed. As with Williams's theory of hegemony, there is little room in Althusser's formulation for the notion of personal agency – 'tasks' are performed according to rules and codes, and it is almost impossible to take an objective view of systems and practices from the 'outside'. This view homogenises individuals into specific 'types', and seems disconnected from a 'real' world in which the relationships between agents, institutions and practices are much more complex. The implications of Althusser's argument are an exclusion of change, and a separation of individual opinion from action. However, this is not always the case, particularly for teachers, whose professional practice shows the influence of theorists operating outside the dominant ideology of the time.

Set against Althusser's theories the story papers are actually playing a much more complicated role in readers' lives than would at first appear. If real school is a tool of socialisation and control, then fictional school worlds are created to function on the same basis, for much the same reasons. But attendance at school is compulsory – reading about school is not. So there is a double concealment, in that readers are subjected to ruling ideology in their daily school lives but also through their chosen reading. Using the story papers as sites of socialisation and control is a much more sinister process, arguably leaving readers more open to manipulation because they have freely chosen to read the stories. The danger here is the 'disabling' effect of an effacing of subjectivity through the reading process, described by Stephens. The temporary location of the self as 'subject' of the text opens up a direct link for the transfer of meanings from story paper world to 'real' world. It is, however, only through the actions of readers in the 'real' world that those meanings are consolidated, and those actions are mediated by the whole range of pressures, conflicts and relationships which construct the daily lives of readers. It cannot, therefore, be assumed that any ideology or meaning can be directly and unproblematically transmitted through the reading process for every reader, however intellectually manipulated those readers may be.

Teachers and readers

There is another key influence on the producer/consumer dynamic that must be taken into account: the role of the teacher. Unquestionably a major figure in both real and story paper worlds, the teacher is one of the main sources of information (knowledge, skills, attitudes) for young readers. A particular tension, however, is created by the fact that many teachers in the inter-war period markedly disliked the story papers. A. J. Jenkinson surveyed teachers' attitudes to story papers in 1938, and found that very few actively encouraged story paper reading, though most would tolerate them as a stepping-stone to 'better' reading:

> A boy has to get a vocab. from somewhere. Errors of style will be seen later and in good time. 'Bloods' are invaluable if one is seeking to illustrate clichés and such like. [Secondary school teacher]

> There are many children of this school who would never read at all were it not for 'bloods'. Therefore I would rather they read those than nothing at all. [Senior school teacher] (Jenkinson, 1940: 132)

Jenkinson notes that these kinds of attitudes towards story papers actually represent a step forward from 20–30 years previously, when teachers would have 'denounced this sort of reading as though it were a deadly sin' (Jenkinson, 1940: 130). This is the result of a gradual tendency in educational theory to 'assert that the child has a right to live his own life, to devote himself to his own interests' (drawing from the work of Rousseau and Dewey, who were very influential during the first 30 years of the twentieth century) (Jenkinson, 1940: 129). Teachers were thus acting as arbiters of change, applying new theories to the practice of teaching, drawing from ideas outside the dominant ideology. These changing attitudes, however, take time to become dominant in their turn; in the meantime many teachers saw the story papers as inferior, and this general attitude must have been obvious to the children. Children's views of story papers are evidenced in the 1937 Mass-Observation survey. Here the tension between the children's love of story papers and their feeling that reading for pure enjoyment was somehow not quite right is very apparent:

> My favourite books are detective or school stories, or some other exciting kind of book. I do not read for the sake of perfecting my English or grammar, or any other kind of thing like that, but only because it is a kind of hobby.

> In books sometimes classed as 'trash', 'nonsense' or some other term there is often some knowledge to be gained by reading them. (Mass-Observation Archive, TC Reading Habits 1937–47, 20/1/B, quotations from E. Waites and J. Borrowdale, respectively)

It is of course important to remember the context in which these responses were made: an authority figure asking children to record their thoughts. It is not therefore possible to be sure that these are honest responses; they are almost certainly coloured by the children's need to 'say the right thing'. The influence of the teacher in the responses is obvious.

This prevailing attitude amongst teachers is an interesting paradox. Following Althusser's theories, as we have seen earlier, the story papers actually represent an effective way of reproducing and re-emphasising ruling ideology. That there were teachers who largely were not aware of this process does tend to underline Althusser's view of the dominance of the 'universally-reigning ideology of the school' (Althusser, 1971: 148). Not only do some teachers fail to 'suspect the work that the system forces them to do', they also do not seem to be able to see beyond the system to the underlying messages of the story papers.

The net effect of teachers' general dislike of the story papers was to increase the likelihood of children wanting to read them. As Jonathan Rose writes:

> the fact that many parents banned such stories [here he is specifically referring to the school stories by Angela Brazil] only enhanced their appeal. John Macadam (born 1903) had to read them in secret, and, forty years later, could still quote freely from them. V. S. Pritchett furtively devoured *The Gem* and *The Magnet* with a compositor's son: both adopted Greyfriars nicknames and slang. Pritchett's father

eventually discovered [the story papers], burnt them in the fireplace and ordered the boy to read Ruskin. (Rose, 2001: 330)

What looks like an act of subversion on the part of the story paper readers in choosing to read the papers in defiance of the rules set down by authority figures is in fact drawing them further into the ruling ideology.

Rose's evidence from published autobiographies of working-class readers shows that children's reading choices were not in fact quite so clear-cut. Many children were so desperate for reading matter that they would read anything and everything, regardless of the quality, and regardless for the most part of what authority figures had to say on the matter. Michael Stapleton was the son of an Irish navvy, and grew up in Clapton in the 1930s:

> I read everything I could understand, and begged twopenny bloods quite shamelessly from the boys at school who were fortunate to enjoy such things. I absorbed an immense amount of useless information, but occasionally a treasure would come my way and I would strain my eyes under the twenty-watt bulb which lighted our kitchen. A month-old copy of the *Wizard* would be succeeded by a handbook for vegetarians, and this in turn would be followed by *Jane Eyre*. *Tarzan and the Jewels of Ophir* was no sooner finished than I was deep in volumes three and four of *The Conquest of Peru* (the rest of the set was missing). I would go from that to *Rip Van Winkle* and straight on to a battered copy of *The Hotspur*. (Rose, 2001: 373)

This wide range of reading matter is also evidenced in Jenkinson's survey. His data showed that boys were reading four to six books a month outside school, and choosing a huge variety of authors from Hans Christian Andersen, Lewis Carroll and John Buchan to Dickens, Erich Maria Remarque and Mary Shelley. (Jenkinson's data on the most popular 'adult' authors amongst boys in secondary and senior schools is shown in the Appendix, Tables A.5 and A.6; those read by girls are shown in Tables A.11 and A.12.) Jenkinson argues that this childish omnivorousness was entirely healthy, and to be encouraged, as an effective way of teaching children to discriminate in their reading. Jenkinson's conclusions seem more in keeping with 1960s liberalist approaches to education than with his own contemporary world, influenced as it was by the mass culture theorists. He argues that, rather than seeking to implant the reading habit, teachers needed to *refine* it:

> The sound reason for letting boys of these ages [12–15] have inferior books is that they get something out of them – some emotional, imaginative, intelligent experience which meets their needs. (Jenkinson, 1940: 156)

In response to the point that boys' private reading is shown by the survey to consist 'largely ... [of] inferior books, magazines and newspapers', he makes some very perceptive comments about power relationships:

> I do not think that this conclusion is a cause for gloom – except in so far as one may doubt the integrity and competence of the purveyors of adolescent literature, whose producing and selling organisations give them rather terrifying (and largely unseen) power. It is natural that juvenile and adolescent tastes should be 'inferior' to adult tastes, and it is also natural that adults should think them worse than they are because they tend to judge them by adult standards. (Jenkinson, 1940: 151)

Interestingly, Jenkinson refers in both of these quotes to the 'inferior' nature of story paper texts – the influence of the mass culture theorists is clearly hard to escape.

Jenkinson concludes that the surest way to put a child off reading is to subject him or her to an exclusive diet of classics. He is in fact arguing for a complete rethink of the 1930s literary curriculum, to try and bring some genuine enjoyment to school reading. Precisely what impact this survey had when it was first published is hard to gauge – but from the evidence of the teachers in the survey his argument does set itself against generally accepted institutional practice.

Autobiographical accounts indicate the range of experiences of school that working-class and lower-middle-class children encountered. In some cases, children saw going to school as an escape. The daughter of a Sheffield flatware stamper (born 1911) wrote that her first classroom was

> sunless and gloomy because it overlooked a prison-like quadrangle surrounded by high buildings. But we did not need the sunshine, for we made our own. School was sheer bliss, and I could not wait to get there. (Rose, 2001: 167)

Rose adds that:

> The Board schools offered what many poor households did not: a structured learning environment, recognition for academic achievements, and (often) sympathetic adults, not to mention proper heating, lighting and plumbing. (Rose, 2001: 167)

This, however, was not the case for everyone. Cannadine et al. point to the fact that although the school leaving age was officially 14, nearly half of English children left at 12 or 13, and 'for many pupils, the last two years in school were wasted, since nothing of significance was taught to those who were anxious to leave' (Cannadine et al., 2011: 63). They also note that the quality of teaching was unsatisfactory, given that few teachers had been given proper training, and in rural areas and inner cities schools were 'cold, insanitary, and unwelcoming places' (Cannadine et al., 2011: 63). If the experience of real school could be so diverse, how did this affect children's reading and understanding of fictional schools? Following Baudrillard's formulation, there is a blurring of boundaries here between the real and the simulation, a narrowing of the gap between actual and fictionalised lives. For some children, 'escape' from the banalities and struggles of home life into the stimulating world of an effectively run school correlates closely with escape into the world of fiction. Similarly, children were also making the transition from the boredom and discomfort of an ineffective school into the 'ideal' fictional school world. Blurring the boundaries between the two allows the codes and behaviours of the simulated fictional world to be transferred back into the real world. Growing up in the 1930s, Bryan Forbes 'devoured every word, believed every word' of *The Magnet* and *Gem*, 'surrendering to a world I never expected to join' (Rose, 2001: 326). Children were drawn in to these fictional worlds, as well as being able to draw out from them ideals and role models on which to develop their own characters:

> How my eight-year-old mind boggled at the heroic antics of Harry Wharton and Tom Merry, and how determined I was to emulate their true blue behaviour by my conduct in the more prosaic atmosphere of St George's [Church School] even if I sometimes wore no shoes and the arse was out of my trousers. (Rose, 2001: 325; the writer here was the son of a Camberwell builder's labourer)

Here, a child reader effectively transcends the hardships of everyday existence by submitting himself to the power of the simulation and by choosing to carry the simulated images and behaviours back into his own world. He consciously and deliberately constructs an identity for himself based on the simulated images and codes, rather than his real-world experiences. This sense of individual agency is central to the experience of story paper reading: child readers exploring meaning-making on their own terms.

Fictional institutions: Greyfriars, Red Circle and *The Hotspur* adventure schools

Frank Richards's Greyfriars was never intended as a true depiction of real life – Richards's knowledge of the public school world was after all drawn from fiction not reality. One of the key features underlying the process of his writing is, rather paradoxically, that he does not spend time building a detailed picture of the institution itself. As we have seen, the story paper genre does not allow room for detailed description – the nature of the format itself meant that each issue of the paper had to stand alone. The writers could not assume that readers were necessarily familiar with the contents of previous issues. Descriptions of buildings, layouts of classrooms or even the structure of the school day are almost entirely lacking from the stories, and it is relatively rare to see boys actually doing any schoolwork. Instead, the focus is on characters and their behaviour – mostly in the 'free' hours outside daily lessons. The effect of this is of course to give the impression that life at Greyfriars (and other fictional schools) is full of endless japes, larks and escapades both within and beyond the school walls. This is common to classics of the school story genre from *Tom Brown's Schooldays* and *Stalky and Co* onwards. P. W. Musgrave quotes from *The Times Educational Supplement*'s reviewers in 1912 and 1915:

> The great difficulty which all writers of school stories have to overcome is the uneventful unevenness which makes up the actual life of a boy at a public school ...
> ... a writer is required to reveal character while he can exhibit it only in certain conventional situations and in persons who – being underdeveloped and under tutelage – are hardly free agents. (Musgrave, 1985: 220, quoting from *The Times Educational Supplement*, 13 December 1912 and 8 December 1915)

The seeming anarchy of school life in the story papers is in fact a much more insidious way of underlining the ruling ideology. Beneath the anarchic exterior of larks and japes, the moral code is intact, but presented in a much less overt and didactic way.

Beyond certain key rules and codes the nature of the institution itself becomes secondary to the action of the stories. Characters behave as they do to a certain extent because they are part of an institution, and also the institution itself and its authority figures give the characters something to react against. 'Real' school lessons only feature in the stories as plot devices, to highlight aspects of character or to set up storylines for later action. In 'Bunter the Ventriloquist!' (*The Magnet*, 12 May 1934), the Remove has a new form master, Mr Smedley, as their usual master, Mr Quelch, is on sick leave. In the extract below, a classroom scene is presented in which the boys are construing Latin, and there is a rare glimpse of the 'real' business of school. The scene shows not only the fact that work must be done in the evenings (prep), but that being kept in after lessons doing lines is also a common punishment. This scene is strongly reminiscent of *Tom Brown's Schooldays*, in which the only mention of schoolwork is the Latin prep the boys do each evening – the 'Vulgus'. In Hughes's story, however, the depiction of boys grappling with Latin translation is accompanied by a typically earnest entreaty to his readers to do their work honestly and not be tempted into bullying others to do it for them: 'a method not to be encouraged, and which I strongly advise you all not to practise' (Hughes, 1997: 216). Frank Richards never moralises as overtly as this, though his message is nonetheless clear.

> 'Cherry! You will construe!' he rapped.
> Bob began on 'con.'
> Bob Cherry was by no means a slacker like Bunter or Skinner; but he was not, on the other hand, a studious fellow like Mark Linley, neither did he find any pleasure in the classics like Wharton. His 'con' was about the average for the Lower Fourth Form – from Bob's point of view, it was just a spot of work that had to be done. Certainly it was not brilliant; Bob's brilliance shone only on the playing-fields. It would have passed with Quelch; but there were plenty of faults for a man to find who wanted to find them.
> Mr. Smedley stopped him, with a gesture.
> 'You have not prepared this lesson, Cherry,' he snapped.
> 'Oh, yes, sir!' answered Bob. 'I did my prep as usual last evening, sir.'

'Unfortunately, you are not a boy on whose word I can rely,' said Mr. Smedley.

Skinner winked at Snoop.

Bob flushed crimson.

He knew that it was the affair of Smithy that was in Smedley's mind. The Head's authority had settled that affair. But it still rankled with Smedley.

'Mr. Quelch would not have said that, sir!' said Bob quietly.

'I do not desire to hear your opinion on that point, Cherry. You may have imposed upon your former master, but you cannot impose on me. You will stay in after class to-day and write out the whole section of the Aeneid given you for preparation twelve times.'

Bob breathed hard as he sat down. ('Bunter the Ventriloquist', *The Magnet*, 12 May 1934: 18)

Hughes also describes the different approaches each boy takes to his work (the 'traditionary' method, the 'dogged or prosaic' method, the 'artistic' method and the 'vicarious' or bullying method (Hughes, 1997: 215–16)). Although there is no written evidence for this, it is hard to resist the thought that Richards used Hughes's description of prep as a reference point, and rarely refers to any other schoolwork because he had no direct knowledge of public school life on which to draw. (Mary Cadogan does make the comment that Frank Richards himself had a passion for learning and a predilection for learning Latin (Cadogan, 1988: 14).)

The action in the stories is driven by pressures and tensions in the relationships between masters and pupils, between the pupils themselves, and between pupils and 'outsiders'. There is a well-understood hierarchy – teacher authority is unquestioningly accepted unless, as in the example above, the teacher is an 'outsider' trying to destabilise the moral equilibrium of the institution. Such 'outsider' characters give authors space to depict story paper characters in confrontational modes, apparently reacting against the authority of the institution, albeit only in small ways. In the example quoted above, Bob Cherry speaks out in a way he would not have done to the 'real' teacher, Mr Quelch. Again, this in fact serves to emphasise institutional power, in that subversive acts are only possible 'outside' institutional boundaries, and resistance to 'real' authority does not succeed.

Institutional control at Greyfriars, and the largely conformist behaviour of its inmates, is counterpointed by the relative degeneracy of pupils from a local rival school, Highcliffe. Highcliffe is a 'slack' school, home to Cecil Ponsonby and his fourth-form friends, who as a group act in a deviant role to draw Greyfriars characters – principally Harold Skinner – away from the safety of the Greyfriars code. Skinner's weakness in the face of this kind of temptation acts in turn to highlight the willingness of the Famous Five to follow the dominant ideology of the school. In the extract below, Ponsonby and his friends are waiting for Skinner in the lane between the two schools, smoking cigarettes, when Mr Quelch walks past. The lane is neutral territory, outside school boundaries, and Ponsonby is bold enough to test his status with Mr Quelch:

> Had it been a Highcliffe master that passed, the cigarettes would have disappeared fast enough. Highcliffe was a slack school; but this sort of thing would not have done, even for Highcliffe. But as Mr. Quelch was a Greyfriars master it amused Ponsonby to shock him, and he quite enjoyed the expression that came over the severe countenance of Henry Samuel Quelch.
> 'Chuck it, Pon!' murmured Vavasour. 'The man's a beak.'
> 'Not one of our beaks, fathead!' answered Ponsonby. 'Stick your smoke in your silly mouth, you ass! Who cares for Greyfriars beaks?'
> 'He might report a man –'
> 'Think Mobby would listen to him if he did?'
> 'No jolly fear!' chuckled Gadsby.
> Vavasour nodded, brought his cigarette into view again, and replaced it in his mouth. The four young rascals smoked, with an air of enjoyment, as Mr. Quelch drew abreast of the stile ...
> Mr. Quelch's face was crimson.
> 'Upon my word!' he gasped. 'If you young rascals were Greyfriars boys I would see you all soundly flogged! I have a great mind to report your insolence to your headmaster at Highcliffe!'
> 'Don't mind us, sir!' said Ponsonby. 'May I offer you a smoke, sir?'
> 'Wha-a-at?'
> 'A smoke, sir!' said Pon, extending his case. 'They're rather good – you'd hardly get anythin' as good at Greyfriars, I think.'
> 'Ha, ha, ha!' yelled Pon's friends, quite overcome by the expression on Mr. Quelch's face as Pon offered him a smoke.
> 'You-you-you impudent young rascal!' exclaimed Mr. Quelch. 'I will not report you at Highcliffe; I am quite aware that it would be useless. But, in the circumstances, I shall take the matter into my own hands!'
> Smack!

'Whooooop!' roared Ponsonby, as the exasperated Greyfriars master boxed his ears. ('The Complete Outsider', *The Magnet*, 5 March 1932: 4)

Interestingly, the Highcliffe boys are spurred on by their certainty that the Highcliffe headmaster would take no notice of a complaint against them brought by a Greyfriars teacher. This skewed sense of values marks Highcliffe out as deviant, and that role is emphasised by the language of the story which identifies Ponsonby and his friends as 'young rascals' three times in the space of one column of text. The Highcliffe boys deliberately insult Quelch, enjoying 'a little necessary and harmless amusement' ('The Complete Outsider', *The Magnet*, 5 March 1932: 4), and expecting no real retribution. As Quelch himself says, 'I will not report you at Highcliffe; I am quite aware that it would be useless.' Quelch, however, in his symbolic role as embodiment of the Greyfriars code, takes the unsuspecting Ponsonby by surprise, swiftly boxing his ears and striding away leaving Ponsonby spinning backwards to fall in the grass. In this case, institutional authority does not simply reside within school boundaries, but transcends those limits in the personality and actions of key figures. The surface message here is a reinforcement of the Greyfriars code and all that the institution stands for, including the institutionally sanctioned use of physical violence. Beneath that is the sense that readers are being pushed towards the transfer of these meanings and practices into their own worlds. Once the Greyfriars code has been seen to function outside the school itself, and to override the seductive rebelliousness of Ponsonby and his friends, the gap between real and fictional worlds is narrowed and it is easier to see how readers could make direct lines of connection between the two. Ponsonby's predictably bullyish response to his humiliation is to take revenge on Harry Wharton, who just happens to be the next person to come along the lane. Harry is quite badly beaten, and his bicycle all but destroyed then thrown in the ditch. A violent response to violence cannot succeed, however, and Ponsonby is not allowed to triumph. Harry is rescued by Vernon-Smith and Redwing, form-mates from Greyfriars, having put up a valiant fight on his own against the four Highcliffe boys, whilst Ponsonby slinks away in cowardly fashion. Ponsonby is further horrified to discover that the smashed bicycle actually belongs to his friend Skinner. Sheer hooliganism here can only lead to humiliation and loss – in this case, Ponsonby's 'punishment' is the seemingly irretrievable break-up of his friendship with Skinner.

The contrast between Greyfriars and Highcliffe is further set in relief by regular references to Cliff House School, a girls' school which operates almost in mirror image to Greyfriars. (Cliff House School was the setting for a series of stories in a companion paper for girls, *School Friend*, which began publication in 1919. The stories were originally written by Charles Hamilton under the pseudonym Hilda Richards, but other writers soon replaced him.) Few details of Cliff House as an institution are offered, but the girls occasionally feature in the Famous Five's adventures, and the boys are periodically invited to Cliff House for tea. In 'The Complete Outsider', Harry is on his way to join his chums at one of these tea parties when he is ambushed by the Highcliffe boys. The description of the tea – which follows directly on from the fight – is remarkable for its almost complete lack of incident. The wholesome scene is only partially disrupted by the unexpected arrival of Billy Bunter:

> Miss Clara Trevlyn, and Barbara and Mabel and several of the other Cliff House girls were already at the tea-table in the school-room, and the juniors joined them – Billy Bunter bestowing fat smirks all round in the happy delusion that spirits rose on all sides at the sight of him ...
>
> It was Bunter's intention to charm the tea-party with a genial flow of easy and witty conversation, but the edibles claimed his attention, and he almost forgot to wag his fat chin. The tea-party, however, did not seem to feel the loss very greatly. Cheery conversation was accompanied by a sound of steady chomping from Bunter. So far from missing his brilliant talk the Cliff House girls and the Remove fellows seemed to forget he was there. ('The Complete Outsider', *The Magnet*, 5 March 1932: 7)

Like the Famous Five, Clara Trevlyn and her friends are willing and diligent followers of school codes, and the tea-party episode is designed to restore the 'natural' order following the emotional upset of the fight and its aftermath. There is no real interaction between the Famous Five and the girls, and not even the slightest frisson of a sexual overtone of any kind. The girls are symbolic of institutional and domestic values, performing a calming function which returns the focus of the story to the established order. Readers are thus drawn away from locating themselves in the mode of revenge which characterises the fight scene, towards the safe boundaries of 'proper' institutional behaviour. Any shades of intellectual manipulation here are, however, muted by the flatness of the tea-party description, which is rather more soporific than inspiring.

The Red Circle School stories in *The Hotspur* have even less institutional background detail than the Greyfriars stories, but, by comparison, have more to say about the lessons that fill the boys' days. The stories are often based in classroom situations; again this is most likely due to the space available to the writers, as maintaining the focus on a familiar classroom situation would leave more space for describing action. The lessons, however, are used as plot devices in the same way as in *The Magnet* and elsewhere. In 'Is it Goodbye to Red Circle?', the real subject of the story is Mr Welks, the rather ineffectual and aged Housemaster of the Third, who is under threat of replacement by a younger man. The fact that he is incapable of classroom control has to be highlighted in order to set up the storyline for him to be 'redeemed' later:

> It was a mutinous Third that went back for Mr Welks' next lesson, which was history. The little master might as well have been taking a class of pillar-boxes for all the attention he got. In fact, pillar-boxes would have been easier to teach, for they would have been quiet, whereas the row that Buzz and his Form-mates made was awful.
>
> Mr Welks tried desperately to keep them in hand. He dished out lines by the thousand, but it was no good. The Third were fed up with Mr Welks, and didn't care. They clattered and laughed and banged desks. Never had the old Master been more thankful than when that lesson ended. ('Is it Goodbye to Red Circle?', *The Hotspur*, 18 January 1936: 75)

By the end of the story, Mr Welks has saved a dying boy, forgiven the ring-leaders of the Third, and effectively taken a stand against the bullying Mr Smugg – enough to raise his status considerably in the boys' eyes:

> 'There has been enough disruption this morning, so let me have no more noise,' commanded Mr Welks, with a new sternness in his voice, though his eyes were bright. 'We will proceed with the lesson.'
>
> But there was no need for Mr Welks to be stern. He had won the respect of his Form for good and all, and from that time further there was no rowdiness in the fag Form. ('Is it Goodbye to Red Circle?', *The Hotspur*, 18 January 1936: 77)

Academic learning takes place in the 'gaps' between the main storylines – readers are left to fill these gaps with their own experiences of classroom learning.

The story of Mr Welks is also interesting for its depiction of power relationships between masters and pupils. Welks is shown as weak, and lacking in the 'proper' authority of a master, his age and short stature acting as physical representations of his lack of status. Welks does not conform to the school-masterly ideal, which in turn allows the Third Form boys to blur the boundaries of 'proper' behaviour. Welks's attempts at control are ineffectual because the boys have negated his symbolic authority by relating to him at their own level. In order to restore that authority, Welks has to legitimise it in the eyes of the boys by taking a leading role in a series of dramatic incidents – exhibiting the characteristics of a leader and hero, attributes to which the boys themselves aspire, and which are part of the dominant view of the masculine 'ideal'. In this case, institutional authority exists only when sanctioned by the boys, and only when the authority figure conforms to a particular moral and behavioural model.

This transfer of power to the boys themselves is a regular feature of stories in *The Hotspur*, in which boys are often shown in anti-authority roles, and where masters are not always the unquestioned source of control. In Red Circle stories, contrast is repeatedly drawn between Alfred Smugg, hated for his snobbishness and his bullying authoritarian behaviour, and Dixie Dale, the handsome and popular games master. Smugg's obsession with institutional rules and codes, and the honour of the school, blinds him to the codes of friendship, loyalty and team spirit which characterise the boys' lives. This obsession leads him into direct confrontation with the boys, as he imposes regular punishment for minor transgressions, often unjustly, and plots to have the worst 'offenders' expelled. Resistance to this concentrated form of authority is both legitimate and constant – the centrepoint of most Red Circle stories. In 'Death in his Guns and Dynamite in his Boots!' (*The Hotspur*, 27 August 1938), Smugg and his brother Weepy Willie, also a master at the school, are horrified at the arrival in school of the three Kelly brothers, the sons of the American outlaw Two-Gun Kelly, who have been given a new start and the 'chance of becoming law-abiding citizens' following the shooting of their father. Unable to see past the 'outlaw' label, the Smuggs immediately begin to plot against the brothers:

> The two hated masters had made several attempts to get the Westerners into trouble, but so far they had not succeeded. Now, with little Pete Kelly at his mercy in the classroom, Weepy Willie thought that here was his chance to vent his spite on the youngster.

'Brought up in Robbers' Roost, the young ruffian can't possibly know a thing about lessons,' gloated the master, rubbing his hands. 'I've only got to show that he's hopelessly ignorant to get rid of him, and that will mean his brothers will leave, too.' ('Death in his Guns and Dynamite in his Boots!', *The Hotspur*, 27 August 1938: 19)

The Smuggs' efforts are thwarted by Dixie Dale, who represents 'true' authority here. Dale is a much more sympathetic character who embodies physical and moral ideals as well as codes of friendship and loyalty with which the boys, and readers, can identify. The contrast with Welks is clear. Dale operates as a guardian and supporter to the boys, and is able to communicate at their level – a point which is signified by the consistent use of his first name: he is always Dixie Dale, and never Mr Dale. Dale has achieved this popular position amongst the boys through his own behaviour and attitudes. He is always shown in a controlling role, unlike Welks, who has allowed the boys to define a role *for* him. With Dale on their side, sanctioning their resistance to the Smuggs, the boys are able to mount effective action, much in the same way as Harry Wharton and his friends do against the bogus master, Smedley, with the support of their games master, Lascelles (see Chapter 2). In the end, however, these are not stories of resistance to or subversion against ideologies, as the institutional order and hierarchy are always ultimately restored. The Smuggs do not succeed in their plots any more than Smedley does at Greyfriars, but the boys learn much about morality, leadership and humility in the 'traditional' mould. Dixie Dale is an example of what Boyd sees as the changing representation of manliness in the story papers of the inter-war period – one which begins to stress values of community above the individual (Boyd, 2003: 119). This aspect of the story papers is explored in more detail in Chapter 4.

Despite the aggressiveness of its title, 'Death in his Guns and Dynamite in his Boots!' is in essence a moral tale which turns 'outlaws' into model citizens through the benevolence of institutional practices and the comradeship of the football field. Jake Kelly proves to be a miraculously gifted footballer, scoring the winning goals in his first ever match despite having been shot in the head by one of his father's enemies on the way to the game. His special talent is an obvious plot device to move the story on, but the ultimate message of the story is clear: those who conform to implicit institutional and social roles will succeed.

Other stories in *The Hotspur* take the school story genre further into new ground, expanding the boundaries of the genre by playing with the definition of school and inventing an enormous variety of rather dubious-sounding institutions. Selecting *The Hotspur* issues from 1934 by way of example, new schools appear almost every week, from those clearly recognisable as based on the traditional model to outlandish organisations which could hardly be further removed from the readers' own experience. These include:

'The Big Stiff' – Septimus Green, teacher and natural hero, tries to change the harsh regime at Brayford Boys' School;
'Dixon's Dog Academy' – a school in north-west Canada, training dogs for all kinds of work, and teaching boys how to manage dogs;
'Tiger Jake' – a school attached to Benger's Mammoth Circus (making a tour of Canada) to educate the circus boys;
'The School with a Kick' – featuring Dellwood House School for Footballers;
'The Eyes They Feared' – evil headmaster Dr Sprigg terrorises Monkhouse College;
'Public Enemies Trained Here' – Rockport School on Long Island, a training ground for international crooks.

These themed institutions have specialist curricula of their own, which neatly sidesteps the problem of how to make the daily life of school interesting, and takes readers further into the world of simulation. This combination of school and adventure stories was genuinely innovative at the time, and the success of this new style of writing is probably due in large part to the diligence of D. C. Thomson's researchers in finding out what their readers really wanted to read. Jenkinson's survey also backs this up: in all of the age groups, the list of books that boys chose to read out of school shows that adventure stories were the most popular (for example, at age 12+, 42.8 per cent of books read by secondary school boys, and 53.3 per cent in senior schools), followed some way behind by school stories (14 per cent in secondary schools and 12.2 per cent in senior schools) and detective stories (7.8 per cent in secondary schools and 5.2 per cent in senior schools) (Jenkinson, 1940: 17; see also Table A.4 in the Appendix). This manipulation of the genre nevertheless manages to keep the moral code intact – these new schools are still founded on team spirit, comradeship, truthfulness and bravery. In every case, key characters (including the dogs at Dixon's Academy) embody the strict moral code of the traditional school story. The school as institution becomes less important here, functioning simply as a base for the development of an adventure story. In almost all cases these are boarding schools which take boys from a safe home environment into a sometimes very alien world where they must learn to cope for themselves. This is 'safe' adventure, protected by the controlling influence of the schools and their role-model masters.

Summary and conclusions

By the 1920s, the school story genre had become enormously popular amongst child readers, and this chapter has set out both to account for that popularity and to show how the authors of stories in *The Magnet* and *The Hotspur* drew on the genre and reshaped it for their own uses. Althusser's description of the school as a key ideological state apparatus helps to show how the school as an institution is a powerful instrument for the transmission of ideologies to what he sees as a vulnerable audience. This role is paralleled in the use of fictional schools to represent ideologies-in-action through the behaviour of schoolboy and adult characters operating within and across school boundaries. As we have seen, however, the direct transferability of ideologies from text to reader cannot be assumed, and that child readers carry a distinct level of agency in this process.

Story papers are ideologically charged texts which invite readers to view the world in specific ways. As Iser has argued, the extent to which these textual realities impact on readers depends on the reader's own level of engagement with the text, in both locating him or herself within the narrative and in actively bridging textual gaps. This readerly interaction with the text also acts as a connector between the separate 'realities' of school and story paper worlds, allowing readers to make journeys into alternate 'realities' and to select the codes and models from them which have relevance to their own daily lives.

Teachers play a key role in the producer/consumer dynamic in the context of inter-war story papers. The predominant attitude of general disdain for this kind of reading matter creates a tension for readers who are drawn towards the pure enjoyment of story paper reading, but are also subjected to criticism for their reading choices. Given the ideological charging of these texts, set within the dominant social character, teachers' attitudes in this case represent something of a paradox.

School stories in the story papers focus on characters and behaviours, rather than the physical description of institutions, buildings and the minutiae of school life. Central to the stories is the depiction of power relationships and hierarchies – between teachers and boys, and between the boys themselves. The various story extracts quoted in this chapter show the different ways in which these relationships are represented in *The Magnet* and *The Hotspur*, and help in drawing some comparisons between the two. Although on the surface the stories in *The Hotspur* would appear to operate on a more subversive level, inviting readers to identify with characters in anti-authority roles, and depicting teachers in correspondingly weak positions, the dominant social order is always restored, and resistance can only succeed where authority figures are themselves shown to be corrupt or subversive.

4
The Imperial Hero: Story Paper Hero-Figures

Whilst much work has been done to explore the culture of the inter-war period through classic works for children, in school textbooks and in the rise of out-of-school entertainment for children, such as boys' clubs and the cinema, relatively little attention has hitherto been paid to the story papers in these connections, despite their huge circulation amongst children at the time. This chapter explores the twin mythologies of the hero-figure and imperialism: in what ways are inter-war story paper heroes underpinned by these ideologies? How do the processes through which cultural myths are constructed and disseminated, becoming embedded in social and cultural life, influence the producers of the story papers and their narrative content? How can evidence from the social history of the time help in understanding the depiction of hero-figures? And was the imperial ethos present in story papers for boys throughout the 1920s and 1930s, in school stories as well as in other publications for children? Analysis of the key figures in *The Magnet* and *The Hotspur* stories reveals that, beneath the very different styles of writing, imperialist influences still have some bearing on both characters and plotlines.

The myth of the hero

Roland Barthes writes of the process by which ideological and political concepts become mythologised to a level at which they can be seen as 'natural' and unquestioned:

> Myth does not deny things, on the contrary, its function is to talk about them; simply, it purifies them, it makes them innocent, it gives them a natural and eternal justification, it gives them a clarity

which is not that of an explanation but that of a statement of fact. (Barthes, 1973: 143)

Myth is a mode of signification, a 'metalanguage' (Barthes, 1973: 115) which functions as a transmitter of meanings developed over time. This meaning-making process is, paradoxically, one which bleaches out historical significance, so that myth functions as 'empty reality' (Barthes, 1973: 143). Myth purifies out the essence of meaning, discarding evidence of its origins in human actions, allowing the seemingly transparent signification of ideologies as facts. Barthes draws on Marxist theory to recognise this process as deeply political; the distillation process of myth depoliticises speech and action:

> The depoliticisation which [myth] carries out often supervenes against a background which is already naturalised, depoliticised by a general metalanguage which is trained to *celebrate* things, and no longer to *act* them. (Barthes, 1973: 144)

This complex layering of meaning builds myth on top of myth, further distancing the celebration of an idea from its roots in human social relations.

Barthes's theories illuminate the processes through which the myth of the hero had by the early twentieth century become 'naturalised'. The heroes of inter-war story papers were shaped against a metalanguage in which heroes had been constructed according to a classical model of masculine bravery, or 'greatness of soul', over many hundreds of years – celebrating the 'natural' superiority of the white Western male. As we have seen in Chapter 3, in the particular context of the years following the First World War, this ideological work carries increased significance. Myth is depoliticised according to particular need (Barthes, 1973: 144), and in this context the hero myth and the myth of imperialism were constructively combined by writers and producers in an attempt to inculcate specific values in the nation's youth.

In Barthes's conception there is no room for dialectics, as the distilling process of myth dissemination also conceals the fact of their original construction in human societies. His formulation, however, is not a closed circle – myth does not go on endlessly reproducing itself, and the deconstruction of myth is not only possible but very necessary. Barthes's own position sets him outside the hegemonic influence of myth, demonstrating the creation of critical space in the same way that Williams does in his exploration of hegemony.

This macro-scale view of the construction and dissemination of myth helps to show the ways in which myth is shaped to particular ends. A contrasting micro-scale view of individual characters and behaviours is presented by Joseph Campbell in his exploration of the hero, which takes a psychological starting point. This work sheds further light on the processes of myth-making, in this case with direct reference to the behaviour patterns of fictional heroes. He develops the concept of 'monomyth', 'a magnification of the formula represented in the rites of passage: separation – initiation – return' (Campbell, 1968: 30). Campbell argues that this pattern is common in stories of heroic adventure across many cultures, and that although such adventure may be portrayed in physical terms through journeys, battles and struggles against injury, the real work of such stories is psychological:

> The first work of the hero is to retreat from the world scene of secondary effects to those causal zones of the psyche where the difficulties really reside, and there to clarify the difficulties, eradicate them in his own case ... and break through to the undistorted, direct experience and assimilation of what C. G. Jung has called 'the archetypal images'. (Campbell, 1968: 17)

The form of the heroic narrative is thus an attempt to make sense of human existence, to clarify and resolve psychological difficulties and to present messages of triumph over internal, as well as external, struggle. This is the metalanguage of which Barthes speaks – a common mode of representation of the fundamentals of human existence. The return phase of the narrative allows the hero to return to 'teach the lesson he has learned' (Campbell, 1968: 20), thus facilitating the continuance and dissemination of myth.

This classic model of monomyth is central to the structure of a school story, where it is applied on two levels. The experience of boarding school operates both as separation from the family and initiation at a basic level into the new world of school codes and rules. The return home is implied, rather than followed through in this case; by implication, the return phase here is a transition to the world of manhood that exists beyond school boundaries. In the context of the story papers the return in this sense can only ever be implied, as the central emphasis of the stories is the initiation stage – characters must remain at the school in order to operate as role models for subsequent communities of new readers. This initiation stage nearly always involves a second level of separation, either through transition to physical spaces beyond the institutional boundary to face adversaries of one sort or another, or by setting the characters in some way outside the school rules to test moral boundaries. At this level, the closure of the return stage is always completed, as boys return safely to the school and its rules, having clearly learned from their experiences.

Dudley Jones and Tony Watkins posit another approach to the deconstruction of the hero myth, which juxtaposes the two theoretical stances presented above: the archetypal approach (which uses Jungian psychology to 'emphasise the transhistorical, transcultural significance of the hero', closely corresponding with Campbell's work); and a more materialist approach which argues that myths are stories drawn from history which acquire meanings according to the society that produces them (which in turn resonates with Barthes's theories) (Jones and Watkins, 2000: 2). Jones and Watkins's theoretical position provides a bridge between these two theories, arguing that the archetypal pattern is modified by a sense of national identity:

> This approach insists that the substance of myth is provided by human 'authors', men and women who fabricate or compose the stories and promulgate them, who bring to the work their needs, intentions and concerns. (Jones and Watkins, 2000: 9)

This approach personalises the mythologising process, building on Barthes's concept of depoliticisation and allowing for greater influence of individual agency. Cultural contextualising is particularly important in the case of children's literature, where authors are creating and promulgating stories not for themselves, or for an audience of peers, but for an audience of 'others' – children. For the purposes of this book, it is also important to situate the discussion in the particular historical period of the 1920s and 1930s. In this context, the Jones and Watkins model needs to be examined further, to show the tensions between the composers and the promulgators, and to emphasise the fact that their needs, intentions and concerns were not necessarily the same. Jones and Watkins concentrate on the substance of story, downplaying the role of economics. However, the publishers' role is as important as the authors', in that the selection and dissemination of ideas is dependent on publishers' decisions. Alfred Harmsworth, Frank Richards and the D. C. Thomson writers were all products of the imperial age, but it was ultimately the publishers who controlled the way ideals were presented to juvenile audiences. In order to expand their business, publishers sought to exploit a new market by combining the accepted ideology of the archetypal hero-figure – drawing on the metalanguage which would have framed their own youthful reading – with the contemporary concern of building nationalist feeling in the context of post-war disillusionment.

The part of consumers in this relationship also needs to be explored. Kelly Boyd argues that story papers allow us to see how elite ideas were repackaged for a child audience. Her stance is similar to that of Jones and Watkins, in that in her view analysis of the narratives can reveal the mechanisms of myth dissemination. Boyd argues that the ideas and opinions reflected in the story papers echoed the conservatism of schoolboy readers eager to understand the world and fit into it rather than reshape it – publishers, editors and readers would, she feels, have argued that the stories were harmless and without a message (Boyd, 2003: 2–3). This view underestimates the power of the cultural experience of story paper reading, and also contradicts her own later assertion that story papers should be seen as 'a point of negotiation between a posited ideal culture ... and culture as it is lived' (Boyd, 2003: 8). This latter notion of reciprocal exchange allows space for individual agency and the transfer of meanings to the lived experience of interpretive communities. Boyd's conception of this transfer focuses on the conservative and conformative aspects of an inter-war culture in which the political system was often under threat, arguing that the stories emphasise recognition of the needs of the community in order to maintain a certain type of class relationship (Boyd, 2003: 72). While this is true to some extent, in that team spirit and comradeship are the cornerstones of the school stories' moral life, it overlooks the potential for subversive and resistant interpretations located in that very gap between the ideal and the lived experience. As Harry Young, a childhood fan of *The Magnet*, writes, part of the appeal of the characters was their sheer affluence and opulence:

> Toast in front of the blazing fire in 'their own study', where incidentally they never studied anything! The 'fivers' from 'Pater'!! All the games, fights and japes. But above all !NO WORK! which we all had to do ... None of the Greyfriars boys was ever going to be anything or do anything. There was never the slightest suggestion that they MIGHT work at something. They were fifteen but the thought of a career or profession just didn't occur. They were parasites, non-workers. (Quoted in Rose, 2001: 332)

A negotiation of meaning is contingent on the social and cultural context of the reader, and an authorial intention to transmit conforming messages of heroism or imperial values does not necessarily transfer directly from the story paper world to the real world. The appeal of these stories lies in the fact that, for a predominantly working-class readership, the hero-figures of the school stories combined the allure of the privileged other with largely class-transcendent representations of the emotional trials of male adolescence, and allowed readers to select and apply meanings appropriate to their own personal contexts.

Boyd argues that the nature of hero-figures in the story papers changes in the inter-war period, to allow young adults to serve as role models, rather than necessarily focusing on the schoolboys themselves. In this sense, stories such as the Red Circle series were more likely to include adult hero-figures, 'who emphasized a type of masculinity which reinforced traditional sources of guidance (fathers, employers, teachers) and which stressed not the individual but the community' (Boyd, 2003: 119; see, for example, the characters of Compton, in *The Magnet*, and Black John in *The Hotspur*, as quoted below). Melanie Tebbutt also notes this change, arguing that teacher heroes were more likely to act as 'companions' rather than rulers, 'playing games with their young charges and encouraging their independence' (Tebbutt, 2012: 51).

The detailed example from *The Magnet* below shows how the mythical qualities of the hero are typically presented and reinforced through the actions of key characters. In 'The Cruise of the Firefly' (*The Magnet*, 26 December 1936), Harry Wharton and his chums accept an invitation to spend Christmas aboard a yacht belonging to Valentine Compton's uncle, on a trip to Spain:

> The long grey ship was a shadow now. But that she was rushing on, in rapid pursuit, everyone knew. Boom on boom came from the great guns. And the juniors realised, with a thrill, that the Spanish gunners were not firing warning shots now. Only the fall of night saved the yacht from the shells that screamed over the sea.
> Harry Wharton & Co., bunched at the taffrail, stared back.
> They were not scared, but they were deeply thrilled and excited. Billy Bunter, buried deep in his bunk, palpitated with funk; but the Famous Five of the Remove were made of sterner stuff. Moreover, as Bob had remarked, there was no cover if they had hunted it. If shells crashed into the yacht, it would not matter much whether a fellow was above or below decks. It was impossible to dodge the danger, if they had wanted to, and they were not going to miss the excitement.
> 'I'm sorry for this, you fellows.' It was Compton's voice, at their elbows, in the darkness. 'I never foresaw anything of this kind. You can guess that.'

'My dear chap, that's all right,' said Bob.

'I never dreamed of danger for you fellows,' muttered Compton, with a shake in his voice – 'never for a moment.'

'Our danger's no more than yours, is it?' asked Harry.

'Eh? No; but –'

'Right as rain,' said Bob. 'Wouldn't have missed this for worlds, and the whole giddy universe! Poor old Bunter's missing it, though he was so jolly keen on seeing something of the Spanish civil war while we're on the spot.'

'It's my fault,' muttered Compton.

'Rot!' said Johnny Bull. 'Like their dashed cheek to worry an English ship! I'm jolly glad the skipper's taking no notice of them. I wouldn't, in his place!'

Boom!

Something whistled over the yacht, and plunged into the sea ahead. Compton set his lips hard.

'Cheeky rotters!' growled Johnny Bull. 'I suppose there's no doubt that was meant for us, Compton.'

'Hardly. I'm glad to see that you've got plenty of nerve,' said the Greyfriars Fifth Former, with a faint smile.

'Not likely to be frightened by a gang of Spaniards!' grunted Johnny.

('The Cruise of the Firefly', *The Magnet*, 26 December 1936: 26–7)

The story features a deliberate double separation used to situate the schoolboy heroes in an initiation scenario. The extract above is part of the culmination of a long-running plotline in which Compton has become entangled with a smuggling ring, which is apparently in the control of his uncle. The chums are instrumental in securing the arrest of the real criminals – after a string of exciting encounters with gun-runners. The tone of the tale is upbeat throughout, giving the schoolboys ample opportunity to show their fighting spirit.

The junior boys' exuberant disregard for their own safety is contrasted with Compton's sense of responsibility for the dangerous situation in which they find themselves. This is an interesting twist on the concept of the action hero, in that ultimately it is Compton's behaviour in setting himself apart from the action which is held up as truly heroic. While Wharton and the others are swept up in the excitement of events, it is Compton who shows leadership and concern for his companions. Contrasted, too, as usual, is the behaviour of the anti-hero, Bunter, who operates in a subplot of separateness and alienation. Choosing to confine himself to his bunk, Bunter avoids any initiation situations.

This is the source of both the humour of his character and his inability to learn from experience: permanently locked in the separation stage, Bunter consistently fails to complete the learning cycle of the narrative. Story paper narratives do not often allow real-world events to intrude on the action, but in this case there are references to the real conflict of the Spanish civil war. The boys approach the situation of war as a huge game, a spectacle to be enjoyed. This is very much in keeping with the traditions of adventure stories and the metalanguage of the hero myth, but here the juxtaposition of the high spirits of the juniors with the reserve of Compton gives the impression that the juniors are simply ignorant of the danger. Compton functions both as protector and as the physical embodiment of school codes in this other space. He assumes the status of hero as teacher, guiding the junior characters through initiation to the successful completion of the return phase. It must be noted here that the fact that a senior should have invited a group of juniors on a trip is very unusual. Clearly this is a rather contrived plot device, which readily reveals the didactic intentions of the narrative. Frank Richards gives only the briefest of coverage to the question of why Compton chooses to holiday with juniors:

> At Greyfriars there was rather a gulf between a Fifth Form man and the juniors in the Lower Fourth. Away from the school, however, that gulf was bridged by Compton's good nature. He seemed to forget that he was a senior among juniors. ('The Cruise of the Firefly', *The Magnet*, 26 December 1936: 7)

What were the influences that informed the work of the story paper writers in their portrayal of heroes, in the particular context of the 1920s and 1930s? Looking in detail at the narratives, we can see that the hero-figures of the school stories had many resemblances to their predecessors in the adventure stories of earlier children's magazines and fiction, by situating examples from the story papers against the metalanguage of the hero narrative, but also that representations of hero-figures are changing in the inter-war period in terms of the portrayal of masculinity and the class basis of key characters. The next sections of this chapter also explore the different ways in which the imperial ethos manifested itself in the two story paper series under discussion. The schoolboy heroes of *The Magnet* and *The Hotspur* may have been constrained by the geographical confines of their schools for much of their time, but their out-of-school jaunts, and the long school holidays, gave them ample opportunity for adventure. Bending the conventions of the genre in this way gives characters space to develop, and to underline the fact that heroic behaviour does not only belong in the school world. The moral code which sets the rules for heroic behaviour is clearly represented as a way of life, not just a school convention to be discarded at the school gates.

Imperial influences

As we have seen in previous chapters, many of the writers, and Frank Richards in particular, drew on pre-war models (Henty, Ballantyne, Hughes and others) for their inspiration. These Victorian writers were in turn heavily influenced by contemporary cults: hero-worship, imperialism and 'muscular Christianity'. Interconnecting and mutually dependent, these concepts can give some interesting background to the development of the story paper characters of the inter-war period. These interlinked obsessions can be seen across many areas of Victorian life, but were particularly promoted through popular culture, children's literature and education. John Mackenzie cites architecture, statuary, public ceremonies, parades, displays and 'all manner of publications' as being 'bent to the ends of promoting new nationalisms' (Mackenzie, 1986c: 3).

These Victorian cults were the culmination of a deep-seated process of intellectual and social change which had begun to take place from about 1850 onwards. As Mackenzie writes:

> In the emergence of the new nationalisms, state, nation and society converged, and the elite which promoted this convergence created new rituals, a whole range of invented traditions and cults through which it could be communicated to the public. (Mackenzie, 1986c: 3)

This is a fascinating process for two key reasons. Firstly, such convergence was symbolised by the coming together of intellectual and popular taste 'to an extent seldom encountered before or since' (Mackenzie 1986c: 4); and, secondly, the fact that these cults and traditions were *invented* by the ruling classes. The invented tradition is clearly a variation of Williams's concept of the selective tradition. As defined by Eric Hobsbawm:

> Invented tradition is taken to mean a set of practices, normally governed by overtly or tacitly accepted rules and of a ritual or symbolic nature, which seek to inculcate certain values and norms of behaviour

by repetition, which automatically implies connection with the past. In fact, where possible they normally attempt to establish continuity with a suitable historic past. However, in so far as there is such reference to a historic past, the peculiarity of 'invented' traditions is that the continuity with it is largely fictitious. (Hobsbawm, 1983: 2–3)

Through repetition, invented traditions evolve towards the status of myth. As with selected traditions, invented traditions are a means by which ruling classes can reinforce the dominant social character. Although just as powerful as selected traditions in this process of reinforcement, invented traditions are paradoxically more vulnerable in that once their basis in fiction has been discovered their power is considerably diminished. It is, however, in the hegemonic nature of traditions, selected or invented, that finding space for objective questioning is problematic – hence invented traditions are very rarely unmasked as fiction (except with the benefit of a suitable distance of hindsight).

As we have seen in Chapter 3, educational institutions are of central importance in reinforcing the dominant social character, and the Victorian public school was the central institution of the consolidation of Victorian ideology (Bratton, 1986: 74). Values were disseminated directly to the boys, by 'righteous', 'arrogant' and 'zealous' headmasters, who 'fostered a passionate adherence to the propriety of imperialism' (Mangan, 1986: 118). Whilst the public schools turned out fine examples of imperialist clones, with the school-leaving age set at 14 it was much harder for state schools to exercise the same level of influence. In this case, fiction was much more effective – boys' magazines, adventure stories and even school history books, which used fiction as a means to put across historical fact, functioned in the transmitting of ideology. Martin Green writes that there was a striking and significant change in children's literature around the middle of the nineteenth century:

> Their literature was ... captured by the aristo-military caste. Adventure took the place of fable; and the adventure took on the characteristics of romance. Children's literature became boys' literature; it focused its attention on the Empire and the Frontier; and the virtues it taught were dash, pluck, and lion-heartedness, not obedience, duty, and piety. (Green, 1980: 220)

Here again is evidence of traditions being invented. By altering the emphasis of fiction published for children – moving away from religion, towards an emphasis on action, bravery and patriotism – the controlling elites (producers) could draw child readers (consumers) into fictional worlds specifically designed to inculcate imperial 'traditional' values. John Springhall describes this shift in emphasis as a fundamental change in the concept of manliness, from the 'strenuous moral earnestness and religion' of Thomas Arnold and Ballantyne, to the tradition of 'sturdy manliness' of Henty (Springhall, 1987: 61). This move towards 'muscular Christianity' is really more muscular than Christian, so that towards the end of the century the more popular fictional heroes, in Henty's novels as well as in the *Boy's Own Paper*, were more likely to represent imperial ideals than religious ones.

The key characters in the inter-war story papers draw very much on this model of lion-heartedness, but set this against a very moral background. The school stories, whilst offering fewer opportunities for the characters to show dash and pluck in adventurous situations, nevertheless underline the key characteristics of muscular Christianity – muscular in their attention to athleticism and competitiveness on the sports field, and at the same time adhering to firm moral standards, albeit not in an overtly religious way. The closed community of school acts as both container and inculcator of muscular Christian values, and key characteristics of the ideal are shared by dominant characters. Bob Cherry of the Famous Five, for example, represents the muscular model most effectively in his language and attitude. His language is consistently hearty and energetic:

> 'Lovely morning!' roared Bob Cherry.
> He tramped down from the windy deck, his mop of hair rather like a busby, his cheeks red as apples and a few snowflakes spattered over him ...
> 'Oh, ripping!', said Bob. 'The jolly old wind goes through you like a jolly old knife through cheese! It gives you a jolly old appetite – what? Blessed if I don't feel I could eat nearly as much as Bunter!'
> ('The Cruise of the Firefly', *The Magnet*, 26 December 1936: 7)

This verbal energy is matched on the cricket field by Harry Wharton's prowess at batting, and Hurree Jamset Ram Singh's keen eye as a bowler. The true star of the Remove on the cricket field, however, is Herbert Vernon-Smith, 'the Bounder', whose muscular physical skills are set in powerful relief by his deeply flawed behaviour off the pitch. In 'The Worst Master in the School', Vernon-Smith is given a chance to prove himself, having been in serious trouble with the school and his father for bad behaviour. When he is put in detention unfairly by Mr Smedley, a temporary form master who has a grudge against him, Vernon-Smith nearly misses the vital match against St Jim's. He escapes detention in time to make 150 not out, and then is called to bowl:

> The Bounder was given the ball for the first over, and the Greyfriars fellows watched eagerly to see how the St Jim's batsmen would fare. They fared ill. A long innings with the willow had not impaired the Bounder's deadly efficiency with the leather. Tom Merry went down in that over, and Blake followed him at the last ball. And the Greyfriars fellows roared:
> 'Bowled! Oh, well bowled!'
> 'Good old Smithy!' ...
> It had been a great game, and a tremendous victory, and Tom Merry & Co. took it cheerfully, like the good sportsmen they were ...
> That night ... there was little prep done in Remove studies. Fellows paraded the passages, cheering. The scapegrace of the school was the hero of the hour. It was Smithy's triumph, and he enjoyed it to the full. ('The Worst Master in the School', *The Magnet*, 2 June 1934: 28)

There is a moral point to be made here, in that Vernon-Smith is only permitted to take up a role as hero because he has been unfairly treated, and because he has been seen to suffer for his misbehaviour. And, as might be expected, Frank Richards takes the opportunity to underline the sporting behaviour of the gallant losers. The military overtones of 'deadly efficiency' combine with the gentlemanly code of sporting conduct to produce the triumphant reward of hero status.

The Hotspur school stories apply traditional heroic qualities to key figures in non-traditional school settings. But here writers begin to develop new strands by presenting an adult as heroic role model. As Kelly Boyd points out, this is a recasting of the hero-figure in that adult characters now operate as guides and mentors for child characters, teaching by example and 'offer[ing] a clear illustration of how readers should act. The ideal they presented urged greater conformity with the structures of society' (Boyd, 2003: 101). This pattern is repeated across hundreds of different settings. In 'The Last School', for example, the role-model hero is Hugh Jarrold, the sole remaining man of principle in a futuristic post-holocaust world which is 'slipping back into primitive conditions'. Education, he believes, will save the world from degenerating into utter savagery, but in fact the boys learn just as much from his heroic actions in resisting the brutal General Smith as they do from their books ('The Last School', *The Hotspur*, 23 January 1937: 87–9).

In 'Black John of the Battles', set in Glengarn School, 1745, the mysterious 'big, dark' teacher Mr Oliphant, 'powerful and soldier-like in his bearing', is revealed as Black John of the Battles, a famous fighter for the Stuart cause. Black John's leadership skills are mirrored in the character of Tom Wade, who, as the son of an English officer, finds his allegiances split between the English and the Jacobites. Politics, however, are less important than strength of character, and Tom is allowed to learn from the heroic behaviour of Black John without being too encumbered by emotional allegiances. The choice of the name Wade is interesting here – Field Marshal George Wade was famous for the construction of military roads in the Scottish Highlands in the 1720s, as part of English precautions against Jacobite insurrection. This gives added resonance to the fact that Tom is the son of an English officer, but it is detail that may not have been picked up by juvenile readers. In the context of a school story (and Black John is still a teacher, despite his double life as a famous warrior), the boy heroes must look first to their teacher as role model, having left the world of family behind ('Black John of the Battles', *The Hotspur*, 27 February 1937: 237–40). Boyd's thesis that 'by the end of the inter-war years manliness constructed in boys' story papers encouraged all boys to accept their allotted place in society, and to conform to the structure imposed by adults' (Boyd, 2003: 101) is demonstrated in both of these stories from 1937. The actions of the hero-figures in both cases are clearly constructed as markers for readers, though it is interesting that in both stories the values are invested in the person rather than the institution of school itself. The stories' intentions are clear, but how far those messages were actually internalised by readers is less easy to demonstrate.

The use of fiction as a means of disseminating ideologies can only work if that fiction is readily available to a wide audience. Towards the end of the nineteenth century, advances in publishing technology (new processes, cheaper paper and so on) rendered cheap books and magazines affordable to all but the poorest of working-class families. The market was soon flooded with 'works which enshrined contemporary hero-worship' featuring explorers, missionaries, military heroes such as General Gordon and the exploits of pioneers in far-flung parts of the Empire (Mackenzie, 1986a: 18). (Henty's novels for children are a good example of this, with such titles as *With Kitchener in the Soudan* (1903), *With Clive in India* (1884) and *Held Fast for England* (1893); 25 million copies of his books had been sold by 1914 (Carpenter and Prichard, 1984: 245).) The Victorian boys' story papers also showed clear signs of imperialist values, often featuring cover pictures of big-game hunters, regimental badges, Union Jacks and Prince of Wales's feathers; and Henty was editor of a boys' paper called *Union Jack* from 1880 to 1883. In the story papers, however, the heroes were not mighty military warriors but boys aspiring to be such. In J. S. Bratton's view:

> The heroes of magazine stories are often described in glowing terms which combine the values of youth, masculinity and fitness with more abstract qualities of high birth, moral worth and racial type ... The implication is that the boy – the idealised self of the reader – is the highest form of life. (Bratton, 1986: 83)

This invitation to the reader to situate himself within the text allows for much greater flexibility in reader/text interaction. Ideals expressed in this way are much more palatable and potent than straightforward didacticism.

In the inter-war period, tracings of imperialism are also apparent in the attitudes of key characters towards those from other cultures, both within and outside the Empire. On the surface, Hurree Jamset Ram Singh is a colonial character who is fully accepted into school life, and becomes part of the key group, the Famous Five. There is, however, more to the relationship than this. As Castle writes:

> [Hurree] is incorporated within the Remove partly through his rejection of the other foreigners and does not fight as they do for a recognition of national indentity. He claims to be 'English' but the boys' descriptions of him emphasise his 'Indianness'. (Castle, 1996: 45)

This is in fact quite a subtle way of reinforcing ideological imperatives. Hurree is accepted partly because of his noble background, and partly because he is Indian, and therefore a citizen of the Empire. He may appear to have equal status with the other boys of the Famous Five, but that position is undermined by his peculiar language, which constructs him as an object for humour rather than respect. His claims to be English also represent the subordination of his own national identity. The English boys therefore have superiority and control from the first appearance of the colonial character. Castle does not take her analysis further to look at characters from countries outside the Empire, but these, too, are almost always figures either of fun or of contempt. The French master at Greyfriars, Monsieur Charpentier, referred to by the boys as 'Mossoo', is an incompetent who is unable to command respect from either the boys or his fellow masters. As with Hurree Jamset Ram Singh,

Mossoo's language is a deliberately silly mix of French and cod-English, and he is consistently described in the narrative as well as in the boys' dialogue as 'the little beast' and 'little ass'. Non-colonial characters seemingly cannot be admired or respected, but are represented as subhuman, described in animal analogies. Those whose countries have not been subdued by the might of the English are allowed no power, but must remain only as objects of ridicule. In 'The Cruise of the Firefly', Spanish sailors are referred to in much the same deprecating way:

> 'They dare not fire on the British ensign,' said Johnny Bull, with a grunt.
> 'Well, I don't know,' said Bob thoughtfully. 'There's a lot of gun-running going on on both sides in that Spanish scrap. And any old gun-runner could fly British colours, if he liked. They've a right to stop us and ask us questions, I believe, in Spanish waters.'
> 'Like their cheek!' grunted Johnny. 'They can see that this is an English yacht, if they've got any eyes in their silly heads. Do they think anybody on this yacht would be mixed up in gun-running?'
> ('The Cruise of the Firefly', *The Magnet*, 26 December 1936: 26)

The boys' sense of the superiority of the English over the Spanish sailors is clear, and underlined by the fact that most of the snobbery is voiced by Johnny Bull, namesake of the archetypal Englishman.

The imperialist ethos in *The Hotspur* stories is if anything even more directly portrayed. The nomenclature of the three houses at Red Circle School immediately gives the non-English characters the status of 'other'. The American characters are depicted as bullies – again, with few redeeming features that could attract any respect from the English characters who dominate the stories – and the only 'Yank' to feature frequently, Cyrus Judd, is described as 'bony', in direct contrast to the sporty and athletic ideal. He is also given stereotypical, gangster-style language to reinforce his bullying behaviour: 'his bony fist shot out and hit Doyle right on the nose. "Say, how do you like that, Wise Guy?"' ('Dead-Wide Dick's Book of Doom', *The Hotspur*, 8 February 1936: 145). As noted earlier, the Red Circle School stories do not make much use of the house system within the school, but it does serve as a useful counterpoint to the Englishness of the Home House boys.

Post-war imperialism

The inter-war story papers must be set against the background of Victorian culture, the culture which informed the writing of Frank

Richards and his contemporaries. By the 1920s much had changed, and the notion of imperialism had taken on a rather different flavour. Mackenzie argues that although in strategic and economic dimensions imperialism was less in evidence after the war it did live on in the popular psychology and in popular culture. He suggests that a truly popular idealistic imperialism, which was interested in defending an existing empire rather than in its acquisition, was even stronger in the inter-war period than in the late nineteenth century:

> There is ample evidence to suggest that the role of Britain as a world power deriving from its unique imperial status continued to be projected to the British public after the First World War. Victory in war had confirmed rather than diminished that status, however much the economic indicators pointed the other way. On the contrary, in the economic storms of the inter-war years it was possible again, as in the late nineteenth century, to depict the Empire as a saviour from decline. Children's literature, educational texts and national rituals directed to these ends were joined by the powerful new media of the cinema and broadcasting. (Mackenzie, 1986c: 8)

There is, however, much disagreement between cultural historians on this point. As Hyam notes, the current debate about the impact of empire on British society is 'between "integralists", who believe that Britain was awash with, or saturated by, imperialism, and "minimalists", who believe its influence has been wildly overstated' (Hyam, 2006: 2, note 4). Mackenzie, an example of the former, argues that imperialism was an obsession for both middle and working classes; Rose and Mangan tend more towards a minimalist position, in arguing that the working classes were largely indifferent to it, and in any case had far too difficult a life to be bothered about ideals of masculinity (or femininity). Humphries argues that some aspects of working-class culture and practices could be more accurately described as resistant behaviours:

> much of the behaviour of working-class subcultures that is conventionally stigmatised as anti-social can alternatively be conceptualised as resistance and viewed to some extent as an indictment of oppressive institutions. (Humphries, 1981: 6)

Porter speaks for the 'minimalists' in launching a 'powerfully devastating attack on the integralists' (Hyam, 2006: 2, note 4). In Porter's view, the working classes were largely indifferent to the Empire and notions of imperialism: 'they did not think much about it. They seem generally not to have identified with it. This is what the imperial propagandists felt, and feared' (Porter, 2004: 225). Taking issue with Mackenzie's sense that imperialist propaganda must have been overwhelming because there was so much of it, he argues that its influence 'could not have been all that persuasive, if the propagandists felt they needed to propagandise so hard' (Porter, 2004: 6). Interestingly, this attitude is in line with what 'intelligent contemporaries' always said was the case – Hyam quotes Noel Annan (born in 1916): 'the country had always been bored with the empire: on this matter a gulf yawned between the mass of the population and the ruling class' (Hyam, 2006: 2, note 4).

Thompson argues a third position, which he labels 'elusivist', which focuses on ways in which the Empire 'reflected and reinforced existing social, economic and political trends' rather than pushing them in new directions (Thompson, 2005: 4). In contrast to the relatively extreme positions of the 'saturated' integralists and the 'indifferent' minimalists, Thompson takes a more balanced view which underlines complexity and flux: 'The effects of empire on the structure of British society, the development of British institutions and the shaping of British identities were complex and (at times) contradictory ... There was never likely to be any single or monolithic "imperial culture" in Britain, therefore' (Thompson, 2005: 5).

In the context of the story papers, Thompson's approach is the most helpful in allowing space for readers to interpret the messages embedded in the narratives and apply them in their own lives. In the end, it is the reception of ideas which is of most importance (Porter, 2004: 6). While the imperial ideology presented in the popular culture of the time may have been carefully constructed by producers, it did not work for all. For many working-class readers there was too much of a contradiction between the rhetoric of imperialism and their own everyday reality. Edna Rich (born in 1910) stopped short of rebellion against imperial ritual, but certainly had strong feelings of resistance:

> I loved poetry, and the school was assembled and they stood me on top of the headmistress's desk and I had a Union Jack draped round me. And I had to recite, 'Oh where are you going to all you big steamers? To fetch England's own grain up and down the great sea. I'm going to fetch you your bread and butter.' And somehow or other it stirred a bit of rebellion in me. I thought, where's my bread, where's my butter? And I think it sowed the first seeds of socialism in me, it really did. (Humphries, 1981: 42–3)

What form did this imperialist ideology take in children's lives of the inter-war period, and how was it transmitted? Mackenzie's suggestion of the interlinked influences of children's literature, educational texts and national rituals is useful here. National rituals (again these are *invented* traditions which operate as tools of social engineering) took on a new importance after the war, and again were particularly popular amongst the middle classes. Hobsbawm defines three overlapping types of invented traditions:

> a) those establishing or symbolising social cohesion or the membership of groups, real or artificial communities; b) those establishing or legitimising institutions, status or relations of authority, and c) those whose main purpose was socialisation, the inculcation of beliefs, value systems and conventions of behaviour. (Hobsbawm, 1983: 11)

He adds that type a) was prevalent, with the other two operating more as subsets of the function of type a). Looking at the position of children in society, however, it seems to me that types b) and c) were equally, if not more, important. National rituals, such as singing the national anthem and saluting the Union flag, were a powerful part of the process of educating children in the ways of imperialism. New rituals were invented at this time with the specific aim of educating the public – and children in particular – about the Empire. As noted above, there is disagreement about how much importance the general public attributed to these rituals; while there is plenty of evidence to show that children were exposed to imperialist ideals, there is also evidence to suggest that they were able to take a critical stance, or even an indifferent one, in the face of propaganda.

The Empire Exhibition at Wembley in 1924–25 was the first great national event after the war, and was designed by its organisers to showcase the wonders of the Empire. It was also the first national event to be broadcast on radio, through a speech given by King George V. Thompson describes it as 'a self-consciously imperial affair ... a miniature model of the empire', which was visited by some 27 million people over two years (Thompson, 2005: 86). It was featured, admiringly, in almost every children's annual for 1924. *The Magnet* also incorporates a visit to the event. Although this story was not written by Frank Richards, but by one of his (unnamed) colleagues, it has all the elements of a Frank Richards tale. The extract below includes: a vivid illustration of Harry's leadership and Bob Cherry's hearty gung-ho attitude; a reminder that school rules still apply beyond the building, as the boys do as 'Quelchy' told them; a reminder that Hurree Singh may be a colonial, but is still one of the 'chums'; and a nicely humorous underlining of the sheer size and influence of the Empire:

> 'Wembley!'
> 'Hallo, hallo, hallo! Here we are at last!' called Bob Cherry eagerly. At Charing Cross the juniors had made a brief halt for lemonade and sandwiches – having decided not to 'blue' cash on a more elaborate meal – before going on to Wembley, and now they had arrived at their destination at last.
> The juniors had recovered some of their cheery spirits by this time, and they lost no time in gaining admittance to the huge grounds of the most stupendous enterprise of its kind ever planned, eager to make the most of their brief visit.
> Having passed through the turnstiles, they purchased programmes and began to study them.
> 'My hat! We'll want a week or two to see this little lot!' grinned Bob Cherry.
> 'We can't see everything, of course,' said Harry. 'We'll have to choose the most interesting – to us. Quelchy told us to be sure and visit the Palace of Industry, so we'd better.'
> 'Ha, ha! Yes!'
> So the juniors made a start by visiting the Palace of Industry. They had scarcely expected to find anything of interest to them here, despite Mr. Quelch's recommendation; yet they did, in the sports and games section.
> 'Now for the Palace of Engineering,' said Harry. 'We must see that, you chaps.'
> The juniors crossed Kingsway and entered the Palace of Engineering, and as they expected, they found the exhibits of wonderful interest, especially in the wireless section. And Johnny Bull, who had a mechanical turn, had to be dragged out of the huge building when Harry gave the word to go.
> 'Over there, my esteemed chums,' remarked Hurree Singh, 'is the pavilion of my own country. Shall we strollfully go there?'
> 'Oh, I don't mind a little jaunt across to India,' said Bob Cherry. 'Afterwards I suggest we take a run over to Canada and Australia. Then I don't think a little tramp through East Africa, South Africa, Burma, Malta and Ceylon would harm us. We could finish up with the West Indies, Newfoundland, Hong Kong and those places after tea, what? Musn't tire ourselves, though.' ('Billy Bunter's Wembley Party', *The Magnet*, 11 October 1924: 16–17)

This description forms part of a long story in which the real emphasis is on unmasking a deception, but the boys' evident delight in visiting the exhibition reinforces the message that this is a major event, Again, here is evidence of imperialist vision being incorporated into the story papers as a means of encouraging readers to conform to the values of the producers. As Pugh points out, however, there is plenty of evidence to suggest that attitudes to the Empire Exhibition were not as clear cut as the visitor figures might suggest. 'Although people enjoyed the spectacles there are grounds for thinking that they saw them essentially as entertainment or escapism, and that their enthusiasm for the imperial cause was rather shallow' (Pugh, 2009: 402). Thompson also notes that there are alternative interpretations of the event, including the 'minimalist' position that the organisers were concerned about public ignorance of the Empire, or the fact that previous propaganda had failed in its task of persuading people of the value of the Empire (Thompson, 2005: 86). William Woodruff recalls his own attitude as a child in the 1920s: 'I had no idea why we had such a big empire except that it was taken for granted that we were better than anybody else' (Woodruff, 2002: 125). Empire Day, a national holiday to take place on Queen Victoria's birthday, 24 May, and instituted by the Conservative peer Lord Meath in 1902, was given new prominence in the 1920s. Meath's aim was to train youth in order to build up an imperial race 'worthy of responsibility, alive to duty, filled with sympathy towards mankind, and not afraid of self-sacrifice in the promotion of lofty ideals' (Mangan, 1986: 130). Through careful strategic marketing, by 1928 the Empire Day movement had grown to the extent that 5 million children had participated in ceremonies across the country, and schools had wholeheartedly committed themselves to it. Mangan writes that

> During Empire week, imperial topics in schools were to predominate. In time, a whole battery of instruments of indoctrination came to exist – schools could choose from among an Empire Service, the performance of an Empire play or pageant, an exhibition of Empire products, film and slide lectures, a school concert, a recitation of heroic English poems, an Empire Day wireless programme, a display of imperial flags in the playground and the observance of the slogan 'Empire meals on Empire Day.' (Mangan, 1986: 132)

The Empire Marketing Board also distributed materials free to schools, on the premise that 'teachers as a whole offered a most promising field for propaganda work' (Empire Marketing Board sub-committee, quoted in Constantine, 1986: 212). In 1932 there were 9000 requests for copies of free Empire Marketing Board posters, and by 1933, 27,000 schools were on the mailing list. Correspondents to the Empire Marketing Board underline the value of these free resources:

> Your posters have been a godsend to us. They vivify and intensify the very impression we wish our pupils to receive with respect to the resources and potentialities of our Empire.
>
> The posters are of real value educationally and nationally and quite fit in with my idea of teaching geography, history and economics. (Constantine, 1986: 213)

For children, however, one of the main attractions of Empire Day was the fact that they were given time off school. As Woodruff puts it: 'the meaning to me was that we got free buns and a half-day holiday' (Woodruff, 2002: 125). Porter describes the 'mild' content of many Empire Day celebrations, which focused on English folk-dancing and dressing up as characters from English history, rather than any specifically imperialist content. In this way, he argues, 'children could enthuse over the trappings of such events without being deeply persuaded' (Porter, 2004: 210). As noted above, attitudes to empire were complex, and child readers did not necessarily wholeheartedly submit themselves to the messages being offered to them.

Alongside these powerful influences was a further cultural force which had grown tremendously in popularity before the war and continued to do so in the inter-war period: the boys' movements, including the Boy Scouts, and the Boys' Brigade. These quasi-military movements were a determined attempt to extend Christian manliness to working-class adolescents. Springhall quotes Baden-Powell's publicity for the Boy Scout movement, which promotes the Scouts as a 'form of training to reverse decadence in the coming generation by restoring manliness and character to the adolescent male' (Springhall, 1987: 53). Baden-Powell's aims for the Scout movement are interesting in that there is an almost direct correlation between his views and the general focus of adventure stories in the story papers. Baden-Powell's ideas on training boys apparently came from Lord Edward Cecil's Boy Scout troop, formed in Mafeking during the siege of 1899–1900, but they are also the culmination of a process of myth-making which sees certain skills as 'natural' to an archetypal male hero. Baden-Powell defined this group as 'men who in peace time carry out work which requires the same type of abilities as in war':

> These are the frontiersmen of all parts of our Empire. The 'trappers' of North America, hunters of central Africa, the British pioneers, explorers and missionaries over Asia and all the wild parts of the world, the bushmen and drovers of Australia, the constabulary of North-West Canada and of South Africa – are all peace scouts, real *men* in every sense of the word, and thoroughly call upon scout crafts, i.e. they understand living out in the jungles, and they can find their way anywhere, are able to read meaning from the smallest signs and foot tracks; and they know how to look after their health when far away from any doctors, are strong and plucky, and ready to face any danger, and always keen to help each other. They are accustomed to take their lives in their hands, and to fling them down without hesitation if they can help their country by doing so. (Baden-Powell, 2004: 13)

As Todd notes, however, the popularity of these movements does not necessarily mean that young members accepted the leaders' philosophy entirely, suggesting that the movements found greatest popularity among the more affluent sections of the working class with children whose parents preferred their leisure outings to be supervised (Todd, 2006: 719).

Stories in *The Hotspur* draw directly on Baden-Powell-type frontier stereotypes – for example: 'Buffalo Bill's Schooldays' (a lumberjack school in North America); 'The School Amid the Snows' (fur trappers in Canada); and 'The Ting-a-ling Teacher of Tarza' (a school for settlers' children in the African jungle). These stories from 1933 demonstrate that imperial values are still current, albeit in a slightly less overtly didactic fashion than in pre-war stories. The stories follow a familiar format – an English schoolboy is sent, for varying reasons, to school in a distant, wild part of the Empire, and struggles to settle in to his new life, against the strangeness of the environment, the wildness of nature and, more often than not, the resistant behaviour of the 'natives'. Colonialist values survive strongly here, with English characters assuming 'natural' superiority over 'others'. In 'The School Amid the Snows', from *The Hotspur*, 6 January 1934, the villain figure is a 'half-breed' (French/ Native American) who attempts to persuade the Native Americans to fight against the fur traders by telling them that the land is rightfully theirs, taken from them illegally by the colonialist invaders. When he is eventually defeated, the colonialists' victory has to be made complete by the humiliation of the Native American chief, who is ridiculed in a very patronising manner:

> 'We've decided to make no report about it this time,' went on the Sergeant, 'but it's got to stop. Not another drop of gin to be drunk in your encampment. Go back at once and tell your men to behave themselves or it will be the worse for them. And before you go, you may as well see the selection of trade goods we have got here ready to exchange for your furs.'
> 'Well done, you lads!' he told the three boys later. 'It was a bright idea bringing the old chap here. He's seen our goods and his soul's burning with envy.' ('The School Amid the Snows', *The Hotspur*, 6 January 1934: 22)

In 'The Ting-a-Ling Teacher of Tarza', Martin Arrow is sent into the jungle by 'the Education Authority for Kenya Colony' to set up a school for settlers' children. As Arrow says:

> 'You can't have your children growing up into young savages. After all, they're white, and they must learn what other white boys learn. The world would be a queer place without education.' ('The Ting-a-Ling Teacher of Tarza', *The Hotspur*, 24 March 1934: 319)

Here again is the dualism of English against 'other', but interestingly in this case there is no attempt to educate the 'others'. The school is a protected enclave of white Western values, attempting to fend off the 'savage' influence of the indigenous population. The implication is that only the white boys are worthy of 'education' – and the story compounds this colonialist ideology by showing Arrow and his boys foiling a threatened attack by 'blacks' by chalking triangles on themselves, an act which scares the 'blacks' into submission.

Summary and conclusions

This chapter has traced the background to and representation of imperialist ideology in the story papers, and in school stories in particular. Exploring the portrayal of hero-figures in the stories has shown how the mythical qualities of the classical male hero are reinforced in the particular context of the 1920s and 1930s in order to present intended messages to child readers. Looking in detail at the ways in which the imperialist ethos had complex and contested influence on the culture and public life of the inter-war years shows that the story paper writers were themselves caught up in a web of cultural myths and invented traditions, and that although there were clear intended moral and imperialistic messages embedded in the story papers, the extent to which children took these on board is difficult to determine.

Though *The Magnet* and *The Hotspur* may appear on the surface to be very different in approach, they are very much the same in their aims – to show boy heroes being tested, but ultimately conforming to a moral pattern and learning from their experiences. Situated against a metalanguage of myth, writers and publishers are part of this value system, and consciously or unconsciously seek to ensure that these values remain dominant.

Imperialist tendencies seem to be reinforced through the context of the stories, with school used as a metaphor for country, and boys' allegiance to the school and its codes of behaviour seen as paramount. School is the centre against which the 'other' is defined, in the same way that England is the 'mother' country in contrast with colonial outposts and 'other' savage places. The schoolboy heroes are always English, but the school itself does not have to be in England – enclaves of 'Englishness' can exist in other places so long as the code of heroic behaviour is maintained.

School stories may seem less obvious vehicles to reinforce imperial values than the traditional adventure story, but in fact they can be just as effective. School gives readers a familiar context in which to apply the rules of the adventure hero narrative.

5
Inter-War Story Papers and the Rise of Children's Cinema

The rapid rise in cinema attendance amongst the general population in the 1920s and 1930s has been well documented as a social and cultural phenomenon. The appeal of cinema was just as strong for children, so how did this expansion of children's cultural lives affect their reading? How are story paper reading habits connected to cinema attendance, and in what ways did the cinema influence the story papers? Making meaning from cultural acts does not happen in isolation – that is to say that story paper reading should not be seen as a discrete act with meaning in and of itself. This chapter explores the ways in which children took messages and meanings from story paper reading in the context of their wider social and cultural lives, bringing together visual (cinematic) and written (story paper) textual experiences. Using film theory and narrative theory it shows how story paper and film narratives of the period intersect and draw from each other, setting up structural parallels. Weekly story papers carry obvious comparisons with weekly cinema serials, but beyond superficial similarities some key points can be drawn out about the roles of producers and consumers, authors and directors.

In researching this chapter I have tried to draw as far as is possible on primary materials. Film archives for this period do exist – for example, at the British Film Institute – but these are not extensive, quite possibly because many of the original serials were not seen as worthy candidates for archiving, and have been lost (a significant commentary on the low status of popular cultural artefacts at the time). There are also issues of appropriate storage space for bulky canisters of inflammable celluloid film, given that film serials generally ran to 12 or 15 episodes. Few complete runs have survived and of those that have, not all are held as 'viewing copies' by archives. However, digital copies of many serials are now available online, for example via www.camelotbroadcasting.com, and many can also be bought in DVD format. For the purposes of this chapter, I have chosen two representative film serials – *Wolf Dog* (1933) and *Flash Gordon's Trip to Mars* (1938) – which will be explored in detail in later sections. *Wolf Dog* is a straightforward example of an action adventure serial, with a teenage boy as the main protagonist, and the added attraction of a dog who accompanies him on his adventures – animals as stars having been a popular plot device from the early 1920s, when Rin Tin Tin featured in a series of Hollywood films. Flash Gordon has iconic status as a comic book hero-figure (first seen in comic-book format in the US in 1934). Staples notes, of an earlier Flash Gordon serial from 1936, that 'everyone who was there remembers [it]' (Staples, 1997: 217).

In the course of my research I also consulted copies of the five reports that were produced in the early 1930s, officially enquiring into the effects on children of their cinema-going habits (Birkenhead Vigilance Committee, 1931; Birmingham Cinema Enquiry Committee, 1931; London County Council Education Committee, 1932; Mackie, 1933; Sheffield Juvenile Organisations Committee, 1932). All five are held in the BFI Library, London. While none of these was particularly lengthy, some did quote children's responses in some detail.

Children's cinema in the 1920s and 1930s

What was the experience of going to the cinema like for children of the period? What sort of films did they see, and what did they think of them?

The 1920s and 1930s saw the vast expansion of popular cinema across Britain. By the end of the 1930s there were nearly 5000 cinemas in operation (up from 3000 in 1926), and annual admissions had risen to over 1027 million by 1940 (Staples, 1997: 43). 'Everyone saw films, even if they were in some cases only the old silent ones that were still being recycled in the mission halls for an admission charge of a penny' (Magee, 2003: 222). A sizeable proportion of these attendees were children, who saved their pennies to go to Saturday matinees and cinema clubs run by the major chains Odeon, ABC and Granada. These Saturday shows were very cheap and very popular – children would pay between two and fourpence (compared with an adult ticket costing a shilling and sixpence), and matinees regularly attracted an audience eagerly queuing in the street. The shows usually consisted of 'a main film, a B-feature, a newsreel, a cartoon and one or two shorts' (Magee, 2003: 222). The first Granada matinees were so popular that over 200 children were left outside, and in Glasgow in 1933, 10,000 children applied for tickets for just two special Saturday shows (Staples, 1997: 43). The films they watched were in the main the same as those the adults watched at other times and were mostly made in America – featuring actors such as Charlie Chaplin, Buster Keaton, Jackie Coogan, Mary Pickford, Douglas Fairbanks or Tom Mix the cowboy. By the inter-war period, American films made up 85 to 90 per cent of the British market (Rose, 2001: 358). Most of the 'B-movies', designed to back up the main film in a double bill, were westerns made for the US market. Short, straightforward and overwhelmingly moral in tone in their simplistic rendering of 'good' versus 'bad', these B films were among the more popular genres for boys (LCC Education Committee, 1932: 4; Birkenhead Vigilance Committee, 1931: 6). The output of B westerns was prolific, with around 1000 produced in the 1930s. Staples notes that 'if all the B westerns ever made had come to Britain, there would have been enough titles to show a different one every Saturday for 20 years' (Staples, 1997: 63). With such availability, it is hardly surprising that children were enthralled by them. In William Woodruff's words:

> Talking pictures opened up a new, exciting world for me ... It is impossible to convey the impression the earliest films made ... My spirit soared across the great plains of America as far as the Rockies. I jolted along in a covered wagon, gun on knee. There were times when, glued to my seat, I feared the red Indian warriors as much as any white settler had done. (Woodruff, 2002: 177)

In 1923, Home Office guidelines led to a licensing agreement which allowed under-16s to see 'U'-rated films, but specified that they should be kept out of 'A'-rated films unless accompanied by an adult. Whilst many areas of England and Wales complied with the agreement, 35 per cent of the licensing areas did not accept the guidelines and consequently many children were able to watch 'A'-rated films on a regular basis (Staples, 1997: 22). That children were given regular access to 'adult' content was the source of some concern, as was the influence of American culture through the language and behaviour of key characters. As Magee points out, 'the '30s was the decade in which Britain came under the dominance of American influences in popular song and talking film – and in both cases it was partly the classlessness of the American approach that invited this and enabled it to happen. We children of the '30s were the first in Britain to grow up with everyday familiarity with things American' (Magee, 2003: 221). Such dominance (and the poor performance of the British film industry) led to the introduction of the Cinematographic Film Act (1927), which imposed a quota system on cinemas, who were legally obliged to make 7.5 per cent of their showings British-originated films, rising to 20 per cent by 1936 (Pugh, 2009: 340). Even so, this would hardly have dented the influence of all things American which still represented 80 per cent of the offering. The 'classlessness' that Magee points to is interesting in that it implies a more inclusive approach to audiences. It is also worth noting here this inclusiveness also applies to the gender of the audience, in that the appeal of the cinema was equally strong among boys and girls. While the publishers of children's fiction were still dividing their output along gender lines, the film industry was not – films were produced to appeal to as broad an audience as possible, with no reference to gender, class or even age, as we have seen.

The five cinema enquiries confirm that over 40 per cent of children went to the cinema one or more times each week. In Birkenhead the figure was over 45 per cent, and A. J. Jenkinson's survey in London reported that between 40 and 50 per cent of secondary school boys visited the cinema once a week or more, and that figure rose to more than 60 per cent among senior school boys (Jenkinson, 1940: 96). (The figures are very similar for girls, with over 40 per cent of secondary school girls attending once a week or more, and 60 per cent of senior school girls.) There was some drop-off in the figures for older secondary school pupils (at the age of 15+), which Jenkinson attributes to rising pressures of schoolwork and homework for secondary school pupils (Jenkinson, 1940: 96). Those 14-year-olds who had left senior school and found work may have had relatively more income to spend on cinema trips; boys aged 15 and over who were not at secondary school would have been either working or unemployed, and Jenkinson's survey did not include this group. In the Edinburgh report, the average weekly attendance figure given was as high as 71 per cent. This survey, however, consulted a slightly older age-group (ages 9–18), and although a detailed breakdown of age and attendance patterns is not given, it seems possible that a higher percentage of older teenagers, who were more likely to have been earning a wage, would have been able to attend the cinema more often.

Once inside the cinema, heat and noise would have added to the general excitement. Sarah Smith quotes Valentine Tucker, who attended Saturday matinees in Dagenham from 1934:

> We all shouted, 'Look be-ind yer!' when the baddie was creeping up on our hero, and in unison with the pounding of the horses' hooves

our enthusiastic feet slithered on discarded bread crusts and empty winkle shells, and paddled in pools deposited by those who had used the floor as a lavatory rather than miss out on any of the excitement. (Smith, 2005: 145)

A report from the 1931 Birkenhead investigation also shows the commitment of the young cinema-goers:

> Cinema A: (1) Hall 70% full, all children from a very poor area. Management quite efficient. A hot afternoon. Disinfectant occasionally sprayed. Films: 'Topical', 'The Finger Points', 'The Cuckoo' (U Talkies). During 'Topical', the children kept up one long babel of shouting and talking. 'The Finger Points' highly exciting, full of hairbreadth escapes, shootings and mêlées. 'The Cuckoo' was composed of leg shows, love scenes and fights. Immediately the leg show part commenced there was silence. The children missed the adult humour of the piece. (Birkenhead Vigilance Committee, 1931: 18)

In these extracts, children's ability to engage with film action is clear, despite the apparent discomfort of heat and disinfectant spray. ('The Finger Points' is a 1931 gangster movie starring Clark Gable as a gambling house boss involved in a bribery plot with a journalist. With a plot centring on gambling, murder, alcoholism and fraud, it's likely that the 'adult' content of this piece was also missed by the child audience.) William Woodruff's experience of the Saturday matinee (which he paid for by handing over two empty, clean two-pound jam jars) was also 'a wild affair where a man kept order with a long bamboo pole. If we were caught blowing rice or rock-hard peas at the pianist, or spitting orange pips from the balcony, or whistling too long at the kissing scenes, we ran the risk of getting whacked – a real hard whack' (Woodruff, 2002: 175).

The children's preference for action adventure over any sort of love scenes is also made clear elsewhere in the Birkenhead report: in answer to the question 'What sort of pictures do you like best?', out of 1440 replies, 303 voted for 'travel/adventure' and only 17 for 'love' films. The other reports give similar results. Boys in Birmingham (in response to the same question) wrote, 'We like any kind but not love' and 'We do not like loveing [sic] pictures' (Birmingham Cinema Enquiry Committee, 1931: 9); and in London, love films were bottom of the popularity list for boys (LCC Education Committee, 1932: 4).

Cinema managers were not slow to pick up on the kinds of films that children enjoyed the most. Sidney Bernstein, an early pioneer of the children's matinee show, and owner of the Granada cinema chain, spoke of children's interest in these special performances at a BFI conference in 1936:

> The gratifying thing about the present shows is that we have been able to achieve a regularity in attendances. One important contributory factor is that we have adopted the policy of showing serial films. The children like the serials because they are action films. For the same reason there is no question that their main preference in feature films is for westerns. (Bernstein, 1936: 31)

Speaking at the same conference, Kenneth Nyman (Chairman of the London and Home Counties Branch of the Cinematograph Exhibitors' Association) listed the components of 'the ideal programme' for children. This would, he felt, be less than two hours long and consist of a slapstick comedy, a cartoon (in particular Donald Duck, which he suggested was a real favourite), a feature of the 'actionful-cum-heroic sort with a minimum of dialogue', about 45–50 minutes long, and an episode of a serial film:

> The serial *in toto* would be approximate in type to the feature film, but the thrills at the end of each weekly episode and the sense of anticipation aroused by the climax at the end of each episode are interesting to and not unhealthy for the children (and are incidentally good business!). (Nyman, 1936: 41)

Nyman articulates what Bernstein hints at – that regular attendances are what makes money for the cinema owners. Attracted to the cinema by the pull of visual pleasure and the shared experience of dramatic action narratives, the child audiences were drawn back week after week to follow the exploits of their serial heroes. This weekly cycle is almost exactly the same as the producer/consumer interaction of the story papers: producers (in this case film-makers and cinema owners) deliberately working to build anticipation and emotional reaction in consumers in order to keep them buying in to the experience, and hence keep the business expanding. This is very much a reciprocal process – producers follow consumers' likes and dislikes, and consumers repay the attention with their custom. The success of serials (visual or written) depends as much on the skill of the storytelling as on what happens in the anticipatory spaces between episodes. The cliffhanger final scene must be compelling enough to sustain a week-long sense of anticipation, and genuine interest in the completion of the action event. How this was done, in the film serials as well as the story papers, will be the subject of later sections of this chapter. That the strategy worked – for producers and consumers – is evident from comments such as Nyman's, that the serials represented a sound business proposition. It is also clear from reminiscences such as the quotations below from Annette Kuhn's and Terry Staples's interviewees, commenting on the pull of the cliffhanger ending:

> That meant we had to go to the cinema thirteen weeks in succession ... But, you know, it couldn't come quick enough! See when you come out of the cinema, on a Saturday afternoon? You'd say to yourself, 'I wonder what'll happen next week? I wonder if he'll get out of that mess he's in.' (Interview transcript from Glasgow (1995), in Kuhn, 2002: 56–7)

> The only titles I remember are *Tarzan* and *Flash Gordon*, but I remember vividly that they all stopped each week at the most exciting moment when everyone was in danger, so we could hardly wait the week out to find out how they came through. The camaraderie of discussing how the hero would escape that week's perils occupied a lot of children, and made school more bearable. (Staples, 1997: 70–1)

Here, the memory of bridging the weekly anticipatory space remains strong, and these respondents are remembering the experience of anticipation rather than the details of the storylines themselves. Even though the hero invariably did escape from his 'mess', audiences seem to have gained as much enjoyment from anticipating the ways in which he would manage to do this as from watching the action itself.

Narrative poetics and film theory

This section explores in more detail the construction of meanings in narratives, and in particular draws some comparisons between structure and meaning-making in film serials and written stories in the story papers.

An 'ideal' narrative can be described as one which begins with a stable situation, which is then disturbed by some power or force (Todorov, 1977: 111). The resulting disequilibrium is then resolved by a force applied in the opposite direction – equilibrium is thus restored. This basic structure can be seen in the film serials as well as in stories in *The Magnet* and *The Hotspur*. In *Wolf Dog*, the three main characters (boy, dog and man) have three separate narrative beginnings, each of which is immediately destabilised (the dog loses his master in a plane crash; the boy finds out his real identity; the man has his invention stolen). In the Greyfriars and Red Circle School stories, stability is signified by the school and all its codes, and storylines work against this as characters either transgress the codes or outsiders are introduced as threats. Equilibrium is always re-established at the end of the narrative – Flash defeats his enemies Ming the Merciless and Azura, Queen of Magic; Greyfriars school rules are always upheld. In short, morality/'good' always triumphs over immorality/'evil'.

An obvious point about serial narratives – written or filmic – is that the moment of resolution is repeatedly delayed. As Cohen and Shires write:

> Serial structures organise several macrosequences, embedding or combining the final point of one sequence with the opening or middle points of another one in order to defer the final moment of closure. (Cohen and Shires, 1988: 54)

Crucially, in order to maximise the effect of the anticipatory space between one episode and the next, the action sequence must be cut before it reaches a final point. Closure of the featured sequence happens at the beginning of the next episode, but is always embedded in the beginning of a new sequence in order to maintain the narrative flow. At the beginning of episode two of *Flash Gordon's Trip to Mars*, for example, the spaceship spins out of the nitron beam (resolving the action event from the previous episode) but then crash-lands, leaving Flash and his friends stranded on Mars (initiating the next sequence).

In film serials, and in some of the longer story sequences from *The Magnet* and *The Hotspur*, the overall effect of this rapid turnover of sequences is a heightened sense of disequilibrium in the viewer/reader. In *Wolf Dog*, rapid sequencing of what Roland Barthes calls 'cardinal' or 'kernel' events, 'initiating, increasing or concluding an uncertainty to advance or outline a sequence of transformations' (Cohen and Shires, 1988: 54), gives viewers little time to absorb and reflect on narrative stasis (to take a narrative breath, as it were) before the next action event provokes further disequilibrium. Kernel events are supported in narrative structures by 'catalyzers' or 'satellite' events, which 'fill in the narrative space' which separates kernel events (Barthes, 1973: 8). In *Wolf Dog* the action runs at great speed, with twists and turns of plot which quite quickly become confusing. In an extended first episode, the story begins with a pilot and his dog setting out on a solo long-distance flight, watched by an assembled crowd. The plane crashes not long into its journey, and the pilot is killed, leaving the dog to fend for itself by joining a pack of wolves. The plot then switches to a teenage boy living with his uncle and grandmother in a backwoods shack. The uncle mistreats the boy, and his grandmother urges him to run away, telling him he is really Frank Courtney, heir to a great shipping fortune. Frank does indeed run away, and encounters the dog on his journey, rescuing him from hunters. They become firm friends, and stow away on a ship belonging to the company to which Frank is allegedly heir. On the ship, they make friends with Bob Whitlock, the ship's radio officer, who has created a 'lightning ray' which he intends to give to the government. The machine is stolen by two thugs, Lang and Brookes, who are in the employ of Norman Bryan, the chairman of the shipping company. Not only does Bryan want to use the ray to his own ends, but he has also heard that Frank is on his way to claim his fortune. Bryan therefore needs to make sure Frank is dealt with, or risk losing the shipping company. Episode one ends with Lang and Brookes escaping from the ship (with the lightning ray) in a speedboat, with Bob and Frank close behind them. All of this action happens within 30 minutes.

The fact that there is so much action in the first episode creates a problem for the beginning of the second – how to summarise all of this for viewers who may not have seen the first instalment. The film producers solve this by adding a lengthy written description, in blocks of text with a music soundtrack (the text is not voiced). A surprising level of literacy – and attention span – is required of viewers here in order to read through this description. To try and alleviate this problem, the serial makes use of flashbacks with great regularity, showing and re-showing earlier sequences to remind viewers of the backstory. This, however, quickly becomes tedious for viewers who have followed the whole serial. By episode four, in which there is a long sequence repeated exactly from episode one (Frank's grandmother telling him about his real identity), the flashback method has become stale and seriously impedes the forward momentum of the story. Interestingly, the producers of *Flash Gordon's Trip to Mars* resolve this issue in a rather different way, presenting the plot summary in the form of a strip cartoon, which appears on a screen operated by one of Azura's guards. The drawings show scenes from the previous episodes, with written captions below. The pictures reinforce the words – and vice versa – giving audiences plenty of opportunity to take in the relevant information.

This dependence on the destabilising power of action events is typical of film serials, and of the style of *The Hotspur* stories in particular. Cohen and Shires use the theory of 'suture' in order to explain why reading a story or watching a film offers pleasure, and their argument can be readily applied to action narratives and serial narratives. They argue that narrative unfolds as a chain of signifiers, and that the process of delaying the final signified 'sutures' or connects the viewer/reader to the chain. Viewing/reading pleasure comes from an interactive process of exchanging meanings:

> Each 'cut' of the text encourages identification with a signifier positioned along the chain, leaving behind tracings of desire (unpleasure) which disrupt the reader/viewer's secure relation to the symbolic order of culture by jeopardising his or her imaginary history as a stable, continuous and coherent subject. In response to this dis-ease, the reader/viewer sutures the text's segmentations, achieving coherence (content) by identifying with the signifier, and attaining pleasure (contentment) as a sutured narrated subject seeking reinsertion in the symbolic order of culture. The suturing process actually increases pleasure when it allows the reader/viewer to repeat the history of previous and orthodox suturings, not only those from earlier points in the text but those from other texts as well. (Cohen and Shires, 1988: 172)

The suturing process enables the viewer/reader to deal with the sense of disequilibrium provoked by the narrative, through identifying with the signifier and actively suturing 'cuts' and 'gaps' in the text. Here, the viewer/reader feels him/herself to be at the centre of the process, actively creating both meaning and pleasure. As Cohen and Shires point out, this process is reinforced by repeated action, and pleasure is increased by making connections with previous viewings/readings. In the context of serial viewing/reading, the process points forward to the next episode as well as backward to previous episodes and to previous serials. The sense of connection to a signifier allows the viewer/reader to imagine future suturings – thinking through the ways in which the signifier will progress towards the final signified – as well as to invoke the memory of previous suturings. In this sense the viewer/reader can make active use of the anticipatory space between episodes and increase his/her pleasure in the experience by drawing not only on knowledge of the macro/microstructure of the serial currently in view, but also on intertextual knowledge from other serial viewings/readings and from an awareness of the external structuring of serials themselves – the knowledge that each episode will be shown/published at a set time, the need to plan forward to be able to afford to attend/buy the next episode, the sharing of meanings with friends.

Each episode of *Flash Gordon's Trip to Mars* finishes with a cliffhanger scene, leaving the audience to speculate on the fates of Flash and his colleagues each week. The summary at the beginning of each episode heightens the tension – prolonging the wait to see how Flash and company have survived. When the action does resume, the resolution of the action event quite often comes as an anticlimax – the pleasure of the anticipatory space then becomes a sense of displeasure at the ordinariness of the resolution. Episode one begins with Flash, Dr Zarkov and Dale Arden returning to Earth from their previous trip to Mongo (the point at which the 1936 serial ended). Scenes of celebration, apparently from stock news footage – cheering crowds, newspaper headlines and tickertape parades – are inter-cut with scenes inside the spaceship as the heroes prepare to land. This offers continuity for viewers who had seen the previous serial, and introduces the characters as intrepid adventurers to those who had not. The villains of the story, Ming and Azura, are shown plotting in Azura's palace on Mars. They transport two men to Earth, who plant a gas-emitting device and then die. The gas begins to cause atmospheric disturbances, and there are scenes of floods and hurricanes around the world (again these are realistic news-footage pieces). Flash and Zarkov work out the cause of the problems, and Zarkov vows to return to Mongo and save the Earth. Flash and Dale insist on accompanying him and they depart, not realising that Happy Hapgood, reporter on *The Dispatch*, has hidden on board, unaware the ship was about to take off. Meanwhile it transpires that Azura is at war with the Clay people on Mars, and needs nitron to power her weapons (the device planted on Earth is extracting nitron and beaming it back to Mars). In the spaceship, Zarkov realises the beam is actually coming from Mars, not Mongo. Unfortunately, the ship's controls malfunction and it falls into the path of the nitron beam. The episode ends with the spaceship plummeting out of control towards Mars. This sets up a tense and exciting anticipatory space, which is straightforwardly (and unexcitingly) resolved at the beginning of episode two when the spaceship simply spins out of the path of the nitron beam and manages a relatively safe crash-landing. At the end of episode two, Flash and his friends are trapped in the cavern of the Clay people, with stalactites descending to crush them, and panic beginning to set in. The beginning of episode three then shows a confident Flash simply shooting a hole in the wall with a nitron gun he stole from the Martians in the previous episode.

Similarly, each episode of *Wolf Dog* ends with a cliffhanger scene, with Frank or Bob involved in some sort of dangerous predicament. In *Wolf Dog*, the dog is quite often used as a device to help the heroes out of their danger, although this does begin to dampen the effect of the cliffhanger, as viewers quickly recognise that the heroes are safe, whatever their trouble, because the dog will save the day. At the end of episode two, for example, Bob is kidnapped by Lang and Brookes and forced to show them how to operate the lightning ray. The episode ends as the machine explodes and demolishes the building. Episode three begins with a reprise of the kidnap scene, but this time we see that the dog has followed, and is on hand to revive Bob in time for him to escape from the collapsing building.

Although the viewer/reader may feel actively and creatively at the centre of the suturing process, the whole dynamic is regulated by producers, 'with an economic interest in maintaining the social structures of power' (Cohen and Shires, 1988: 173). Both film and story paper production follow this pattern, producing narratives aimed at a specific audience, designed to embed specific ideologies.

The position of the spectator within this cinematic ideology is also an important consideration. Laura Mulvey argues that watching a film produces a sense of separation for the spectator:

> Although the film is really being shown, is there to be seen, conditions of screening and narrative conventions give the spectator an illusion of looking in on a private world. Among other things, the position of the spectator in the cinema is blatantly one of repression of their exhibitionism and projection of the repressed desire on to the performer. (Mulvey, 1989: 17)

She goes on to say that the cinema has 'structures of fascination', strong enough to allow the spectator temporarily to forget their own world – 'I forgot who I am and where I was' – as they are drawn into the illusory film world (which also echoes William Woodruff's feeling of being drawn in to the action of the film, as quoted earlier). This interconnects with Cohen and Shires's suturing theory; it is the structure of fascination which elicits the suturing process. There is therefore a dual process of separation and involvement in the film narrative – spectators look in on a separate, private world at the same time as identifying with the key figures within it. This sense of engagement increases with familiarity – in the case of film serials, for instance, spectators' ability to identify with the key character would have improved as the story progressed from week to week, and as they became more familiar with cinematic conventions, both physically, in the act of going to the cinema/experiencing the film, and cognitively, in learning the conventions of film narrative. This process is very similar to that of experiencing written narrative and identifying with key written story characters. Without a visual stimulus beyond that of the limited illustrations in the story papers, identifying with a written character involves a strong imaginative skill, but contemporary and later autobiographical accounts show that readers were able to enter into narrative worlds as completely as they did to film worlds. Child readers and viewers were very easily able to draw meanings from both film and story and to bring these into their own play:

> When the show was over we came out, still intoxicated by the excitement of the story and ... we galloped off home – up Broughton Road, across Broad Street, down Hankinson Street, then up Ellor Street, smacking our buttocks as we went, no longer Salford kids of the street. We were the goodies riding our trusty steeds against the baddies. (Wynne, 1997: 6)

> Invariably, after seeing a particularly exciting movie, I would reenact the hero's exploits. Thus, as Fred Thomson or Tom Mix, I would make a hundred 'indians' bite the dust; or as Captain Blood ... I would perform miraculous piratical exploits with a toy pistol and a wooden sword. (Mayer, 1948: 17)

> When I recall the absorption of self into the games I played and even into the stories in those boys' comics I cannot believe that my imagination was stunted in its growth ... Every child has in common the construction of a private world of fantasy, compounded of a variety of extravagant wishes which he can fulfil in his games. What we loosely call reality – meaning the bread and butter facts of life which are the burden and responsibility of parents – impinges upon a child's life only lightly except in the most grievous circumstances. (George Scott, quoted in Rose, 2001: 328)

Graeme Turner writes that the blurring of boundaries between the imaginary and the real is at the centre of the cinema experience, and it seems that it is also central to the experience of story paper reading. Turner quotes Christian Metz's description of the film image as 'the imaginary signifier', which refers to 'the fact that the reality which the filmed images call up is always absent, "present" only in our imaginations' (Turner, 1993: 111). The film spectator is effectively doubly removed from reality through the medium of film (Figure 5.1).

In order to engage effectively with the film narrative, the spectator must situate him/herself at the level of film reality, either critically separating him/herself from the rest of the continuum, or being genuinely unaware of it. Mulvey describes this as the three different 'looks' of cinema: the camera (as it records the pro-filmic event); the audience (as it watches the film); and the look of characters at each other within the screen illusion. She argues that the success of any film narrative depends on its being able to deny the first two 'looks' and subordinate them to the third, thus preventing the audience from being aware of their own 'reality' as consumers of cinema (Mulvey, 1989: 25).

Again there are obvious connections here with the reading experience, and the way in which readers situate themselves relative to the narrative. Here, though, the continuum is shorter and readers are, paradoxically, closer in one sense to reality than they are in the cinema experience, which carries an extra level of illusion (Figure 5.2).

Christian Metz takes this argument one stage further, in describing 'indexes of reality' in film:

> on the one hand there are the real data for which the film reproduces an incomplete perception (respecting the visual appearance of objects – or more generally, bodies – but not their tactile reality or solidity, etc); and on the other hand the data whose perception is as rich in the cinema as in life and which therefore enter the film without an amputation of one of their phenomenal dimensions; these are (1) the visible *movement* of bodies and (2) the set of auditive data. (Metz, 1981: 54)

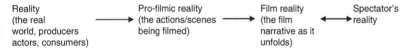

Figure 5.1 Film/reality continuum

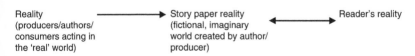

Figure 5.2 Story paper/reality continuum

Because film involves real bodies and real sound (regardless of whether or not the sound/voice is in reality produced by the body/actor on screen), the semblance of reality feels closer to the real for the spectator. Without a visual/aural dimension there can be no index of reality in written fictional narrative. Authors must rely on the powers of written description and the strength of the reader's imagination in order to create their illusions. As Metz writes: 'The novel is a narrative that organises itself into a world, the film is a world which organises itself into a narrative' (Metz, 1981: 64). This crisply balanced sentence is an excellent summary of the relative experiences of film and story narratives, but it does unfortunately exclude the reader/viewer. Story and film worlds are only effective if or when the reader/viewer brings meaning to them.

Adult responses to children's cinema

Adult responses to children's story paper reading habits were mixed, but on the whole more or less condemnatory of the content of the story papers. Teachers and social commentators warned about the potential effects of an addiction to 'low-standard' reading matter; parents variously condoned, ignored or banned it, but rarely encouraged it. Adult responses to children's cinema-going habits were similarly mixed, but there was seemingly a more widespread general concern amongst institutions and individuals who worked with children that the cinema might be doing more harm than good. This general concern is the impetus behind the five reports on the cinema commissioned in the 1930s, and it seems to have been driven in large part by worries about the effects of 'indexes of reality'. Because the filmic illusion is made up of real bodies and sound in an imitation of real events, adults worried about children's abilities to distinguish between the real and the imitation of the real, to separate themselves from imaginary signifiers. J. P. Mayer argued in 1946 that, without regulation, 'children's films must ... remain haphazard, if not dangerous to the child mind' (Mayer, 1972: 4). The Birmingham Cinema Enquiry Committee was convinced that cinema could be a 'tremendous and inexhaustible source of recreation and education', but was in need of regulation:

> [we are] determined to persist in our endeavour until the abuses and dangers – intellectual, physical and moral – particularly for children and adolescents, which at present make what might be

an instrument of good into an instrument of incalculable and irreparable harm, have been extirpated. (Birmingham Cinema Enquiry Committee, 1931: 4)

As with the other four committees, the Birmingham committee was made up of representatives from schools, churches, children's groups such as the Scouts and Girl Guides, and other local dignitaries. Reading between the lines of the reports, it is possible to detect a certain amount of fear of the growing power of the cinema, which these authority figures felt was alarmingly beyond their control. Calls for censorship and other forms of regulation are an attempt to regain that control.

The five reports fail to substantiate in any meaningful way any of the worries which gave rise to the investigations. Although all five try to emphasise the fact that children were frightened by film experiences, the percentage of children agreeing that they were indeed frightened is relatively small – in London only 10 per cent agree (although in one school it was as high as 55 per cent, perhaps as a result of the majority of children having seen one particular film), and in Birkenhead 16 per cent. In Birmingham, the figure was 24 per cent, and the report quotes the reactions of some children to their viewing:

> My friend was frightened to go to her bedroom, so her mother had to go with her and they had the light on all night. It was after 'The Phantom of the Opera'. I will admit I was rather afraid.

> The pictures have often kept my sister and myself from sleeping after by causing us to go hysterical. (Birmingham Cinema Enquiry Committee, 1931: 11, 13)

Some of the reports also specifically questioned teachers as to what they thought of cinema for children, and what influence they felt cinema-going had on children's schoolwork. In London, it was reported that many teachers were surprised at the part films played in children's lives:

> In the ordinary nature of school life, [film] influence is often not suspected. It was reported, for example, that the influence of cinema on composition was negligible, and that school stories which children read are more frequently a source of inspiration. But in conversation, children became more voluble on the subject of cinema. (LCC Education Committee, 1932: 5)

This comment is interesting from the point of view of children's literacy development – the London respondents seem to imply that children were able to transfer knowledge of written language conventions and narrative structure from their reading to their writing, but were unable to do so with visual narratives. Spoken language did, however, apparently benefit from the visual/aural experience of cinema.

In the Edinburgh report, 55 per cent of the 649 teachers questioned felt that children's schoolwork did suffer as a result of their cinema-going habit, but the majority blamed loss of rest and sleep rather than any debilitating intellectual effect of watching films. Some responses did bemoan children's tendencies towards 'passive acceptance of what was put before them' and worried that 'seeing takes the place of thinking', but there were positive responses too. Twenty-seven per cent of the Edinburgh respondents felt that children had made active gains in schoolwork as a result of watching films: 'They get a wider view of life and are bound to see some good stuff amongst the welter of rubbish thought suitable for children' (Mackie, 1933: 43).

Seen together, the reports present a very interesting snapshot of adults' and children's responses to a rapidly growing phenomenon. They present contemporary evidence which shows not only children's real enjoyment of cinema but also that adult worries were in the main unfounded. They also show that children did actually learn from their viewing experiences, from the serious and thoughtful responses:

> My common sense has told me that I couldn't be a poor girl and suddenly be whirled into London and New York society. (Birkenhead Vigilance Committee, 1931: 11)

> Pictures showing Nature show us a great deal more than teachers could tell us. (Birmingham Cinema Enquiry Committee, 1931: 8)

to the unintentionally hilarious:

> [I have learned that] when a boy has a banana if a monkey is near he would take it of him [sic]. (Birmingham Cinema Enquiry Committee, 1931: 13)

The Edinburgh report concludes that children could readily distinguish between real life and the fictitious life of film, though the report does not provide any concrete evidence for this. E. H. Fielder's enquiry into the influence of gangster films on children in Manchester in 1932 also came to the same conclusions. Having asked his interviewees what they had learned about nature, life in other lands, life in the higher rank of society, life in the underworld, and the ways of living of ordinary men and women in the films they had seen, he was told 'we don't go to the pictures to learn' (Fowler, 1996: 132). As Fowler notes:

> [Fielder] found that very few boys (or girls) were attracted by the idea of the underworld – 'the majority look upon it as horrible and dangerous'. He was forced to conclude that 'films do not consciously have a bad moral effect on adolescents ... often the adolescents recognise films as poor stuff; they are distinctly critical of what they see. They claim to be unaffected because they feel that the life depicted on films is unreal ...' (Fowler, 1995: 133)

The intertextual influence of film on story paper style and content

Throughout the 1920s and 1930s the popularity of cinema was increasing at a dramatic rate – in direct competition with story papers for the pennies in children's pockets. Including direct reference to cinema codes, practices and narratives was one way for the story paper writers to demonstrate that they were keeping up with children's interests. It is also possible to detect the beginnings of a move away from the gender-based approach of the story papers in that the audience begins to be seen as children in general rather than just boys – although this does not extend to the inclusion of any female characters in the stories. This section looks closely at some examples from the story papers, to demonstrate the ways in which the writers/publishers responded to the cinema's new threat to their market. In particular, it builds a comparison of the different styles of response of *The Magnet* and *The Hotspur* in this context.

In 'Bill Hawkins and his 60 Dunces' (*The Hotspur*, 6 August 1938: 15–17), a cinema visit forms part of the narrative. This is one of a series of stories about ex-plumber Bill Hawkins, who has been given the job of teaching the 'toughest boys in the district', Class 6 at Cokehampton Central School. The entertainment value of this scenario relies on readers' ability to juxtapose it intertextually with the rules and contexts of both real and fictional schools, as do many of *The Hotspur* stories. Bill's 'unorthodox' teaching methods contrast both with other teachers in the school and with the experiences of 'real' school. His inclusive and collaborative approach sets him firmly on the side of the boys, as one of the 'gang' (indeed, this is his own term for the boys in his class), and for this he is both disparaged and excluded by the other teachers. When Bill is asked by the headteacher to concentrate on the geography of northern India, because the school is expecting an important visitor from that part of the world, Bill sets out to find novel ways of collecting useful information that will really interest the boys:

> The best way to learn about a country, he muttered to himself, as he walked along, is to go to it. But I can't take the gang to India, so what's the next best thing? At that moment, a large poster caught his eye. He was passing the Cokehampton cinema. The poster was about the film that was showing, and it read:
> Now Showing: ELEPHANT HUNTER
> A vivid, smashing drama of tropical India. (*The Hotspur*, 6 August 1938: 16)

The whole class then spends the afternoon at the cinema, much to the consternation of the headteacher.

This is an intriguing plot development for a number of reasons. By taking the children out of school premises, Bill is further separating them from recognised authority and sanctioning 'subversive' behaviour. He is also legitimising what children would see as a leisure activity (and one often frowned upon by teachers, as we have seen), by implying that there is educational worth in watching popular films. 'How dare he waste the boys' time on films when they should be studying geography', snorts the outraged head when he hears what has happened – the expected reaction of an institutional figure. However, as Bill is not a 'real' teacher, the message is more complicated. The event is undershot by the sense that 'learning' does not really belong in this out-of-school context, and that knowledge gained here is somehow of less value than classroom study. Interestingly, Bill is disappointed by the experience:

> The film hadn't been a very good one, and it certainly hadn't taught him anything about the geography of India or the habits and customs of the people. (*The Hotspur*, 6 August 1938: 16)

There is a further level of intertextuality at play in this example, in that child readers in 1938 would have been well aware of the contemporary, very successful film *Elephant Boy*, produced by Alexander Korda in 1937 and starring 'Sabu', a 13-year-old Indian boy. The film was co-directed by Zoltan Korda and the documentary film-maker Robert Flaherty, with an unusual mix of dramatic plotlines, and real footage of animals in the wild. As Staples points out, Sabu was the only international child star that the British cinema produced in the 1930s, and after only a few films he began to appear in children's lists of their favourite actors (Staples, 1997: 76). In the story narrative, the authors have deliberately added an intertextual reference which would have resonated with readers, even if they had not actually seen the film. Looked at in this way, Bill's assertion that the film had nothing to say about the 'real' people of India becomes an exercise in critical literacy, encouraging readers to deconstruct the artifice of the film narrative. In Metz's terms, this is underlining the existence of indexes of reality, showing that the realistic bodies/movements/sound of the film are representations of an imagined reality.

This effect is further emphasised when it appears that there *is* something to be learned from the newsreel that the boys have seen after the film, telling them that the Rajah of Banpore is visiting the country. This is qualified by one boy who has read in the local paper that the Rajah is actually visiting Cokehampton – evidently the really useful information still has to come from a printed source. Films, then, are for entertainment purposes only; newsreels have some educational value; print sources are the best for factual information – the implication being that print does report/represent reality in a way that film does not. The critical message apparently stops at this point, leaving written text critically unexamined. Whilst it is not possible at this distance to determine exactly what contemporary readers made of this story, it is just feasible that D. C. Thomson and his authors were attempting to encourage children to reflect on their cinema-going habits, and to remember the value of reading.

The Hotspur's first issue appeared in 1933, at a time when the cinema was already well established and at the height of its popularity amongst children. D. C. Thomson and his writers made it their business to survey children's opinions and would have been well aware of the influence of cinema on children's popular culture for both boys and girls. For this reason, the writing style of *The Hotspur* combined the 'traditional' school story with adventure/action narratives in an attempt to draw together the pleasures of serial viewing and serial reading. Stories in *The Hotspur* – some more effectively than others – mimic the rapid turnover of action sequences seen in film serials, playing with the readers' sense of dis/equilibrium in order to hold interest, breaking the text repeatedly into kernel and satellite events to encourage readers to situate themselves in the narrative by means of the suturing process.

'Wild Bill Hickok's Schooldays', 'the big thrill of 1939', is a good example of a fast-moving action narrative which draws inspiration from the popularity of the western film genre (*The Hotspur*, 18 February 1939: 2–7 and 14). It also revisits an earlier story serial about the adult Bill Hickok – as the cover of issue 286 states: 'Wild Bill Hickok was the hero of one of the most popular and amazing stories ever published in *The Hotspur*. Here is this great character again in an amazing story of his boyhood.' Reading pleasure, for those who remember the previous serial, is thus increased by 'the memory of previous suturings' to this character, and by the enjoyment of intertextual tracings between the written western genre and the filmic version. Reinventing the character of Bill Hickok as a boy is a shrewd move by the story paper writers, allowing readers to identify directly with their hero from the outset.

The story begins with the youthful Wild Bill Hickok practising his shooting in a clearing in the woods. He is discovered by his father and soundly beaten for missing school. (Henry Hickok is a tax collector, specifically charged with collecting the school taxes – money to keep the village school running.) Bill remorsefully trudges back to school where Buck Lubbock, the school's only teacher, threatens him with another beating. Bill's response to this is to get out his guns and force the teacher to drop his birch. Bill then calmly sits down for the rest of the lesson. The kernel event of Bill's meeting with his father establishes not only the strength of the father/son relationship but also the moral boundaries of the story. Paternal authority is to be obeyed unquestioningly and even the toughest of rebels have to go to school. The satellite event enchained to this – Bill's intimidation of the teacher – mirrors Bill's encounter with his father but reinforces Bill's individuality. Lubbock is a 'small, sandy-haired, weak-looking man' who is comedic rather than authoritative (in contrast to Henry, who is 'short and thickset ... with a grim glint in his eyes') (*The Hotspur*, 18 February 1939: 2, 3). Bill's rebelliousness is sparked off by the comparison of Lubbock with his father, who, 'hardy old pioneer as he was, had taught him everything he knew' (p. 3). (It is interesting to note here that Bill does not remember his mother – she is an irrelevance, as are any 'feminine' qualities which she might have been able to teach him. Here is one point at which the 'inclusive' audience of children rather than boys is momentarily forgotten.) Not only is school an irrelevance to Bill, but Lubbock himself is totally inadequate for his role. The messages for readers here are quite complex, pulling in different directions which could be seen as both pro- and anti-Establishment. Bill is operating within a moral framework ('good' against 'evil', education against anarchy), and yet he is conducting a personal rebellion against the schoolmaster, and apparently succeeding. He has learned all he needs from his father, but this is not as subversive as it sounds, given that Henry embodies Establishment values in his role as tax-collector. The moral framework is therefore reinforced, even though it appears that Bill is acting outside authority. The other children in the school are quiet and studious, despite the failings of the teacher – underlining Bill's difference as hero-figure.

The story moves swiftly on to the next kernel event: Bill's discovery of his father's dead body, shot in the back and dumped by the side of the road. In the moral world of the story, and in the western film genre, this is a triple crime: the murder of an authority figure; a shooting in the back, which is a cowardly offence against the rules of fair play; and the abandoning of the body, which offends against basic humanity. Bill's response is studiedly unemotional ('Wild Bill was not the crying kind'), and he swears revenge:

> Over his father's dead body he swore a grim vow. He would not rest until he had discovered his father's murderers. He would not rest until he had made them pay for their crime. (*The Hotspur*, 18 February 1939: 3)

This is the key event of the story, on which the rest of the action hangs. Bill determines not only to find the murderers, but also to take over his father's tax-collecting job in order to keep the school going, and preserve what his father had worked so hard to maintain. Bill thus becomes the force for stability in the story – he may be outside 'authority', but he is responsible for restoring the moral equilibrium. The repetitive language of his vow underlines the power of his moral strength.

Bill's vow is taken so literally that he sets off on his search immediately, pausing only briefly for his father's funeral, which is dealt with in two lines. He rides to the Circle 6 Ranch, home of the Mexican Marcos Sabini – tax defaulter and one of the key suspects in the murder. Sabini refuses to pay his taxes, but Bill then disguises himself and returns to demand the money at gunpoint. In keeping with the moral boundaries of the story, Bill takes only the amount owed in tax and leaves the rest of the money behind. He then does exactly the same thing at Comanche Geary's ranch (Geary being the other prime murder suspect), again leaving behind the rest of Geary's money having taken out the tax which is owed. As we have seen earlier, 'evil' characters in the story papers are generally depicted as 'other' – in this case Sabini is a Mexican, while Geary has a Native American background. That this semic coding is immediately understood, without further detailed description from the narrator/author, shows the depth of cultural coding at this period.

There are two axes of influence at work in the story at this point. At the level of action, the narrative represents a drama of revenge in which Bill's violent actions are justified through his basically moral motivation. This message is underlined by his determination to continue his father's work and to keep the school going. Underneath this surface narrative are the mechanisms of suturing, through which readers identify with the character of Wild Bill Hickok 'suturing the text's segmentations' in order to achieve subjective coherence. Readers actively have to bridge the gaps in the text in order to piece together Bill's emotional life, which is entirely absent from the narrative. This is the point at which the two axes meet to create meaning, where Bill becomes 'real' in readers' minds. Without this active involvement, the story remains a flat succession of action events. By setting Bill's actions within a clear moral framework, the story's authors construct a definite space towards which readers are led by the suturing process. This moral space in turn frames readers' meaning-making, guiding readers towards the moral messages the authors hope that readers will take from the narrative.

The first episode of this story uses a cinematic cliffhanger denouement: Bill is left perched on the roof of his own shack, in the dark, watching two of Commanche Geary's men dragging a bound and gagged hostage on to his doorstep. The hostage is Sabini's son – the two ranch-owners being deadly rivals, Geary has had Sabini's son kidnapped and plans to kill him, making it look like Bill is the murderer:

> The prisoner had refused to walk. His eyes were rolling with terror, but he could do no more than grunt behind his cruel gag. They were carrying him between them, his feet clear of the ground.
>
> 'Right over to the door, so there's no doubt about it!', whispered one of the gunmen. In his hand was the knife he would use to slit those bonds before he and his pal killed their prisoner on Wild Bill's doorstep! (*The Hotspur*, 18 February 1939: 14)

From the evidence of Bill's sharp-shooting at the beginning of this episode, and from intertextually referencing knowledge of the adult Bill's exploits, readers would quite easily have been able to fill the anticipatory space between this and episode two with imagining Bill shooting his way out of the problem. In fact, episode two opens with Bill shooting both of Geary's men in the arm, using a gun in each hand,

and deliberately shooting to disable, not to kill. The suspended action event from episode one is thus very quickly resolved, leaving 'filling-in' of the plot for readers who missed the first episode until page two. Reading pleasure is sustained by the restoration of equilibrium – Bill easily defeats his opponents – and swift progress to the next kernel/satellite event.

Cliffhanger endings are a regular feature in the story papers, as they are in cinema serials, but are used more sparingly. A significant number of stories – Red Circle School in particular, and most of the Greyfriars stories – are complete in one issue. This style makes use of suturing in a different way, in that readers are invited to identify with the same characters week after week, suturing the gaps between episodes by imagining Red Circle School/Greyfriars as parallel worlds 'visited' by the story papers each week. In this sense action in the worlds of these stories is potentially continuous, whereas cliffhanger endings suspend action at a defined point. The dis-pleasure readers feel at this rupture heightens the anticipation of the resolution of the action event in the next episode. The fact that this narrative device became a staple of film serials, and is one of the main reasons for that genre's popularity, invites the question as to why story papers did not use the cliffhanger ending more consistently. This may be one contributory factor in the decline in story paper popularity in the 1940s, as child readers were drawn more and more to the visual pleasures of cinema and the pure excitement of action serials.

The Magnet's response to the growing influence of cinema was more overt, as Frank Richards made repeated efforts to demystify the film world for his readers. Perhaps motivated by the worries increasingly voiced by other adult commentators and institutions, he attempted to provide sufficient factual information about the workings of cinema to equip his readers with a critical insight into cinematic illusion. In 'Billy Bunter: Film Star!' (*The Magnet*, 18 March 1922), Bunter is mistakenly identified as a film actor, and is taken on as the star of 'The Wood Nymph', a silent film 'photoplay'. In the course of the story, there are several asides detailing film-making practice:

> [The photoplay] consisted of four scenes, three of which were interiors, the other 'on location', as an exterior scene is called in the film world. This exterior scene, which was to be filmed in Friardale Woods, appeared as scene three, but as far as the actual filming went, it was to be left until the last. There is no need for the scenes of a film to be taken in strict rotation. As a rule, the scenes that can be taken inside of the studio are filmed first, and the exteriors last.

> The camera was set up in position, and Mr Pecker ran two converging tape lines from the tripod of the camera to a bush which stood a few yards away. The film producer did this for the benefit of the members of the company, so that they would not stray out of the focus area during the filming of the scene. (*The Magnet*, 18 March 1922: 7, 16)

This metafictive description demands that readers make their way through two levels of fiction (the fiction of a Greyfriars story, and the fiction of the photoplay within the story) in order to reach and understand it. Richards manages the separation of fact from fiction in the first extract by a change of tense – signifying a shift from omniscient narrator role into objective commentator and 'friend'. The present tense transfers readers' attention from the fictional to the 'real', allowing them to be aware of their own position outside the story. Richards's aim is to encourage readers to be similarly objective in the cinema experiences.

The Magnet also presents straightforward factual information outside the stories. The 'editor's chat' page offered an opportunity for writers to talk directly to their audience. Over the years this evolved into an even more personal approach, with the column retitled 'Come Into the Office, Boys', combining a direct invitation with a feeling of authority. In the edition for 2 November 1935, this changes again, to 'Come Into the Office, Boys and Girls', in direct acknowledgement of the growing readership amongst girls. Rather surprisingly, there is no comment on this change in the column itself.

By 1930, when the 'talkies' had increased cinema's popularity still further, cinema had begun to feature regularly on the editor's page:

> What do 'Talkies' cost? is the question which Michael Lawton of Warwick asks me. To install the American equipment costs anything from £1,710 to £3,600 according to the seating accommodation. But at the present time there are about twenty different English systems available, at much lower costs, and, as additional improvements take place, it is certain that the cost of installing 'talkies' will be greatly reduced. In fact, I am informed it will not be long before 'Talkies' are so cheap that it will be possible for us to have them in our own homes, and to take our own talking films! (*The Magnet*, 5 April 1930: 2)

The answer given is concerned only with the physical mechanisms of showing the films, not with making them – an indication of the power of the American film producers and the fact that the majority of films shown at this time were US imports. As far as the question itself is concerned, it is not possible to tell whether this is a genuine enquiry from a reader, or if the producers simply decided to provide information about films in the hope of raising readers' interest, and further demystifying the cinema phenomenon.

It is possible to chart in *The Magnet* a change in attitude towards films, from the early 1920s to the 1930s. There are two particularly revealing examples from *The Magnet* issues in 1921–22. In January 1921 *The Magnet* launched a 'Douglas Fairbanks Competition' for boys and girls:

> As you have all heard, Douglas Fairbanks is appearing in his wonderful screen version of The Three Musketeers – that greatest of all stories by A. Dumas – showing twice daily at Covent Garden. Because he believes that every boy and girl – as well as every grown-up – should see and learn much from this splendid film, Douglas Fairbanks is offering a large number of valuable prizes for essays on just *one* of the many admirable qualities the story illustrates, such as LOYALTY, VALOUR, CHIVALRY, KINDNESS, DEVOTION, etc. (*The Magnet*, 31 January 1921: 9)

Here readers are positively encouraged to take meanings for their own lives from a cinematic fiction. Behind this invitation is a collaboration between the publishers and the film producers/cinema owners which not only draws children in to the cinema experience but also tries to legitimise this by underlining the possible educational value of this apparently very moral cinema narrative. Entry to the competition is conditional on cinema attendance – entry forms are to be given out in the theatre, and the essay must focus on 'an incident in the story *as shown in the film*'. Reading the original book is not encouraged; buying into the cinema experience is what matters. The prize for the winning essay is £25, a quite enormous sum of money for the time (which would equate to over £1000 in today's terms, according to the Bank of England's inflation calculator at www.bankofengland.co.uk). This real monetary reward, and the implied personal involvement of Douglas Fairbanks himself in the competition, situates the children's reality not only as spectators but as active participants in the cinema experience. By offering them a role in the process beyond that of mere consumers, the producers (publishers/film producers/cinema owners) consolidate their own positions, increasing ticket/story paper sales. In effect, the competition asks children to view the film objectively, and works against the 'structure of fascination' – cinema, it implies, is not about illusion but about seeing beyond this to make real meanings in real lives. This conjunction of two interests (film producers and cinema owners) attempts to persuade readers, and, importantly, their parents, that cinema is not as damaging a distraction as authority figures might believe. It also promotes the position that there might be positive benefits, particularly moral and educational ones, to be gained from the cinema experience. Clearly there is primarily an economic imperative at work here on the part of the producers, but readers are offered real gains too, valued in terms of money as well as pleasure.

This encouragement to be objective continues into the story narratives. The second example, from 1922, is 'Bunter the Crook!' (*The Magnet*, 10 June 1922). This story uses the character of Billy Bunter to show the effects of an inability to distinguish between film fiction and everyday reality. As the story begins, Bunter is keen to persuade the Famous Five to go and see 'The Clutch of the Crook', a new 'thrill-a-minute' film starring the actor Snicker Snaggs. Bunter is completely film-struck, but from the outset the Famous Five are scathing about the attractions of cinema. Harry Wharton declares that 'that kind of rot won't do you any good, Bunter', establishing clearly that the main hero-figure in the story has little time for such frivolity. When the boys do eventually see the film, the action is described by the narrator in damningly sarcastic terms:

> In unexplained ways the cold-blooded crook appeared at high windows and on roofs, or in the strong-rooms of banks; for no discoverable reason he was seen racing in big motor cars; and, apparently as a variety of 'physical jerks' he climbed along telegraph wires and swung himself into tree-tops from high window-sills.
>
> Why he did all these things was not explained in the sub-titles, and could not be guessed from the pictures; but the impression given was that the crook with a clutch led an exceedingly exciting life, full of variety ...
>
> ... Billy Bunter had the kind of brain that is greatly impressed by the 'pictures' and it was quite certain that the sensational rubbish he had been watching was not likely to do the fat junior any good. (*The Magnet*, 10 June 1922: 4)

Bunter is so impressed by the pictures that he spends the rest of the story fantasising about crimes and getaways, and finds himself in severe trouble when he steals Mr Prout's old revolver and attempts a 'hold-up' in the Famous Five's study. Bunter's status as comic anti-hero underlines the message here that only the irredeemably silly and self-obsessed would allow themselves to be taken in by cinema narratives in such a way. The Famous Five are, by comparison, models of level-headedness who can see through film illusion, and feel concern and pity for Bunter. Frank Richards consistently reinforces the message, using other characters to ridicule Bunter's behaviour:

> It was not an uncommon thing for fellows to be affected by the pictures, but it was rather startling to see the influence of the films carried to the lengths of 'Clutching Bill'. Skinner remarked that he'd read of such cases in the newspapers, and said that there were lots of Bunters in the juvenile prisons, and opined that William George would arrive there sooner or later. Other fellows were of the opinion that Bunter was more likely to arrive in a home for idiots, or a lunatic asylum. (*The Magnet*, 10 June 1922: 15)

This extract is strongly reminiscent of the attitudes of the investigating committees of the 1930s, in suggesting that cinema narratives were not only ridiculous but also positively harmful. By 1930 this critical tone had changed to one of acceptance. *The Magnet* was by then providing factual information about the cinema (see 'What do Talkies cost?', quoted above, p. 140), and in the issue for 1 March 1930 a new column began:

> A QUICK-ACTION STORY IN DIALOGUE, SUITABLE FOR AMATEUR ACTORS AND ENTERTAINING TO ALL.
> **The MAGNET TALKIES**
> *This week*: THE BULLION HOLD-UP!
> Here's a change from Dicky Nugent's usual 'shocker' – a novel feature by William Wibley, of the Remove, based on the popularity of the 'Talkie' films. Wibley has certainly brought a smile to the faces of the editorial staff, so we confidently place his first 'Talkie' effort before you – ED. (*The Magnet*, 1 March 1930: 14)

The story is written entirely in dialogue, matching the language of the popular western films of the time. From the producer's point of view, this is a parody, presented for sheer entertainment value. From the readers' point of view, however, the editor/authority figure is not only sanctioning the entertainment value of the language/narrative, but also legitimising readers' own involvement in the experience by suggesting they should use it as a playscript. The fact that the piece is 'written' by a Greyfriars schoolboy further sutures readers to the reading (and enacting) experience, giving them space to identify with the 'writer', and inviting them to add their own real bodies/sound to the narrative. Drawing directly on cinema's structures of fascination, this looks like a deliberate attempt to compete on straight terms with the attractions of the talkies.

Summary and conclusions

In the 1920s and 1930s, the dramatic rise in popularity of the cinema presented a direct threat to the story papers in the children's entertainment market. In effect, it was a rather one-sided battle. The majority of films – at least in the 1920s and early 1930s – were US imports, and it is unlikely that American producers had any knowledge of or interest in the UK story papers or their popularity amongst British schoolchildren. From the story paper producers' point of view, the threat was a serious one and they were not slow to respond, including cinema-related storylines and changing the style of narrative presentation to focus on a succession of action events mimicking the speed of cinematic storytelling.

Children's fascination with cinema was a source of worry to authority figures in institutions, children's societies and education, as well as to story paper producers. Commentators in the inter-war years were concerned that children might be unable to situate themselves outside such structures of fascination, but the succession of reports in the early 1930s found no evidence to support the concern. Both boys and girls used cinema fictions in their play in the same way as they used story paper fiction, and the predominantly moral framing of cinema narratives – just as with story paper narratives – meant that identifying with screen hero-figures was more likely to have a positive effect on children's character development. J. P. Mayer quotes what he calls a 'perfect' example of the effect of films on the behaviour of a boy of 14, who had been 'extremely unruly and aggressive'. The youth club leader working with him discovered an 'astounding change' in his behaviour on her return from a holiday:

> He helped her to take off her coat, got a chair for her, and was extraordinarily polite in his speech. Commenting on his changed behaviour, she jokingly asked him what had come over him; the reply was that he had been to see a film showing his favourite star, who had played the role of a gallant hero. The boy had decided to model himself on the star. (Mayer, 1972: 82)

The critical point here is that this altered behaviour pattern is the result of a conscious decision process – the viewer has selected specific codings and meanings from the filmic reality and applied them in his own world. This sense of agency implies a deeper level of engagement with the film narrative than was perceived by authority figures at the time.

The story paper producers attempted to encourage a more critical approach to cinema in their readers, but by the 1930s this stance had developed a softer edge. As authority attitudes in general became much more accepting of the new medium, story paper producers recognised that to position themselves as anti-cinema did not represent good business.

By the beginning of the Second World War, story paper popularity had begun its terminal decline. Among the many reasons for this (not least of which was the war itself and the resulting economic difficulties faced by business in general), the popularity of the cinema must have had definite effect. Ultimately a written medium which required efforts of intellect, memory and visualisation could not compete with a medium whose illusion was based on reality and which functioned on visual fascination rather than written literacy.

6
Story Papers as Cultural Artefacts: Contexts and Content

In what ways can a detailed exploration of the physicality of the story papers, their paratextual elements (cover, illustration, advertising, editors' columns and so on), help to frame an understanding of the stories themselves and the ways in which children interpreted and used them? And might a more macro-scale view of the story paper as artefact help in building a picture of child readers and their reading lives, and open up further the discussion of embedded ideologies? This chapter draws on the concepts of cultural production, cultural/social use-values and symbolic capital (see Bourdieu, 1993) and also looks at the changing space and place of reading, exploring story paper production in social and historical context. In the first part of the chapter we will focus on these broad cultural contexts and values. The second part explores texts and paratexts (Genette, 1997), and draws on concepts from reader response and cultural theory (Iser, 2000; Williams, 1961, 1977) as well as from marketing and advertising theories.

The field of cultural production

In order to analyse cultural production effectively, it is necessary to look at 'the class base of control and also the general economic context within which this control is exercised' (Ryan, 1991: 6). Murdock and Golding propose two levels for this kind of analysis: a normative level, 'which links the content of a culture to particular occupational practices'; and the second, a focus on 'the conditions linking work situation and market situation', for example, how the need of the commercial media to maximise audiences drives them towards 'concentrating on the familiar and formula which are as similar as possible to the tried and tested' (cited in Ryan, 1991: 7). These two levels correspond roughly to Bourdieu's formulations of *habitus* and *field*. In this section, we will look at these levels/formulations in more detail and apply them to the context of story paper production in the 1920s and 1930s.

Bourdieu uses the term 'symbolic capital' to talk about the values generated by social actions within fields. For Bourdieu, there are three forms of symbolic capital: economic capital (literally, the possession of money, wealth); social capital ('a network of lasting social relations'); and cultural capital (which is defined as 'a form of knowledge, an international code or a cognitive acquisition which equips the social agent with empathy towards, appreciation for or competence in deciphering cultural relations and cultural artefacts') (Johnson, 1993: 7). All three of these forms are relevant to this discussion. Economic capital is important to producers, who generate it, and consumers, who both accumulate and spend it – the economic field is a structure of relationships between producers and consumers, based on the shifting values of economic capital. Social and cultural capital are less easily quantifiable, but are equally influential on social relations.

One further concept from Bourdieu is helpful for the purposes of this discussion – the notion of social activity as game. To enter a specific field is to 'play the game', that is, to submit oneself to be bound by the particular rules and practices of that field. As Randal Johnson explains, in order to play the game effectively, an agent must possess both the habitus that predisposes him/her to enter that field/game in particular, and a minimum amount of knowledge, skill or 'talent' to be accepted as a legitimate player:

> Entering the game ... means attempting to use that knowledge, skill or 'talent' in the most advantageous way possible. It means, in short, investing one's (academic, cultural, symbolic) capital in such as way as to derive maximum benefit or 'profit' from the game. (Johnson, 1993: 8)

It would appear from this description that agents are in control of the game, or at least aware of the nature of its rules. This is not necessarily the case, however, as the defining principles of any field 'are only ever made partially explicit, and much of the orthodox way of thinking and acting passes in an implicit, tacit manner' (Grenfell and James, 1998: 20). As with habitus, there are conscious and unconscious levels within this formulation, and it is this combination which allows Bourdieu to account for the fact that there are 'good' and 'bad' players of the game in any given field.

There are problems, however, with using this kind of approach to analyse literary artefacts from historical contexts. As Bourdieu points out, the major difficulty is in 'reconstruct[ing] the spaces of original possibles' (Bourdieu, 1993: 31). If both habitus and field operate on both conscious and unconscious levels, so that even agents themselves are not able fully to define the 'rules' which affect their actions, how can critics reconstruct the relations of habitus/field that shaped specific historical periods and works of literature? Bourdieu acknowledges that ignorance of the 'mood of the age' leads to 'derealization' of works, but is less clear on possible ways to address the problem.

Part of Bourdieu's answer is to posit a concentration on both the material production and the production of the value of the work. (See the later section in this chapter, on value, pp. 150–2.) This situating of text in context works up to a point, but still does not connect with the lived experience of the time. Raymond Williams has tried to address the same issue, and his formulation 'the structure of feeling' which looks to understand the shared values of a culture or society seems to me to be a more fruitful line of analysis. Williams emphasises the selective nature of the historical record – what survives is only a selected part of the full lived experience of a given historical period. It is therefore necessary to look beyond the historical record to recover the voices of the excluded and silenced in order to approach the structure of feeling of that period. By contrast, Bourdieu's focus on the work itself, on its material and symbolic production, does not seem to take enough account of the process of selectivity. His focus on cultural production explores the ways in which values are invested in specific works, but does not really explain how this process changes and develops meanings and values over time as works are by turn selected or excluded.

Bourdieu's theories also seem to devalue the role of the reader, or consumer, of the work. The producers of the meaning and value of the work, are, in his view:

> critics, publishers, gallery directors and the whole set of agents whose combined efforts produce consumers capable of knowing and recognising the work of art as such, in particular teachers (but also families, etc). (Bourdieu, 1993: 37)

This implies that readers are themselves 'produced', and are not therefore able to make and take meanings from texts except by direction from others. In my view, the work of the reader response theorists is more helpful here, in that it proposes a more open-ended meaning-making process, allowing readers to bring multiple meanings to texts. This situates the reader more firmly in a dynamic relationship with the text, balancing the influences on the producer–text–reader continuum. (For more on this point, see below, in the section on texts and paratexts, pp. 155–79.)

Story paper contexts

Applying Bourdieu's theories to the context of children's reading and children's cultures in the 1920s and 1930s, it becomes possible to argue that the cultural phenomenon of the story paper grew out of and was shaped by the habitus of producers and consumers, acting in interconnected fields. From the producers' perspective, the aim of publishing is to maximise economic benefit (profit) from investing economic capital (cash) and cultural capital (authors' creative output) in the fields of cultural production/economics. In other words, producers deliberately target as large an audience as possible in order to make as much money as possible by selling as many copies of a product as possible. This business imperative is the key rule in playing the game of the economic field, but the ways in which players/agents operate in this game are themselves shaped, constructed and influenced by the habitus of each individual.

Alfred Harmsworth's approach to publishing for children was the product of habitus and field. At a basic level, his attitudes to children's cultural artefacts – his dislike of 'bloods' for instance (see Chapter 1) – were informed by his own childhood experiences (home, family, school) as well as the economic conditions of the time, in that by 1908, the year in which *The Magnet* was first published, it was evident that there was good money to be made from publishing for children. The influence of class is important in this context – Harmsworth's upper-class upbringing would have inculcated specific dispositions of habitus, as would his schooling – but, as Ryan points out, class positions and relations are only part of the map of relations, and it is important to consider the 'entire circuit of production and circulation and consumption of cultural commodities' (Ryan, 1991: 45). Players in the economic field necessarily include producers and consumers, indeed the field is structured by the shifting relations between the two, but class is much less important in this process than the possession of hard cash (economic capital). These two forms of capital are obviously interlinked, but as only small amounts of money are involved in this particular process of consumption, anyone – of any class – can play.

Habitus informs the ways in which producers enter the field of cultural production. It could be argued that the specific form of the

Harmsworth story papers, with their emphasis on school stories and adventure yarns, draws directly from the habitus of Harmsworth and Frank Richards – Harmsworth's own school background and the predominance of adventure stories in his own childhood culture, together with Richards's sense of having missed out on childhood experiences (as noted in the Introduction). In this sense, Richards's is a kind of negative habitus, negating his own experiences in favour of imaginary worlds. This, however, is only one aspect of the structure of cultural relations. In Bourdieu's definition, the field is a dynamic concept, 'in that a change in agents' positions necessarily entails a change in the field's structure' (Johnson, 1993: 6). Similarly, structural relations are not static, 'rather they are in flux ... forming and reforming themselves' (Grenfell and James, 1998: 24). As Harmsworth's publishing expanded into the production of story papers for children, so the field of production was restructured: tastes and values were altered and other producers found that their products became less valued in comparison. (Evidence for this can be found in both A. J. Jenkinson's 1940 survey and Joseph McAleer's survey of the field (see Chapter 1 and the Appendix) which show the relative decline in popularity of the *Boy's Own Paper* during the interwar period, from its previous position as market leader.) This in turn prompts new producers and consumers to enter the field as a result. Harmsworth's economic success with *The Magnet* and *The Gem* drew D. C. Thomson to enter the field, aiming to maximise his share of economic capital. This shifted values and relations again: the popularity of the D. C. Thomson papers' different style prompted both concern about economic profit for Harmsworth and discussions about the format of the Harmsworth story papers. As Drotner writes, very quickly after the first boys' story paper from D. C. Thomson appeared (*Adventure*, in 1921), 'new Amalgamated Press periodicals were soon copying their Scottish rivals' (Drotner, 1988: 189). *The Champion*, first issued in 1922, was designed to compete directly with the D. C. Thomson 'big five' papers – and in total Amalgamated Press produced 28 new story papers during the 1920s and 1930s. Interestingly, by the time of Jenkinson's survey (conducted in 1938 and published in 1940), the 'big five' were all still rated as most popular, above any Amalgamated Press paper. (See Appendix for detailed statistics.)

From the consumers' point of view, entering the field of cultural production is about investing economic capital (the price of the story paper) in order to maximise benefit in terms of symbolic capital (the enjoyment of reading, the cultural and social value of possession). This is a complex relationship given that children are necessarily novice players in any field, their economic capital is limited, and the structural relations of value and taste are at their most fluid. Bourdieu writes that in order to recognise the value of a work of art (such as a story paper), the analysis must take account of both its material and symbolic production; that is 'the production of the value of the work or ... of belief in the value of the work' (Johnson, 1993: 37). This is particularly important in the context of the story papers, in that the enormous success of the genre was fuelled by the exchange of papers between individuals and groups of children. Readers invested symbolic value in the story papers through their willingness to enter into story paper worlds. Exchanging views about the stories, structuring creative play around key characters and re-enacting storylines built belief in the value of the work. Physically exchanging copies of the story papers themselves increased their symbolic value. A high symbolic value interconnects with high economic value, in terms of increased sales. By its nature, however, symbolic value is impossible to predict, and this is the risk producers take in putting any new product on the market. Harmsworth's was a calculated risk, expertly judging the timing of developing his story papers, entering the field just as it was primed to expand – although the rapidity of its expansion and the growth of symbolic value must have surprised even him. By comparison, D. C. Thomson's economic risk was less, as the child consumer market and its mechanisms for investing in symbolic value were well established by the 1920s.

Bourdieu argues that the ultimate source of valuing is the field or group in which individuals are placed: 'knowledge can only receive power and value by being recognised as legitimate' (Grenfell and James, 1993: 23). In the context of the story papers, knowledge of the genre, characters and storylines is the prerequisite for entry into the 'game', and this knowledge is in turn legitimised by the group. New players are valued both for their knowledge and for their possession of story paper editions (in terms of exchange value). The concept of 'playing the game' is particularly interesting in this context as it resonates on a number of levels. At a meta-level, children are entering the economic field as consumers, and are largely unaware of the rules of this game beyond the simple exchange of money for their story paper. The relations between consumers and producers, or authors and publishers, do not figure in this transaction, as the consumer is simply focusing on the product. Buying a story paper, however, is the symbolic transition into a game at an individual level, and here the rules are more overt. Without knowledge, the game does not work – 'good'/valued players are those with the most knowledge. This game pattern and value system is mirrored in the stories themselves (in a context where 'playing the game' has its own separate resonances and meanings), as characters explore the parameters of the field (school), both being structured by and contributing to the structure of the rules of the 'game'. There are 'good' and 'bad' players here, too, in the form of popular characters – with high symbolic value both in the context of the story and in the real world of the child readers (e.g. the 'Famous Five', or Dead-Wide Dick of Red Circle School) – and 'others' whose position is on the fringes of, or outside, the 'game' (e.g. Billy Bunter, 'foreign' characters such as members of Colonial House at Red Circle School). These 'others' have symbolic value which may or may not have been recognised by child readers, in that they function specifically as counterpoints to the key players – deliberately placed by their creators to highlight the 'desirable' attributes of the key characters.

There is a further dimension to this argument, which is to do with value over time. Story papers were produced on a weekly basis, and whilst their economic value remained largely static with little scope to increase the cover price without seriously affecting their affordability for the widest market, their symbolic value varied according to age. The urge to buy the latest editions was strong, as was the impulse to swap the story paper once read for another (newer *or* older). This value was recognised as legitimate at the level of consumers (readers) and producers (authors/publishers), but not in the wider field of cultural production (educators, critics). From a twenty-first-century viewpoint, it is possible to articulate a value continuum, charting the legitimisation of symbolic value from its peak amongst consumers in the 1920s and 1930s, through a deep trough after the Second World War, when production had ceased and symbolic value existed only in the memories of the now-adult child readers, to the beginnings of a renaissance in the late 1990s/early 2000s, when academic attention turned to the cultural and historical value of the story papers.

Children as consumers: the changing space and place of reading

Barrie Gunter and Adrian Furnham write that child consumers are in many ways similar to all other consumers:

> Children want to purchase things to satisfy various needs. Satisfaction may be gained from the act of purchase itself, rather than solely from what is purchased. (Gunter and Furnham, 1998: 7)

As we have seen in the previous section, part of the motivation to buy story papers came from wanting to 'play the game' – to join their peers in the shared experience of story paper worlds. This seems to have been as much, if not more, of an impetus than the desire simply to read the stories themselves. Gunter and Furnham's point about the act of purchase is also important in this context. Story papers were amongst the first products to be aimed directly at child buyers, designed solely with a child readership in mind, and cheap enough for children to buy with their own money. The act of purchase is thus of far greater significance to a child in the early twentieth century than it would be to a twenty-first-century child. Buying a comic/story paper thus becomes an act of personal expression, symbolising both freedom of choice and the growth of consumer power. Books, although read by children, were very rarely bought by children at this time. Much more expensive to buy, they were principally given as gifts or prizes, or provided by schools – or, more occasionally, borrowed from libraries. In a world bounded by the rules of home/family and school, the act of buying a story paper is one of the few genuinely free choices of entering a field that children had in the 1920s and 1930s.

Mitchell and Reid-Walsh's study of children's popular culture refers to twentieth-century settings, but their findings are nevertheless relevant to the early days of emergent children's culture. In their opinion,

> children's engagement with popular culture is often determined by the child, not the adult, so the space of popular culture may exist as a pocket of resistance with and against a larger space of quality culture.
> (Mitchell and Reid-Walsh, 2002: 15)

This posits another level to the satisfaction gained from the act of purchase, that of resistance to the adult-orientated worlds of school and home. Looked at in this way, the field of children's popular culture, in which children as consumers interact with producers, is more than just a subfield of the general field of cultural practice, but is rather a positive space actively structured by children, in which they are allowed to construct and transform meanings outside adult influence.

The availability of story papers for individual purchase also creates new spaces for reading in children's lives. In Jenkinson's survey of children's reading patterns, children report 'surprising' levels of story paper reading – an average of 4 per month for boys in senior schools and 2.3 per month for secondary school boys. As there is very little sanctioned space for reading story papers in school – other than in a handful of schools in the report – this reading is restricted to spaces legitimised by children themselves in homes and streets. C. E. B. and L. M. Russell wrote in 1932 of the ways in which working-class boys found spaces for reading in the context of their daily work:

> Who has not seen the reading errand boy, basket on arm, moving slowly down the street, leaning against a lamp post or more comfortably disposed on a doorstep, eyes fixed on a green, blue or pink-tinted paper? The 'nipper' in the waiting van may be similarly engrossed. The office boy has a bulging pocket, suggestive of printed matter surreptitiously enjoyed in moments of solitude. (Quoted in Richards, 1988: 19)

Here again is the sense of reading as a subversive act, something which children actively chose to do in times and places defined by them, and which carried an importance beyond that of tasks imposed by authority figures in school or work. According to Jenkinson's report, most secondary schools prohibited story paper reading in school, with teachers operating tight control of reading choices. Even here, though, there was occasionally space for resistance (and note here that 'bloods' is the generic term used for story papers in the report):

> Any bloods that appear are exchanged and sometimes read when possible, e.g. when a teacher is away, and in private study. (Secondary school boy, quoted in Jenkinson, 1940: 59)

In senior schools there was less direction of reading choice, and 'even the vilified bloods were recorded several times as quiet reading' (Jenkinson, 1940: 59). Jenkinson argues that part of the reason for such high levels of story paper reading, especially in senior schools, was the inadequacy of school libraries and the lack of choice of anything else interesting to read. Although this may indeed be part of the explanation, Jenkinson's view is a purely educational one which does not take account of children's wider cultural lives. The disparity in story paper reading levels between secondary and senior school boys is also interesting, something which Jenkinson points out but does not attempt to explain in any detail. In the absence of specific survey or autobiographical data it is not possible to account for the disparity definitively, but using Bourdieu's terms it is possible to argue that habitus plays a part. For secondary school boys, drawn largely from the middle classes, the habitus of home and school was one which tended to exclude, or deride, the more 'popular' versions of culture. The act of buying or reading a story paper was thus for them a more overt act of resistance, and fewer boys had the disposition to take that risk. Conversely, the less academic ethos of senior schools, uncluttered by the rigours of the exam syllabus, meant that popular reading was rather less likely to be regulated. In both senior and secondary schools, however, some teachers in Jenkinson's survey admit to allowing story paper reading as one means of helping to build a reading habit in their pupils:

> Attempts to repress them would certainly fail; they do very little harm, and it is better to have boys reading in their own time than never reading. (Secondary school teacher, quoted in Jenkinson, 1940: 132)

> The home conditions of many pupils in this class are not conducive to home-reading or study, and so whenever interest is shown in *any* type of boys' literature, I encourage it by tolerating it. (Senior school teacher, quoted in Jenkinson, 1940: 133)

The following section picks up on these ideas of habitus and field, the child as consumer, the space and place of consumption and the interplay of various textual and paratextual elements in the story papers.

Texts and paratexts

The making and taking of meanings involves the interaction of readers in specific social and cultural contexts with stories in specific textual contexts – framed within the broader relationship of producer and consumer. This section unpicks the physical context of the stories within the story papers and shows how the architecture and layout of the story papers, and the mix of textual styles between advertisements, editors' columns and stories themselves contribute to overall meaning-making.

Gérard Genette's work on paratexts builds an understanding of the function of extra-textual elements. As he explains:

> A text is rarely presented in an unadorned state, unreinforced and unaccompanied by a certain number of verbal or other productions, such as an author's name, a title, a preface, illustrations. And although we do not always know whether these productions are to be regarded as belonging to the text, in any case they surround and extend it, precisely in order to *present* it, in the usual sense of this verb but also in the strongest sense: to *make present*, to ensure the

text's presence in the world, its 'reception' and consumption in the form of a book. (Genette, 1997: 1)

Paratexts can thus operate in a number of ways in relation to a text: to adorn, to reinforce/support/surround, to accompany, to extend and to present or make present. These operations represent various levels of functionality. Whilst adornments and accompaniments might be seen as optional extras to meaning, a reinforcing/supporting or extending function interacts more directly with the text. For example, a decorative border around a cover illustration might function solely as an adornment, and its removal would alter little of the ways in which that cover illustration might be interpreted by readers. The cover illustration itself, however, operates as a signifier of the story inside, introducing a key event from the story, heightening readers' anticipation of the reading experience, and setting a level of expectation (in conjunction with the other textual elements of the cover). It might also function as an attraction for new readers, the persuasive push that prompts a reader to pick up and buy a story paper for the first time – in Genette's terms, announcing the presence of the story within.

Interestingly, Genette describes the paratext as a 'threshold', suggesting that it operates as 'a "vestibule" that offers the world at large the possibility of either stepping in or stepping back' (Genette, 1997: 2). This sense of connecting text and reader is important, particularly in the context of weekly story papers, where readers did not necessarily keep up with storylines week by week and new readers could pick up an issue at any time, without the necessary background knowledge to make sense of the stories. In this sense, paratexts operate as ways into the story paper worlds, by offering starting points and references for meaning-making through pictures, explanatory titles and straplines. As Genette explains:

> The paratext provides an airlock that helps the reader pass without too much respiratory difficulty from one world to the other, a sometimes delicate operation, especially when the second world is a fictional one. (Genette, 1997: 408)

This metaphor is extremely vivid, but has the unfortunate effect of both underlining the separateness of real and fictional worlds, and implying that readers must consciously and actively bridge the gap between the two. From a position of outside observer, this is in effect more or less what readers are doing; but from the point of view of readers themselves, the process may not be so overtly functional. As we have seen in previous chapters, child readers were readily able to enter into story paper worlds and to carry meanings from stories to their own lives. For many of these readers the strength of the story was such that the crossing of thresholds was effected almost without their notice.

Paratexts can be both textual and non-textual. Cover text (titles, straplines) as well as illustrations function as paratexts, but so too do typographical choices, and, in the story papers, advertisements, competitions and editorial text. Genette also cites factual information as paratexts – in his definition this covers the historical awareness of the period in which a work was written. For inter-war story paper readers, factual paratexts would have included knowledge of the story paper genre, their previous readings of school stories or series stories, the exchange of ideas and information with friends, and the status of story papers in contemporary culture – that is, the fact that they were deemed less than acceptable by authority figures such as parents and teachers.

Genette describes the basic characteristics of paratextual messages in 'spatial, temporal, substantial, pragmatic and functional' terms; in other words, he looks at location (*where?*), date of appearance or disappearance (*when?*), mode of existence (*how?*), the sender and addressee (*from/to whom?*), and the functions that the message aims to fulfil (*to do what?*) (Genette, 1997: 4). Again, there is a solid emphasis on the functional here, which concentrates on physical characteristics. The missing question is *why?*, and this is only partially covered by the pragmatic and functional elements of his taxonomy. In his largely descriptive work he does not engage fully with the relationship between producers and consumers. In the context of the story papers, the relations of power between producers and consumers, and their parents, are particularly important and an exploration into *why* paratexts function, or are manipulated, is as relevant as the where and the how.

Whether consciously recognised by the reader or not, paratexts form part of the overall process of meaning-making, and contribute at various levels to the reader's ability to fill the gaps and spaces in narrative forms. A very obvious example of this is the use of illustrations in the story papers. Although these are used sparingly, they offer supporting information to the narrative, depicting key scenes from the action of the story. In particular, they supply locational details, picturing the insides of classrooms, or key spaces in and outside the school, which helps to situate meanings in context. Similarly visual representations of key characters – and their mode of dress, physical appearance, gestures and expressions – support the very basic descriptions supplied by the narrative.

The 'undefined zone' between the inside and outside of the text, situated between text and reader, and author and text, encompasses those paratextual elements which relate directly to the text itself – titles, subtitles, pictures and straplines. These may or may not have been deliberately placed by the author (perhaps more likely by the author and publisher working together), but their effects are deliberate in terms of reinforcing/supporting/extending functions. In the context of the story papers, it is also necessary to add another level of influence, encompassing factual paratexts – those elements of the story papers not immediately related to the narratives. These contribute to the overall reading experience, beyond that of the story narratives themselves. They are designed by producers – in this case, publishers, advertisers, or other third parties involved in sponsoring competitions – and appeal directly to real readers. They function as economic levers in the power relationship between producers and consumers, in most cases designed to increase circulation or as a straight financial exchange between publisher and advertiser. Some of these elements also have an educational value, such as the editors' columns in both *The Magnet* and *The Hotspur*, and the question-and-answer running heads which appear in *The Hotspur*. The publisher and authors are situated outside the paratext, but the parent is within its field of influence. Factual paratexts in the story papers, and advertisements in particular, situate parents in the role of consumer, allowing for the fact that parents arbitrated reading choice for the majority of children. Some adverts were aimed directly at parents, thus assuming a direct interaction of parents with their children's reading matter. A similar assumption applies to educational elements, in that it is possible to argue that these are placed by publishers as much to appeal to children as to show their parents that story papers have educational value. In this sense, educational paratexts appear to be a deliberate attempt to legitimise story papers as acceptable reading rather than pure escapism.

Paratextual elements in the story papers

Advertisements

Advertisements in the story papers fall into two categories: 'internal' advertising – that is, those referring to other story papers and books produced by the same publisher, as well as trailers for stories due to appear in the same paper in forthcoming issues; and 'external' advertising, placed and paid for by other producers in order to sell their products.

Both types vary from small (around one-eighth of a column) text-only pieces, to full-page, illustrated adverts.

In his discussion of advertising and children's popular culture, Stephen Kline refers to Williams's work:

> Williams talks about advertising as if it were a modern 'magic system' in which products do not represent things so much as the potential transformation of our experience ... Advertisers choose not to discuss goods as materials things, but rather as motivated social systems nested in stories about everyday life. (Kline, 1993: 42)

In the 1920s and 1930s, the concept of advertising directly to children was just beginning to develop – the practice grows much more slowly than advertising to the general public largely because the concept of children as consumers is itself only just developing. Advertisers had very little knowledge of children as consumers, hence early advertisements for products aimed at children tended to use the established mode of address to the parent. In the story papers of the period, internal advertising is in large part addressed directly to child readers/consumers, often to both boys and girls, whereas external adverts show a mix in styles of address. In most advertising, of both types, it is possible to see Williams's 'magic system' at work, as advertisers attempt to persuade consumers of the transformational properties of their respective products.

The internal advert for *The Gem*, shown in Figure 6.1, builds on an implied collegiality amongst readers of *The Magnet*. Written in the approachable and friendly style of the editor's column, the text carries the implied authorial weight of the editor, in his role as 'chum' and adviser to the reader. The implied reader is a homogeneous 'ideal' *Magnet* fan, devoted to his favourite characters. Embodied in this short text is a Bourdieuian sense of playing the game: if *The Gem* is something that 'every' *Magnet* reader will want to read, it must connect with the rules of the game of being a *Magnet* reader. By implication, reading *The Gem* would make a *Magnet* reader a better player of the game; 'every "Magnet" reader' is a heavily loaded phrase which draws directly on peer pressure – to be without this story paper, it implies, would be to be outside the game. Real readers, of course, may not be aware of these undercurrents, and descriptive language is employed to function on a more obvious level: 'rollicking ... fun and frolic ... It's a scream!' The transformational power at this level is pure fun, and *Gem* readers (like *Magnet* readers) are never bored.

Figure 6.1 Internal advertisement, *The Magnet*, 2 June 1934, p. 20

Internal adverts for *The Hotspur* operate on a similar level, advertising both future issues of *The Hotspur* and its sister papers in the 'big five' as well as other D. C. Thomson products. The internal advert from *The Hotspur* shown in Figure 6.2 invites readers to imagine themselves as detectives. Again the loaded term 'every boy' is used, drawing readers into believing this free gift is the key to acceptance by their peers. The picture used on the front of the free book is of an adult, Sherlock Holmes-type of detective. Reading this free book, and, by implication, *The Hotspur* itself, is therefore to access an otherwise closed-off adult world. Real readers might not be taken in by this seductive transformational message, but the clever combination of hooks in the text which juxtaposes the practical ('how to') with the descriptive/informational ('how') allows the more cynical of readers to enjoy the book for its more educational qualities.

Story Papers as Cultural Artefacts 161

Figure 6.2 Internal advertisement, *The Hotspur*, 26 August 1939, p. 3

This contrasts interestingly with an internal advert from an early edition of *The Hotspur*, shown in Figure 6.3. In this advertisement, the emphasis is purely on value as *The Hotspur* tries to establish itself in competition with other story papers for children's money. The descriptive language is sparing – *The Hotspur* is 'packed' with stories, but there is no mention of what kind of stories these are. Readers are left to fill the gaps here, with a mental image of the stories they would like to see. The implied reader in this case is one who is careful with money and looks for the added value of jokes and news as well as stories. This type of advert does not survive for long in *The Hotspur*, perhaps because the alternative elements (one page of jokes, news and comic strips) are not the main selling point of the paper.

External adverts in the story papers involve more complicated relationships between producers and consumers. These paratexts operate as thresholds to experiences in readers' real lives, and are connected to story paper worlds only through their physical proximity to the stories.

The Paper
 For Value
THAT'S
THE HOTSPUR

Every week you get 26 packed pages of stories, and a page of jokes, news, and comic strips.

Don't miss next Friday's copy, with the great complete story—

'Who's To Be Captain of Red Circle?'

Figure 6.3 Internal advertisement, *The Hotspur*, 30 September 1933, p. 94

In some cases these are direct appeals to children; in others parents appear as intermediaries; and some have an interesting dual focus directed at both child and parent.

The Quaker Oats 'puffed wheat' advert shown in Figure 6.4 appeared in both *The Magnet* and *The Hotspur*. It combines the lure of a free gift with an appeal to an implied mother figure and her implied 'natural' nurturing instincts. The free gift offer draws the reader into the imagined transformational experience of playing with the glider. Implied in this audience are the other members of the *Magnet/Hotspur* reading game – the 'everyboy' (and girl) whose acceptance in the field of story paper reading depends on his ownership of this associated commodity as well as his knowledge/experience of story paper worlds. Having hooked the child reader, the advert then has to transfer its appeal to the mother, who acts as buyer/consumer in this instance.

The advert's authors (product producers) make the assumption that child readers will show the advert to their mothers, who will then be drawn into the transformational experience of improving their sons' health and wellbeing. Not only are well-nourished and energetic children implied here, but it is also assumed that they will grow into the kind of men who are proud to fight for their country: Puffed Wheat and Puffed Rice are 'the foods shot from guns'.

The dual focus of this advert, seen from a twenty-first-century viewpoint, makes it feel somewhat misplaced in a children's story paper. It is not the product itself but the free gift which appeals to the main reader, however much the advertisers try to point out how 'irresistible' the product is. Ryan explains the process of an advert's appeal to a consumer:

> If potential consumers are to be attracted to a commodity, then its purpose and properties must be specified. Some rationale must be provided as to why it should be purchased. The commodity must promise to satisfy potential purchasers by fulfilling their specific wants and needs; what marketers speak of as consumer benefits. (Ryan, 1991: 189)

In this case the child reader's need to be entertained – and to keep up with his or her peers in mutual possession of the same toy – is greater than the need for nutritional breakfasts. Hence the purpose and properties of the glider almost override the description of the commodity the advert is designed to promote. The product producers take the risk that the glider's appeal will be sufficient to lead the child reader to the

Figure 6.4 Quaker Oats advertisement, *The Hotspur*, 13 July 1935, p. 51. This advertisement also appeared in *The Magnet* issue for the same week

'real' consumer. Another example from *The Hotspur* in the same year (26 October 1935: 11), also for Quaker Oats, is directly addressed to boys and girls. It features a free book of magic tricks, in return for 'the quaker figures cut from two packets of Quaker Oats'. Here the emphasis is squarely on the free book, with very little reference to the product. My spot check on issues of *Schoolgirl's Own* and *Schoolgirls' Weekly* from 1935 revealed that there were no external advertisements at all – clearly the advertisers were aware that girls were avid readers of the boys' papers, but that boys would very rarely read a girl's magazine (see Jenkinson, 1940: 217). Tinkler argues that the near absence of advertising in the girls' story papers reinforces the fact that the intended readership is working-class schoolgirls, who were less likely to have money to spend (Tinkler, 1995: 47), but this overlooks the fact that working-class boys and girls are clearly targeted in the boys' papers.

Advertisements for commodities aimed directly at child consumers are more likely to make use of what Ryan calls 'the significance-of-the-commodity-in-its-context-of-use' (Ryan, 1991: 194). The Fry's Chocolate Cream advert from *The Magnet* and the Wrigley's advert from *The Hotspur*, shown in Figures 6.5 and 6.6, are good examples of this. Both images draw from the recognisable discourses of school (linking both to story paper worlds and real schools), and the comradeship of peer relations. Both products signify cultural capital. Fry's Chocolate Cream's value comes from the possession as much as the consumption. Ownership of a bar, the advert implies, will lead to increased popularity – not consuming is thus as important as consuming. Readers are invited to resolve the tension by filling in the symbolic story of the advert: would the real reader eat it himself, or share it with his chums? The Wrigley's advert similarly loads added significance on to the product by juxtaposing it with sporting imagery and language. Wrigley's gum is for 'good' footballers, and by implication is a contributing factor to footballing talent. Implied effects count for more than the experience of consumption – the taste appears almost as an afterthought at the end of the text. The product is thus imbued with the cultural and social capital of the star sportsman, as well as resonating with the role of the sporting heroes of the school playing field so often portrayed in the stories.

Placing product adverts in story papers has additional benefits for producers in that symbolic capital is transferred from the story paper to the product. As we have seen in the first part of this chapter, story papers accumulated symbolic cultural capital through exchange as well as through associated social rituals of discussion and play amongst

Figure 6.5 Fry's advertisement, *The Magnet*, 5 May 1934, p. 21

readers. Locating a product within these value networks allows it to share in a reciprocal relationship of value accumulation. The repeated appearance of certain product adverts – in particular the Wrigley's gum adverts which are a regular feature in *The Hotspur* – indicates the success of these value relationships. Some small adverts appear week by week in exactly the same format in both story papers, over a period of years (see Figure 0.1 for an example of an advertisements page). These are typically advertising products to alleviate physical and social problems such as lack of height, blushing, stammering and bullying. Although to an adult reader they might seem highly dubious in their claims, they clearly had some success amongst child consumers: repeated appearance implies at least some level of positive response. The reverse of this is also true, in that certain adverts are published only once or twice in the story papers, the producers apparently having misjudged their market and failed to elicit a response. This is more evident in earlier editions of *The Magnet*. For example, 'Don't Wear a Truss!' (in *The Magnet*, 22 October 1921) advertises 'Brookes' new scientific appliance ... made

Figure 6.6 Wrigley's advertisement, *The Hotspur*, 8 April 1939, p. 9

for men, women and children'; and a half-page advert in *The Magnet*, 1 May 1925, advertises expensive oak and mahogany wireless cabinets. Neither advert makes any attempt to orientate the product towards a child readership, directly or indirectly. Bad product placement fails to take account of cultural capital.

Other forms of factual paratexts: editors' columns and running heads

Editors' columns in the story papers are a point of intersection between real world and story paper worlds. The editor himself is an amalgam of fact and fiction: the real writer is anonymous, and may or may not actually fulfil the role of editor of the story paper text. As implied author, he inhabits a fictional role as 'chum' and confidant of the child reader, both implied and real. Real readers corresponded regularly with the editor, writing to a real person, but addressing their comments to the fictional figure. Correspondents sent in questions about stories and characters as well as general queries to be answered in the editorial column. Both papers use editors' columns as a regular feature, although in *The Magnet* the column does not appear every week. In earlier issues, from the 1920s, the column is called 'Editor's Chat', and has a rather more formal tone. This is transformed through the early 1930s into a more conversational piece with the regular title 'Come into the Office, Boys!' (later, this becomes boys and girls). This informal style invites readers into an imagined relationship with the editor, which can then connect with the real through the publication of readers' questions in the paper (along with their names), and the receipt of personal replies or prizes. (*The Magnet* offers a reply to every letter on receipt of a stamped, addressed envelope; *The Hotspur* offers a postal order to those whose 'puzzles, tricks and catches' are published in the 'Sez You!' column.) *The Hotspur*'s editorial columns invariably appear on the inside front cover, thus operating on a physical/locational level as a threshold to story paper worlds in addition to their mediating role through the fictional editor. In *The Magnet*, the editor's column is apparently inserted wherever there is space in the paper, its transience somewhat undermining its status and message.

Editors' columns operate on a number of levels, from the relationship-building function, to advertising stories and features in the papers, to providing educational content. The *Magnet* columns generally fill half a page, allowing room for all of these levels to operate; in *The Hotspur* they are sized to a more compact quarter of a page and focus largely on the educational, but are supported by an additional quarter page 'Sez You' element which focuses attention on the reader. The example shown in Figure 6.7, from *The Magnet*, shows the editor using the authority of his implied author role to offer moral advice embedded in a blatant plug for an Amalgamated Press publication. Reading the *Holiday Annual*, it implies, is good for one's health. As with the other forms of advertising discussed above, this allegedly transformational experience is a cultural transaction for readers (reinforcing cultural and social capital through knowledge and possession) as well as an economic one for producers trying to sell more books. The educational, general knowledge element of this column takes up roughly half of the space, although this balance does vary in different

COME INTO THE OFFICE, BOYS AND GIRLS!

Your Editor is always pleased to hear from his readers. Write to him: Editor of the MAGNET, The Fleetway House, Farringdon Street, London, E.C.4. A stamped, addressed envelope will ensure a reply.

NE of my chums who has written to me this week has set me

A PROBLEM!

He asks me what time a boy should arrive home in the evening. Frankly, I think this query is one that should be settled by a boy's parents.

With very few exceptions, I am sure, parents will give a reasonable time for returning home. It may be that some boys think their parents want them to be home too early. But let me assure any boy who feels inclined to grumble that late hours are not good for one's health. There are many ways of passing away the long winter evenings which do not involve being out late. The ideal way, of course, is to get a copy of the "Holiday Annual." This world-famous book, on sale everywhere, is packed from cover to cover with rollicking fine school stories of Greyfriars, St. Jim's and Rookwood, humorous articles, sparkling verses, and many other bright features. It costs only five shillings, and is a real bargain at the price. Get the "Holiday Annual" to-day and I'll guarantee you won't want to stay out late. You'll want to get home early to read it!

Have you ever heard about the woman who gets

SEASICK BY WIRELESS?

You would imagine that anyone sitting safely at home in an easy-chair would be the last person on earth to suffer from sea-sickness. Not long ago, however, a South African woman was listening to a broadcast from the liner Stirling Castle when she was suddenly taken seriously ill. A doctor was sent for immediately, and diagnosed the trouble as seasickness! He said that it was the sound of the waves and the thud of the engines that had brought on an attack of seasickness by wireless!

ALL GOOD THINGS COME TO AN END!

Whenever one of our popular features comes to an end I generally get letters from chums who want to know why I have discontinued it. This, of course, is a great compliment to the features in question. But there is another side. Popular as they may prove to be, I am sure that few of you would like them to go on for ever. And, after all, variety is the spice of life! I believe in giving every feature a run and then replacing it with something just as good, if not better. In this way the MAGNET is always fresh and bright. You will have already noticed that our "Greyfriars Interviews" have come to an end. Well, to make up for this, our long-haired poet is writing a series of verses dealing with "The Stately Homes of Greyfriars," which will be as interesting as they are amusing. Look out for No. 1 of this new series very shortly, chums!

Here is a selection of

RAPID-FIRE REPLIES

to queries sent in by various readers:

When was Nelson's Column Built? (O. H., of Wandsworth): It was erected in the year 1843, and cost £28,000. The bronze lions at the base were not added until the year 1867.

Do Crocodiles Ever Shed Tears? ("Curious," of Brighton): No. They can't, because they have no tear ducts. The expression "crocodile tears" simply means that a person is only pretending to cry.

Which is the Loneliest Gold Mine in the World? ("Aussie Reader," of Melbourne): The gold mine at Portland Roads, Queenstown. The mail is carried to it by packhorse from the nearest post office, three hundred miles away. The gold ore is carried by packhorse to the coast, sixty miles away, and has to be rowed out to steamers, as there is no anchorage. Sixty people live at the mine.

Where did "Houdini" Get His Name? ("Conjurer," of Kingston): Houdini, the famous escapologist, took his name from Robert Houdin, a Frenchman who was, perhaps, the greatest magician of his time. The original Houdin died in 1871, and his American follower adopted a slight variation of the name.

Figure 6.7 Extract from editor's column, *The Magnet*, 28 November 1936, p. 27

Figure 6.8 Editor's column, *The Hotspur*, 23 March 1935, p. 1

issues. The 'rapid-fire replies' answer seemingly random questions sent in by readers, supplying concise but authoritative-sounding information. By comparison, the 'Sez Me!' column, shown in Figure 6.8, takes a more narrative approach in its presentation of facts. Again this is a seemingly random choice of subject, but the storytelling style is much more likely to hold the reader's interest. It is, however, difficult to separate out the elements of fact and fiction here, which rather undermines the educational value of the information. Drawn in by the narrative style, readers are asked to equate the bear's cunning with the fictional behaviour of the boys of Red Circle School, and by implication with their own behaviour. This complex process of constructing meaning is further complicated by the pure entertainment value of the jokes and comic strips on the rest of the page, which draw attention away from the text. This mix of voices mutes the educational message of the editor's column so much as to render it almost valueless.

Factual paratexts do feature elsewhere in *The Hotspur*, however, in the form of running heads which appear consistently throughout the paper's run of publication. These nuggets of general knowledge appear across the top margin of a double-page spread – question on the left, answer on the right. They range from mundanely straightforward historical/geographical/scientific facts to the extraordinary. For example: 'Who was the founder of the US Navy? It was founded by a Scotsman, Paul Jones'; 'What load can a camel carry? A fully-grown camel can carry as much as 1500lbs'; 'What amazing trick can an American Negro perform? He can hold two billiard balls and two golf balls in his mouth' (from *The Hotspur*, 28 February 1939, pp. 16–17; *The Hotspur*, 17 April 1937, pp. 60–1; and *The Hotspur*, 26 August 1939, pp. 4–5). These are set physically outside the text, separated from the body of the text by a thick dotted line, but the bold type and the headline positioning attract attention. These are not throwaway lines, but are meant to be seen, read and enjoyed; the question-and-answer format also suggests readers might use them to quiz their chums, or even their parents. There is no attempt to connect the facts to any of the stories, but their physical proximity to the main text again points towards the blurring of fact and fiction. The addition of these running heads is an attempt to add value on the part of the producers, situating the story paper as the provider of knowledge as well as entertainment.

This form of factual paratext attempts to bridge the gap between child reader and parent, increasing the symbolic value of the paper for the parent by making educational connections, albeit somewhat randomly. It is an effective use of what would otherwise be 'dead' space on the page. By contrast, *The Magnet*'s producers do not make consistent use of running heads, and those which do appear are shoutlines advertising the paper itself and its sister publications. These are effectively extensions of the editor's column, communicating directly to the reader. The following examples come from *The Magnet*, 23 January 1925: 'Introduce a new chum to The Magnet! Thanks!'; 'Our Motto: Clean, Wholesome Literature!'; 'Don't miss our special football supplement next week!'; 'Seen this week's bumper number of The Gem?' Editorial authority gives these instructions added weight, as, again, does the headline positioning and the bold full-capitals typography. The fact that these are not used consistently – in issues from 1934, for example, no running heads at all are used – indicates that the producers are not convinced of their value.

Covers and illustrations

One of the striking things about inter-war story papers is their reliance on the medium of text. Stories are presented in three-column small-print format, typeset in the dense fashion of a broadsheet newspaper of the period. The fact that the major story paper producers were also newspaper publishers is significant. Using existing design (and presumably the same designers) will have led to economies of scale for the producers. This does, however, also imply that the producers were not particularly interested in whether or not the design of the story papers appealed to their child audiences, or in creating designs specifically orientated to child readers. Conversely, the density of text allows for more stories to be fitted into the available space, and may have been seen by children as an indicator of value for money. In comparison with the reading matter offered to twenty-first-century children, story papers are predominantly monomodal. With the exception of specially designed picture books, the illustration in children's books was largely subordinate to the text – illustrations functioned as adjuncts to the text, whilst the text carried the main emphasis for meaning-making. These early multimodal texts were organised as 'hierarchies of specialist modes integrated by an editing process' (Kress and Van Leeuwen, 2001: 2). In other words, it was the editor's role – in conjunction with the publisher – to create multimodality by bringing together text and paratext, in the form of illustration. In the story paper genre, by the 1920s, illustrations had become an accepted element both as the major feature of the front cover and on the inside of the story paper to support the stories themselves. While the quality of illustration in both *The Magnet* and *The Hotspur* is uniformly high, there is in many cases a lack of connection between text and pictures which means that opportunities for meaning-making are missed, and often the disconnection actually disrupts the narrative flow.

The cover of *The Hotspur* from 4 April 1936 (Figure 6.9) carries a large picture of one of the masters from Red Circle School, Mr Smugg, emerging on hands and knees, and in a very dishevelled state, from what looks like a tent. There is no textual indicator of the story to which this picture relates, except for a notice, apparently pinned to the tent canvas, which advertises 'all-in wrestling exhibition inside'. This text invites the reader in two directions: to the imaginary space implied inside the tent, symbolised by the black space which readers are invited to fill, behind the key character; and to the stories inside the paper itself. That the picture should illustrate the denouement of the story is unusual, but this does in fact help to appeal to new as well as to established *Hotspur* readers. Those readers familiar with the Red Circle series would readily have recognised Mr Smugg as the most hated teacher in the school. The picture thus builds strong expectation in readers who will relish Smugg's long-awaited comeuppance. Those readers new to *The Hotspur* would have been drawn in to the story by the reversal of authority which this illustration depicts. Smugg has managed to retain his mortar board, which acts as a symbol of his position of authority, despite the extreme raggedness of the rest of his clothing. Readers are thus hooked in to discover what this teacher has done to find himself in such unexpected circumstances.

This particular paratext works hard to invite readers across the threshold into the story, operating at various levels to connect readers to the narrative. Once inside the magazine, however, the reader is confronted with a range of texts and paratexts to work through in order to reach the story which connects directly with the picture. The Red Circle story starts on page 8 with the title, 'When the Fifth Form Went Crazy', and a picture of a classroom in complete chaos (see Figure 6.10). There are three more paratextual thresholds here, each of which plays with readers' knowledge of the school story genre by subverting the recognised rules of the 'game'. Both the running head and the title imply deliberate anarchy – although this is anarchy in a contained and controlled form, with the two lines of text acting as a frame and boundary to the picture of wild disorder. The reversal of established classroom order connects with the cover image: in both, teachers are clearly shown in situations in which they are without authority. The combination of effects of the two images and their accompanying texts raises further expectation in the reader, which the text then struggles to fulfil. The classroom anarchy of the picture is described in two short paragraphs,

Figure 6.9 Front cover of *The Hotspur*, 4 April 1939

Figure 6.10 'When the Fifth Form Went Crazy', *The Magnet*, 4 April 1936, p. 7

and then order is restored – leaving the reader to fill in the textual gaps with an imagined simulation of transgressive behaviour. In the story, the 'crazy' disruption is a deliberate but very temporary affair – Smugg has declared that the best behaved boy will be given the honour of acting as his 'assistant' in arranging the forthcoming school fête, and the boys take drastic action to avoid being selected for the role. Anarchic behaviour is thus legitimised as a means to an end, but normal order is swiftly restored once the role has been assigned to Horace Glossop, the class swot.

Turning the page of the story paper, the reader is immediately drawn to the picture in the centre: a large and muscular wrestler is hoisting Smugg in the air, in the middle of a wrestling ring which is surrounded by cheering boys (see Figure 6.11). This is a severe disruption to the flow of the narrative: the incident shown in the picture does not occur in the story until the final column of the following page, when the story describes how Smugg, in trying to stop what he sees as a vulgar display of fairground sideshows inappropriate to a 'serious and dignified event', finds himself accidentally caught up in a wrestling bout. The reinforcing function of this paratext is therefore weakened by its location as separate from the text to which it relates. It does, however, act to reinforce

Figure 6.11   Mr Smugg and the wrestler, *The Hotspur*, 6 April 1936, p. 8

readers' expectations of the events to come, and as such operates in support of the cover image.

The image itself also reinforces the story's theme of challenge to authority. Within the double boundary of the circus tent and wrestling ring, Mr Smugg's rules of order do not apply. His symbol of authority, the mortar board, has been displaced and floats free, and his look of horror seems as much directed at the hat and its loss, as to his painful predicament. He also has no shadow: the boundary of the picture cuts off the wrestler's shadow at the shoulders, which serves to emphasise the wrestler's bulk and to minimise the 'presence' of Mr Smugg. Strength and showmanship are most valued here, in a space where the symbols and rituals of school have no power. This comedic reversal is underlined at the end of the story, when Smugg, still in his tattered and bruised state, is presented with a charitable donation by Lord Yodell, 'the star guest of the day', 'tall and distinguished' and clearly representative of established order. Lord Yodell has enjoyed the 'show' immensely:

> 'Great show! Amazing! Don't know how you thought of it, Smugg! Your fooling in the ring with that man Parelli was the hit of the century! Perfect clowning, old boy!' ('When the Fifth Form Went Crazy', *The Hotspur*, 4 April 1936: 10)

This exchange manages quite cleverly to combine an extension of the comedy of the further humiliation of Smugg, with the beginnings of a resolution of order. Lord Yodell sanctions Smugg's presence in the circus tent, and offers him a route back into the order of the school world. The fact that the story ends at this point, in an open-ended way which leaves readers to imagine Smugg's return to the classroom, is significant, in that it allows readers to enjoy the feelings of anarchic disruption after the story has finished. In this case the illustrations add to that enjoyment, supporting and reinforcing that strand of narrative.

Cover images and those within the stories generally depict action events. The events chosen for illustration, however, are not necessarily the key action points of the stories. In both *The Magnet* and *The Hotspur*, cover images are chosen for maximum comedic impact. The cover of *The Magnet*, 9 June 1934, for example, shown in Figure 6.12, shows Billy Bunter falling into the river, having apparently tried to get into a boat. The boy in the boat is deliberately using his oar to move the boat out of Bunter's reach. The strapline, 'A bath for Billy Bunter!' implies that this is a central incident in the story, but in fact it happens in chapters 1 and 2, and is all but forgotten by the beginning of page 4. The incident itself, then, has little bearing on the subsequent development of the narrative, but the image gives Bunter a central status which is important to the story. Bunter is the essential link point in the kernel events of the narrative: when Mr Smedley is looking for Vernon-Smith, Bunter lets slip that he has gone out of bounds; when Vernon-Smith is in danger of being caught out of bounds by Smedley, it is Bunter who, albeit accidentally, alerts Vernon-Smith's friend Redwing to the danger, in time for Redwing to save him; and when Mr Smedley forges a letter, trying to implicate Vernon-Smith in a theft, Bunter manages to avert the plot by (again accidentally) dropping the letter in the river. The cover image thus sets up a level of expectation of Bunter's role in the story – expectation which will be enhanced for regular readers by their knowledge of Bunter's role as Greyfriars' clown.

Figure 6.12 Front cover, *The Magnet*, 9 June 1934

As with the example from *The Hotspur* above, the various elements of this *Magnet* cover design combine to 'present' the story text inside the paper, and to invite readers in. The line of the oar and the slanted title text in the bottom right-hand corner act as vectors to draw the eye towards the leading edge of the cover, and, by implication, towards the content of the story paper. Similarly, the four keywords in bold full capitals along the top of the cover draw the eye in stages towards a final emphasis on the word 'inside', announcing key elements of the story paper content and building readers' expectation of enjoyment. The oar also acts as a point of connection between the boy in the boat and the jetty on which his chums are standing, creating a space between the two groups into which Bunter falls. Bunter is stepping into an undefined space, away from the safety of the jetty and the other boys. Bunter may be the centre of attention here – an impression which is heightened by the halo-effect of the splash of water – but his separateness and difference are clearly highlighted.

Even with 28 pages of space to play with, *The Magnet's* designers seem to have had difficulty positioning illustrations at suitable points in the narrative. In this story, illustrations appear in each case at least two pages before the text to which they relate: Bunter dropping the letter in the river is pictured on page 13, but related text is on pages 17–18; Smedley's confrontation with Vernon-Smith is pictured on page 19, but related text is on page 22. The cumulative effect of this is to destroy any sense of suspense: the images present events so far in advance that it becomes difficult to bridge the gap between image and text.

Summary and conclusions

This chapter has explored the relationship between the macro-view of story papers in their social-historical context and the micro-view of the function of separate elements of the papers. Bourdieu's theories of cultural production have helped towards an explanation of the ways in which the story paper genre developed, and the shifting pattern of values attributed to them by their producers and users.

Story papers carried symbolic value for their readers as much in the acts of purchase and possession as in the consumption. The purchase of a story paper, designed and produced purely for a child reader market, represents an important step in the development of the child as consumer. Such a purchase is a symbol of autonomy – in that a child is making his or her own decision to exchange economic capital for cultural/social capital, and also in that it can be seen as an act of subversion, through buying an artefact which is on the whole disapproved of by parents and teachers. Knowledge and ownership of story papers also transferred symbolic capital to readers, giving them status amongst their peers: both the knowledge and the physical artefacts could be exchanged between readers as part of the 'game'.

Any analysis of the story paper genre must take into account the importance of paratextual features as well as the story narratives. Readers' understanding of the stories would have been framed, consciously or unconsciously, by the combination of paratextual elements in text, design and illustration. Story papers must be viewed as complete texts, the influences of text and paratext functioning jointly in the meaning-making process.

The notion of multimodality is useful here in exploring the ways in which texts and paratexts work together. There is a sense, however, that story paper producers did not fully understand this process, and that elements in the papers did not combine effectively in a consistent way. The misaligned location of illustrations is a good example of this. Story papers are not multimodal in the full sense of Kress and Van Leeuwen's concept, and this might perhaps go some way towards explaining their decline in the face of competition from more obviously multimodal texts in the form of comics.

Conclusion

This book has both shown the central role that story paper reading played in the reading and cultural/social lives of working-class and lower-middle-class children, and mapped the scale of influence of the genre in terms of the business of publishing for children. The success of the story paper genre changed the nature of children's publishing, shifting the focus to children as purchasers as well as readers, and correspondingly moving towards a diminishing of the role of parents as arbiters of reading choices. By operating a reciprocal model drawing on children's own patterns of valuing and taking account of their interests in developing narratives and content, story paper producers were able to translate cultural capital into commercial and economic profit, restructuring the field and attracting the investment of new players, both producers and consumers.

Throughout this book I have argued for the situating of the story papers in their cultural and historical contexts. This critical positioning is essential in order to connect the dominant social character of the time to the functioning of narratives and their embedded ideologies. It also informs the exploration of value systems, and the ways in which patterns of valuing, amongst producers and consumers, shift over time. From the evidence of contemporary adult commentators as well as later historians of children's literature, it is clear that the genre was held in low regard. The story paper attracted contempt as well as a certain amount of moral panic from those critics worried about literary standards and the rise of mass culture. The critical stance of the mass culture theorists, however, takes a simplistic view of the texts, valuing them according to a strict literary-critical code which privileges certain kinds of classic texts and discards others. This approach is as much a product of the dominant social character of the time as are the texts themselves, and it is only with the benefit of historical distance that alternative modes of valuation are possible.

Drawing together the work of Williams, Bourdieu and the reader response theorists facilitates a critical positioning which brings to the fore the lived experience of readers whilst also offering formulations through which to explore the process of meaning-making through texts. Using this predominantly new historicist approach, it is possible to map a network of interconnecting economic, social and cultural value patterns contingent on author/producer–text–reader relationships. To these Bourdieuian symbolic values I would also add historical value, in that this critical re-evaluation seeks to restore a role and status to the story paper genre in the context of the history of the development of children's literature. All of these value patterns must be interrogated according to their specific historical, social and cultural contexts – in Williams's terms, with respect to the structure of feeling of the time – but such interrogations must also be recognised as informed by the habitus of the interrogator.

In economic terms, story paper publishing came to represent a sound financial investment, bringing in substantial profit even in times of national economic downturn in the 1930s. For the producers, the impulse to profit acted as a strong motivator for entry into the field. Both Harmsworth and Thomson diversified their already successful newspaper and periodicals publishing operations into the children's story paper market, thus minimising their economic risk and maximising economies of scale in production practices. In D. C. Thomson's case, the decision to publish children's story papers was carefully timed to take advantage of a fast-emerging new market, which had already been primed by the Amalgamated Press papers. Economic exchange clearly involves consumers as well as producers, and, as we have seen in Chapter 6, story papers were among the first commodities developed to be bought by children for themselves. The success of the story paper genre was therefore dependent on the extent to which child readers were prepared to attribute symbolic value to the papers in exchange for the 2d. cover price, and the skill of the producers in managing the balance of this exchange.

An understanding of the ways in which these symbolic values were developed, in terms of social and cultural capital, is in my view key to explaining the overwhelming popularity of the story paper genre. Entering the story paper field can thus be seen as much more than simply a reading experience, or a straightforward engagement between text and reader. The connected acts of purchase and ownership carried value in themselves, symbolising new status for the child consumer both in the economic field and amongst his or her peers. Knowledge of characters and storylines carried as much validity as currency for exchange under the rules of the game as did the physical copies of the papers. Layers of symbolic value overlaid on the narrative pleasure of the reading experience combined to create a uniquely powerful pull to consumers.

Although the producers were completely in control of story paper content, and took pains to ensure this appealed directly to readers, they cannot have predicted, nor in any way have been able to manipulate, the symbolic valuing of the story paper as a commodity by its consumers. This offers a new perspective on the producer–consumer dynamic, indicating a rather more balanced power relationship than might previously have been assumed. The child audience is often characterised by critics as powerless and vulnerable, but here it is possible to discern both agency and power, through the structures of value which children built for themselves. This process became genuinely reciprocal as producers began to take account of these new patterns. Underlying these relationships is Nelson's concept of the producers' key imperative to find a balance between the impulse to profit and the impulse to improve (Nelson, 1997: 15). To this must be added the consumers' impulse to be entertained and to learn, without which the reciprocal transaction cannot be completed.

Interpreting the story paper phenomenon in this way presents an empowering view of producer–consumer relationships in which child readers play an active part. This is not a framework for the direct transmittal of specific ideologies, rather it is a process of exchange of meanings through which child readers were able to adapt and apply meanings in their own cultural contexts. The messages of authority were thus filtered through the child's view of both real and fictional worlds, and the perceived interconnections between the two. The implementation of these mechanisms of meaning in children's lives is readily apparent from the evidence of contemporary readers who describe the sheer pleasure of story paper reading interactions, and in those of adults recalling the life-long effects of childhood reading.

Story paper reading largely took place in children's personal space, in the home or in the street, beyond the gaze of authority figures. This enhanced sense of personal ownership was given an added frisson of subversion for readers by the knowledge that many parents and teachers disapproved of such reading matter. This disapproval had an ironic edge given the profoundly moral aspirations of the authors and publishers, but its effects are nonetheless clear in terms of increased symbolic value amongst readers. Just as the stories themselves offered space for children to explore notions of transgression and conformity within safe parameters, so the act of buying/exchanging and reading a story paper represented an opportunity for a minor act of subversion, a form of self-expression which tested the boundaries of adult authority.

Each of these layers of symbolic value is important to developing readers making sense of their world. The depiction of characters who consistently transgress the rules of school and of moral behaviour served both to increase entertainment value for child readers locating themselves as subject but also to reinforce those boundaries through always-moral resolutions. The thrill of identifying with nonconformity was balanced by the restoration of moral order, in the same way as child readers' subversive acts in the real world were contained within the overall pattern of adult–child power relationships.

The complexity of the structured relationship between producer, text and reader is further complicated by the school story setting, which defined characters and actions against institutional boundaries, both physical and moral. From the author/producers' point of view the school as institution offered a ready framework for the representation of moral values and behaviours, in a genre already familiar and understandable to child readers. The institutional setting underlined the portrayal of authority and conformity, scaffolding a structure through which an author could aim, as a D. C. Thomson editor put it, 'to impose his ideas on the reader' (McAleer, 1992: 188). Following Althusser's formulation of the school as ideological state apparatus, the institutional setting could be said to operate in a parallel role, in representing ideologies-in-action, and 'imposing' key values on the reading subject. This, however, assumes an overly simplistic process of transmission which overlooks both the readers' own critical faculties and the social/cultural context of reading. Clear moral messages were embedded in the stories, but by taking ownership of the reading process and evolving patterns of behaviour through play and peer interaction, child readers were able to select and interpret those messages, tailoring them to individual lived experiences.

The nature of the ideologies, mythologies and moral structures incorporated into the stories was the product of the dominant social character of the time, an inter-war milieu in which the imperial hero myth was accepted as 'natural'. Against this background the stories defined ideal versions of masculinity, which focused on codes of conduct, sportsmanship, loyalty and comradeship. Here again, however, it is important to note that text–reader relationships were not as straightforward as this description would imply. The status of the story papers as series publications and their physical structure combining stories, pictures and other elements, served to complicate these relationships, undermining the imposition of ideas and potentially offering space for subversive readings. The serial format necessarily introduces gaps in the narrative which readers were invited to fill in order to sustain storylines between issues. These anticipatory spaces served to heighten narrative expectation and enjoyment, but they also disrupted the potential for ideological manipulation by permitting alternative imagined resolutions. A cliffhanger ending in which action was suspended with a character left in a transgressive situation carried a vicarious thrill which could resonate across the week-long gap to the next issue. The intended moral resolutions to such stories might not have been picked up by every reader, given the ephemeral nature of the story papers and the ease by which an issue might have been missed for economic, social or cultural reasons. Anticipatory spaces are an important element in the patterns of consumption of the story papers, in that it is in these spaces that readers were able to connect the separate realities of school and story paper worlds, and to transfer meanings for themselves between the two. Serial reading over time consolidated those links, allowing readers to become more proficient players of the game, and helping them to blur distinctions between the two worlds. This active mode of reader response is evident in the testimonies of readers who speak of incorporating actions and behaviours of key characters into their own play.

The structures of fascination of story paper worlds elicited a suturing process which both drew readers in and assisted in their identification with key characters and their filling in of gaps in the text. This sense of connection was particularly apparent through children's engagement with serial narratives in both story papers and the cinema. As shown in Chapter 5, the mechanisms of suturing operated in similar ways in both genres, allowing readers/viewers to locate themselves as subjects in fictional worlds. The similarities between the two genres were not accidental, as narrative pleasure was firmly centred at the core of each. The appeal of the visual experience of cinema represented a major threat to the story paper business, and producers responded by reshaping the story paper genre more closely to resemble the narrative style of the cinema serial. That sales of *The Hotspur*, and the other 'big five' papers, outstripped by so far those of *The Magnet* is arguably attributable in the main to the cinematic style of storytelling and the overt ways in which the D. C. Thomson writers exploited children's fascination with cinema. Drawing on film narratives and conventions in this way also represented a shift in focus, moving away from an emphasis on child and parent as audience, to the child in his/her own right. The rise in popularity of cinema was accompanied by the same kind of moral panics as had surrounded the appearance of the Victorian 'penny dreadfuls', with parents and concerned adults deeply worried by its imagined effects on the nation's youth. This sense of moral alarm, however, did nothing to stem the flow of children towards the picture houses, and it was the D. C. Thomson writers' recognition of this change in parental authority which helped to fuel the explosion in popularity of the 'big five'. By focusing on the child consumer, the D. C. Thomson papers effectively diminished the role of parents as arbiters of reading choice. Here, the impulse to profit was balanced by the child readers' impulse to be entertained – the impulse to improve being concealed behind directly orientated structures of fascination. The Amalgamated Press papers, by comparison, set their approach slightly too far in favour of appealing to parental approval and a more overt impulse to improve, and consequently were less able to compete for children's attention.

This reluctance to evolve is part of the reason for the decline in sales of the Amalgamated Press papers, but the genre as a whole suffered decline from the early 1940s for a number of reasons, not least of which was the increasing competition from other magazine formats and leisure activities. Jenkinson's data show the continuing popularity of the D. C. Thomson papers in the late 1930s, though his questioning was designed to indicate the number of papers *read* rather than bought. The economic value of the story paper business may have been beginning to decline, then, but their cultural value remained buoyant. The strength of this cultural capital, and reader loyalty, was sufficient to sustain all but one of the 'big five' through the trading difficulties of the war years: *The Hotspur* remained in publication until 1959; *Wizard* until 1963; *The Rover* and *Adventure* until 1961; while only *Skipper* ceased publication during wartime, in 1941 (Drotner, 1988: 250–1).

The Hotspur evolved with the changing tastes of its readers, maintaining its popularity as new generations of readers entered the story paper-reading field. By comparison, where once Frank Richards's writing skill had enthralled child readers, the reliance on one author over so many years seems to have contributed to a spiralling decline for both *The Magnet* and *The Gem*, both of which went out of print in 1940. *The Champion* is an interesting example which neatly underlines the atrophied qualities of Frank Richards's output by the late 1930s. *The Champion*, an Amalgamated Press paper originally launched in

1922, was reworked with a new style modelled on the D. C. Thomson papers in the 1930s. When *The Magnet* went out of print in 1940, with a circulation of 80,000 copies weekly, *The Champion* had almost double that audience, with 150,000 copies circulating every week. This is again supported by Jenkinson's data, which show *The Champion* as the most popular paper outside the 'big five', although 15-year-olds in secondary schools and 14-year-olds in senior schools place *The Magnet* above *The Champion* (see Tables A.1 and A.2).

Orwell's *Horizon* essay, published in 1940, focused critical attention on the Amalgamated Press model which was by then already being superseded. The essay does point to the growing influence of the D. C. Thomson papers, but does not recognise the significance of other developments in the field which were influencing the genre – although clearly hindsight allows a much more direct view here. The D. C. Thomson company produced another major innovation in the 1930s in the form of the comic weekly, notably *The Dandy* (first issued in 1937) and *The Beano* (first issued in 1938). Kline argues that comics developed on a parallel trajectory with the story paper genre, originating from early comic strips in late nineteenth-century daily newspapers – and hence aimed at an adult readership (Kline, 1993: 98). *The Dandy* and *The Beano* represent the *rapprochement* of those trajectories. This highly visual mode of representation located a shift from the monomodality of story papers to a multimodal form which drew on cinematic storytelling and visualisation techniques, and which set a pattern for children's entertainment which continues today. Text became one part of an integrated multimodal narrative.

The combined effects of competition from other cultural activities, and the appearance of new visually orientated modes of storytelling in print were difficult to overcome for the story paper producers. As the emergent concept of the child as consumer became more dominant in the 1930s and 1940s, so more producers entered the field with products specifically designed for this market. Although the shaping and constructing function of the structured relationship between producers and consumers allowed the D. C. Thomson papers to continue for some years, continually reshaping themselves in response to changes in consumer taste, the genre itself had evolved, and the traditional format of predominantly text-based narrative had all but disappeared by the 1960s.

The story paper genre may have been relatively short-lived, but it performed an important role in the lives of generations of child readers. To dismiss story papers simply as 'terrible trash', or as damaging 'tools of social control', or to describe them as pure entertainment designed to give readers 'a feeling of cheerful security', is to underestimate their value to child consumers, their complexity as cultural artefacts and their place in the history of children's literature. Story paper value can be demonstrated at economic and cultural levels for both producers and consumers. For the producers, as I have shown, the economic impulse to profit was balanced by the cultural impulse to improve, but it is the value to the consumer that has tended to be overlooked by critics.

My revaluation of the genre is based on an examination of author/producer–text–reader interactions, and on restoring a voice to neglected and silenced child readers. Although the story paper narratives may not rate highly on any critical scale of literary value, my exploration has argued for an equal validity for alternative modes of valuation through the cultural and social aspects of readers' lived experience. Revaluing the genre in these terms repositions the story paper phenomenon, situating it at a pivotal point in the history of the development of children's literature, and according it new status as a primary element in the evolution of the concept of the child as consumer. By restoring the balance, in privileging the voices of children within the relations of power between producers and consumers, the critical space in which the genre can be discussed is reshaped.

Appendix: Boys' and Girls' Story Paper Reading

Table A.1 Most popular story papers read in one month by secondary school boys, 1937

Age 12+ (304)	Age 13+ (211)	Age 14+ (250)	Age 15+ (171)
Wizard: 150	*Wizard*: 87	*Hotspur*: 68	*Wizard*: 37
Hotspur: 145	*Hotspur*: 86	*Wizard*: 63	*Hotspur*: 20
Skipper: 114	*Skipper*: 57	*Rover*: 44	*Magnet*: 19
Adventure: 97	*Adventure*: 52	*Champion*: 37	*Modern Boy*: 14
Champion: 74	*Champion*: 50	*Adventure*: 33	*Boy's Own Paper*: 9
Modern Boy: 52	*Modern Boy*: 37	*Magnet*: 32	*Champion*: 8
Pilot: 43	*Magnet*: 37	*Modern Boy*: 21	*Rover*: 8
Magnet: 40	*Pilot*: 28	*Pilot*: 19	*Scout*: 6
Gem: 28	*Gem*: 18	*Boy's Own Paper*: 13	*Skipper*: 6
			Adventure: 5

Source: Jenkinson, 1940: 68–9.
Note: Numbers in brackets indicate the total numbers of boys in each group.

Table A.2 Most popular story papers read in one month by senior school boys, 1937

Age 12+ (279)	Age 13+ (287)	Age 14+ (68)
Wizard: 173	*Wizard*: 173	*Wizard*: 41
Hotspur: 139	*Hotspur*: 149	*Hotspur*: 36
Rover: 138	*Rover*: 140	*Rover*: 35
Skipper: 132	*Skipper*: 130	*Skipper*: 29
Adventure: 124	*Adventure*: 112	*Adventure*: 22
Champion: 60	*Pilot*: 66	*Magnet*: 14
Pilot: 52	*Champion*: 53	*Champion*: 13
Magnet: 32	*Magnet*: 47	*Pilot*: 12
Chips: 29	*Mickey Mouse Weekly*: 28	*Chips*: 7
Larks: 29	*Chips*: 25	*Funny Wonder*: 6
Butterfly: 28	*Larks*: 25	*Butterfly*: 5

Source: Jenkinson, 1940: 70.

Table A.3 Number of story papers read in a month by boys

Age	Secondary school boys	Senior school boys
12+	3.7	4.2
13+	3.0	4.0
14+	2.0	4.0
15+	0.8	(no boys of this age in school)

Source: Jenkinson, 1940: 64.

Table A.4 Boys' reading preferences by genre

	School stories %	Detective %	Home life %	Adventure %	Love %	Historical %	Collections %	Technical %
Secondary schools								
12+	14.0	7.8	11.5	42.8	0	0	8.1	0
13+	10.0	15.4	14.9	41.8	0	0	0	0
14+	6.7	17.6	8.3	39.9	0	6.1	0	6.7
15+	5.3	18.2	–	36.2	6.8	9.6	0	9.8
Senior schools								
12+	12.2	5.2	7.5	53.3	0	6.6	7.1	0
13+	12.4	6.7	7.3	54.6	0	5.4	5.1	0
14+	11.5	7.8	11.5	51.6	0	0	7.2	0

Source: Jenkinson, 1940: 16.

Table A.5 Most popular 'adult authors' at succeeding ages in boys' secondary schools

12+	13+	14+	15+
Lewis Carroll	John Buchan	R. D. Blackmore	R. D. Blackmore
Daniel Defoe	Daniel Defoe	John Buchan	John Buchan
Charles Dickens	Charles Dickens	Warwick Deeping	G. K. Chesterton
Arthur Conan Doyle	Alexandre Dumas	Daniel Defoe	Joseph Conrad
Zane Grey	Zane Grey	Charles Dickens	Charles Dickens
Thomas Hughes	L. Rider Haggard	Arthur Conan Doyle	Arthur Conan Doyle
Charles Kingsley	Thomas Hughes	Alexandre Dumas	L. Rider Haggard
Rudyard Kipling	Charles Kingsley	Walter Scott	Rudyard Kipling
Walter Scott	Rudyard Kipling	R. L. Stevenson	Jack London
Anna Sewell	Jack London	H. G. Wells	Baroness Orczy
R. L. Stevenson	Baroness Orczy	P. G. Wodehouse	Walter Scott
Mark Twain	Walter Scott		R. L. Stevenson
H. G. Wells	Anna Sewell		H. G. Wells
	Mary Shelley		P. G. Wodehouse

(*continued*)

Table A.5 Continued

12+	13+	14+	15+
	R. L. Stevenson Lawrence of Arabia (Thomas) H. G. Wells P. G. Wodehouse		

Source: Jenkinson, 1940: 50.

Note: The standard of popularity is judged at 12+ as authors named 5 times by the group; at 13+ authors named 4 times; at 14+ authors named 4 times; and at 15+ authors named 3 times.

Table A.6 Most popular 'adult authors' at succeeding ages in boys' senior schools

12+	13+	14+	15+
John Buchan	(Arabian Nights)	(Arabian Nights)	(No boys of this age in school)
Daniel Defoe	Daniel Defoe	R. D. Blackmore	
Charles Dickens	Charles Dickens	John Buchan	
L. Rider Haggard	Thomas Hughes	Lewis Carroll	
Thomas Hughes	Charles Kingsley	Daniel Defoe	
Charles Kingsley	R. L. Stevenson	Charles Dickens	
R. L. Stevenson	Jonathan Swift	Arthur Conan Doyle	
	Mark Twain	Thomas Hughes	
		R. L. Stevenson	
		Jonathan Swift	

Source: Jenkinson, 1940: 52.

Table A.7 Most popular story papers read in one month by secondary school girls, 1937

Age 12+ (171)	Age 13+ (207)	Age 14+ (188)	Age 15+ (153)
Schoolgirls' Own: 58	*Schoolgirls' Own*: 75	*Schoolgirls' Own*: 40	*Schoolgirls' Own*: 16
Schoolgirls' Weekly: 42	*Schoolgirls' Weekly*: 69	*Schoolgirls' Weekly*: 39	*Schoolgirls' Weekly*: 15
Crystal: 39	*Crystal*: 57	*Crystal*: 26	*Schoolgirls' Own Library*: 9
Schoolgirl: 28	*Hotspur*: 28	*Girl's Own Paper*: 24	*Girl's Own Paper*: 8
Girl's Own Paper: 23	*Rover*: 21	*Schoolgirl*: 22	
	Schoolgirl: 17		

(*continued*)

Table A.7 Continued

Age 12+ (171)	Age 13+ (207)	Age 14+ (188)	Age 15+ (153)
Schoolgirls' Library: 20	Schoolgirls' Library: 15	Schoolgirls' Library: 13	Magnet: 6
Wizard: 18	Wizard: 15	Guide: 11	Crystal: 5
Hotspur: 12	Girl's Own Paper: 14	Hotspur: 11	Guide: 5
Magnet: 11	Adventure: 10	Wizard: 10	Hotspur: 5
Schoolgirls' Own Library: 9	Skipper: 9	Adventure: 9	
Adventure: 9	Mickey Mouse Weekly: 6	Magnet: 9	
Rover: 9		Skipper: 9	

Source: Jenkinson, 1940: 214.
Note: Numbers in brackets indicate the total numbers of girls in each group.

Table A.8 Most popular story papers read in one month by senior school girls, 1937

Age 12+ (260)	Age 13+ (298)	Age 14+ (53)
Schoolgirls' Own: 84	Schoolgirls' Own: 113	Schoolgirls' Own: 25
Crystal: 53	Schoolgirls' Weekly: 74	Schoolgirls' Weekly: 14
Schoolgirls' Weekly: 41	Crystal: 67	Crystal: 14
Wizard: 38	Wizard: 60	Miracle: 14
Red Letter: 33	Miracle: 50	Oracle: 13
Miracle: 30	Rover: 43	Wizard: 13
Oracle: 29	Oracle: 41	Red Letter: 12
Red Star Weekly: 26	Skipper: 41	Rover: 11
Hotspur: 21	Red Letter: 39	Secrets: 10
Skipper: 18	Adventure: 32	Adventure: 9
Betty's Paper: 18	Hotspur: 31	Hotspur: 9
Rover: 16	Mickey Mouse Weekly: 31	Skipper: 9
Secrets: 16	Red Star Weekly: 25	Flame: 6
Chips: 16	Betty's Paper: 15	Film Fun: 4
Flame: 15	Family Star: 15	Mickey Mouse Weekly: 4
Comic Cuts: 15	Secrets: 15	Funny Wonder: 6
Mickey Mouse Weekly: 14	Butterfly: 15	Red Star Weekly: 3
Larks: 13	Funny Wonder: 15	Comic Cuts: 3
	Larks: 15	

Source: Jenkinson, 1940: 215.

Table A.9 Number of story papers read in a month by girls

Age	Secondary school girls	Senior school girls
12+	2.0	2.7
13+	2.0	3.3
14+	1.3	4.2
15+	0.6	(no girls of this age in school)

Source: Jenkinson, 1940: 211.

Table A.10 Girls' reading preferences by genre

	School stories %	Detective %	Home life %	Adventure %	Love %	Historical %	Collections %	Humour %
Secondary schools								
12+	22.3	0	33.5	17.6	7.9	6.1	5.6	0
13+	16.6	10.0	23.0	22.3	12.6	0	5.0	0
14+	12.4	10.0	18.0	24.7	16.9	8.7	0	0
15+	0	11.8	15.5	22.5	19.6	13.3	0	6.3
Senior schools								
12+	24.9	0	30.0	21.8	5.8	0	11.6	0
13+	26.3	0	26.8	20.2	7.6	5.7	9.4	0
14+	23.2	0	25.5	16.2	11.4	9.6	9.2	0

Source: Jenkinson, 1940: 174.

Table A.11 Most popular 'adult authors' at succeeding ages in girls' secondary schools

12+	13+	14+	15+
J. M. Barrie	(Arabian Nights)	Jane Austen	Jane Austen
R. D. Blackmore	J. M. Barrie	R. D. Blackmore	J. M. Barrie
Charlotte Brontë	R. D. Blackmore	Charlotte Brontë	R. D. Blackmore
Lewis Carroll	Charlotte Brontë	John Buchan	John Buchan
Miguel de Cervantes	Emily Brontë	G. K. Chesterton	Charlotte Brontë
G. K. Chesterton	John Buchan	Warwick Deeping	John Buchan
Daniel Defoe	G. K. Chesterton	E. M. Dell	G. K. Chesterton
Charles Dickens	Charles Dickens	Charles Dickens	Joseph Conrad
Alexandre Dumas	Arthur Conan Doyle	Arthur Conan Doyle	Warwick Deeping
Kenneth Grahame	Kenneth Grahame	Alexandre Dumas	Charles Dickens
L. Rider Haggard	Zane Grey	John Galsworthy	Arthur Conan Doyle
Thomas Hughes	L. Rider Haggard	Kenneth Grahame	Alexandre Dumas
Washington Irving	Thomas Hughes	Zane Grey	John Galsworthy
Rudyard Kipling		L. Rider Haggard	Oliver Goldsmith

(continued)

Table A.11 Continued

12+	13+	14+	15+
Baroness Orczy	Charles Kingsley	Charles Kingsley	Kenneth Grahame
G. S. Porter	Baroness Orczy	Rudyard Kipling	Zane Grey
Walter Scott	G. S. Porter	E. Bulwer-Lytton	L. Rider Haggard
Anna Sewell	Anna Sewell	B. Nicholls	Thomas Hardy
R. L. Stevenson	R. L. Stevenson	Baroness Orczy	Rudyard Kipling
Harriet Beecher Stowe	H. G. Wells	G. S. Porter	S. Leacock
Mark Twain	P. G. Wodehouse	Walter Scott	C. Mackenzie
		R. L. Stevenson	W. Somerset Maugham
		W. M. Thackeray	Baroness Orczy
		Mark Twain	G. S. Porter
		H. G. Wells	J. B. Priestley
		P. G. Wodehouse	D. L. Sayers
			Walter Scott
			W. M. Thackeray
			Lowell Thomas
			Mark Twain
			Hugh Walpole
			H. G. Wells
			P. G. Wodehouse
			Ellen Wood

Source: Jenkinson, 1940: 201.
Note: The standard of popularity is judged at 12+ as authors named 5 times by the group; at 13+ authors named 4 times; at 14+ authors named 4 times; and at 15+ authors named 3 times.

Table A.12 Most popular 'adult authors' at succeeding ages in girls' senior schools

12+	13+	14+	15+
John Buchan	(Arabian Nights)	(Arabian Nights)	(No girls of this age in school)
Lewis Carroll	R. D. Blackmore	Charlotte Brontë	
Charles Dickens	Charlotte Brontë	Charles Dickens	
Kenneth Grahame	Lewis Carroll	Baroness Orczy	
Thomas Hughes	Daniel Defoe	R. L. Stevenson	
Charles Kingsley	Charles Dickens	Harriet Beecher Stowe	
Baroness Orczy	Thomas Hughes		
R. L. Stevenson	Charles Kingsley		
Jonathan Swift	Walter Scott		
	Anna Sewell		
	R. L. Stevenson		
	Harriet Beecher Stowe		
	Jonathan Swift		

Source: Jenkinson, 1940: 204.

Bibliography

Primary sources

The Magnet, selected issues 1920–39

'Billy Bunter: Film Star!', *The Magnet*, 18 March 1922, pp. 2–28.
'Billy Bunter's Wembley Party', *The Magnet*, 11 October 1924, pp. 2–28.
'The Boy with an Enemy', *The Magnet*, 5 December 1936, pp. 2–28.
'Bunter's Body Guard', *The Magnet*, 8 September 1928, pp. 2–28.
'Bunter the Crook!', *The Magnet*, 10 June 1922, pp. 2–28.
'Bunter the Ventriloquist!', *The Magnet*, 12 May 1934, pp. 2–28.
'The Complete Outsider', *The Magnet*, 5 March 1932, pp. 2–28.
'Contraband!', *The Magnet*, 28 November 1936, pp. 2–28.
'The Cruise of the Firefly', *The Magnet*, 26 December 1936, pp. 2–28.
'Douglas Fairbanks Competition', *The Magnet*, 31 January 1921, p. 8.
'Editor's Chat', *The Magnet*, 7 February 1920, p. 2.
'The Magnet Talkies', *The Magnet*, 1 March 1930, p. 14.
Vignette no. 42: Arthur Woodhead Carne, *The Magnet*, 7 February 1920, p. 9.
'The Way of the Transgressor!', *The Magnet*, 12 December 1936, pp. 2–28.
'What do "Talkies" Cost?', *The Magnet*, 5 April 1930, p. 2.
'The Worst Master in the School', *The Magnet*, 2 June 1934, pp. 2–28.

The Hotspur, selected issues 1933–39

'3rd Form Brains v. 5th Form Beef', *The Hotspur*, 11 April 1936, pp. 36–8 and 42.
'6 Yellow Knife Men', *The Hotspur*, 30 December 1933, pp. 429–32.
'The Big Stiff', *The Hotspur*, 9 September 1933, pp. 31–3.
'Bill Hawkins and his 60 Dunces', *The Hotspur*, 6 August 1938, pp. 15–17.
'Black John of the Battles', *The Hotspur*, 27 February 1937, pp. 237–40.
'Black Wolf', *The Hotspur*, 18 November 1933, pp. 311–14.
'The Champ from the Swot Brigade', *The Hotspur*, 13 January 1934, pp. 31–2.
'Dead-Wide Dick's Book of Doom', *The Hotspur*, 8 February 1936, pp. 143–6.
'Death in his Guns and Dynamite in his Boots!', *The Hotspur*, 27 August 1938, pp. 18–26.
'Doom from the Desert', 10 February 1934, pp. 154–8.
'Is it Goodbye to Red Circle?', *The Hotspur*, 18 January 1936, pp. 71–6.
'The Kids of Caravan College', *The Hotspur*, 23 December 1933, pp. 473–6.
'The Last School', *The Hotspur*, 23 January 1937, pp. 87–9.
'The Master in the Purple Mask', *The Hotspur*, 10 February 1934, pp. 150–3.
'Red Circle in Wartime', *The Hotspur*, 21 October 1939, pp. 78–81 and 88.
'The School Amid the Snows', *The Hotspur*, 9 December 1933, pp. 395–8, and 6 January 1934, pp. 19–22.
'The Son of Scarface', *The Hotspur*, 9 September 1933, pp. 34–7.
'The Swooping Vengeance', *The Hotspur*, 25 April 1936, pp. 78–81.
'The Teacher from Dartmoor', *The Hotspur*, 9 December 1933, pp. 399–401.

'Tiger Jake's Academy', *The Hotspur*, 10 February 1934, pp. 143–6.
'The Ting-a-Ling Teacher of Tarza', *The Hotspur*, 24 March 1934, pp. 317–21.
'Too Tired to Work – Too Lazy to Play!', *The Hotspur*, 25 April 1936, pp. 87–90.
'When the Fifth Form Went Crazy', *The Hotspur*, 4 April 1936, pp. 8–10.
'Wild Bill Hickok's Schooldays', *The Hotspur*, 18 February 1939, pp. 2–7.
'The World's Toughest Teacher', *The Hotspur*, 20 January 1934, pp. 59–62.

Other primary sources

Bernstein, Sidney (1936) 'Attempts Made by the Film Trade to Meet the Problems and the Difficulties Encountered', in *Report on the Conference on Films for Children, November 20th and 21st, 1936*, ed. British Film Institute (London: BFI).
BFI (ed.) (1936) *Report on the Conference on Films for Children, November 20th and 21st, 1936* (London: BFI).
Birkenhead Vigilance Committee (1931) *The Cinema and the Child: A Report of Investigations, June–October 1931* (Birkenhead Vigilance Committee).
Birmingham Cinema Enquiry Committee (1931) *Report of Investigations, April 1930–May 1931* (Birmingham City Council).
London County Council Education Committee (1932) *School Children and the Cinema* (London: LCC).
Mackie, John (ed.) (1933) *Being an Investigation Conducted into the Influence of the Film on School Children and Adolescents in the City* (Edinburgh Cinema Enquiry).
Mass-Observation Archive, TC Reading Habits 1937–47, 20/1/B: 'Why I read books'.
Nyman, Kenneth (1936) 'What Might Be Done', in *Report on the Conference on Films for Children, November 20th and 21st, 1936*, ed. British Film Institute (London: BFI).
Sheffield Juvenile Organisations Committee (1932) *A Survey of Children's Cinema Matinées in Sheffield* (Sheffield Juvenile Organisations Committee).

Secondary sources

Aldcroft, Derek (1983) *The British Economy Between the Wars* (Oxford: Philip Allan Publishers).
Aldgate, Anthony, and Richards, Jeffrey (1999) *Best of British: Cinema and Society from 1930 to the Present* (London: I. B. Tauris, first published 1983).
Althusser, Louis (1971) *Lenin and Philosophy and Other Essays*, trans. Ben Brewster (London: NLB).
Arizpe, Evelyn, and Styles, Morag (2003) *Children Reading Pictures: Interpreting Visual Texts* (London: Routledge).
Arnold, Matthew (1960) *Culture and Anarchy*, ed. J. Dover Wilson (Cambridge University Press, first published 1869).
Ashley, Bob (ed.) (1997) *Reading Popular Narrative: A Source Book* (London and Washington: Leicester University Press).
Auchmuty, R. (1992) *A World of Girls* (London: The Women's Press).
Avery, G. (1975) *Childhood's Pattern: A Study of the Heroes and Heroines of Children's Fiction 1770–1950* (London: Hodder and Stoughton).
Baden-Powell, Robert (2004) *Scouting for Boys*, ed. Elleke Boehmer (Oxford University Press, first published 1908).
Barker, Martin (1989) *Comics: Ideology, Power and the Critics* (Manchester University Press).

Barnes, James (n.d.) 'Depression and Innovation in the British and American Booktrade, 1819–1939', in Robin Myers and Michael Harris (eds) *Economics of the British Booktrade 1605–1939* (Cambridge: Chadwyck-Healey).
Barthes, Roland (1966) *Introduction to the Structural Analysis of Narrative* (University of Birmingham Centre for Cultural Studies).
Barthes, Roland (1973) *Mythologies*, trans. Annette Lavers (St Albans: Paladin).
Barthes, Roland (1977) *Image, Music, Text*, trans. Stephen Heath (London: Fontana).
Baudrillard, J. (1988) *Selected Writings*, ed. Mark Poster (Stanford University Press).
Beaven, B. (2005) *Leisure, Citizenship and Working Class Men in Britain* (Manchester University Press).
Beer, Patricia (1968) *Mrs Beer's House* (London: Macmillan).
Benjamin, Walter (1970) *Illuminations*, trans. Harry Zohn (London: Cape).
Bennett, Tony (ed.) (1990) *Popular Fiction: Technology, Ideology, Production, Reading* (London: Routledge).
Benton, M., Teasey, J., Bell, R., and Hurst, K. (1988) *Young Readers Responding to Poems* (London: Routledge).
Best, Stephen (1994) 'The Commodification of Reality and the Reality of Commodification: Baudrillard, Debord and Postmodern Theory', in Douglas Kellner (ed.) *Baudrillard: A Critical Reader* (Oxford: Blackwell).
Bettelheim, Bruno (1989) *The Uses of Enchantment: The Meaning and Importance of Fairy Tales* (New York: Vintage).
Bingham, Adrian (2004) *Gender, Modernity and the Popular Press in Inter-war Britain* (Oxford University Press).
Bloom, Clive (ed.) (1993) *Literature and Culture in Modern Britain, Vol 1: 1900–1925* (Harlow: Longman).
Booth, Wayne C. (1991) *The Rhetoric of Fiction* (London: Penguin, first published 1961).
Bourdieu, Pierre (1977) *Outline of a Theory of Practice*, trans. Richard Nice (Cambridge University Press).
Bourdieu, Pierre (1986) *Distinction: A Social Critique of the Judgement of Taste*, trans. Richard Nice (London: Routledge).
Bourdieu, Pierre (1993) *The Field of Cultural Production: Essays on Art and Literature*, ed. Randal Johnson (Oxford: Polity Press/Columbia University Press).
Bourdieu, Pierre (1995) *The Rules of Art*, trans. Susan Emmanuel (Stanford University Press).
Boyd, Kelly (2003) *Manliness and the Boys' Story Paper in Britain: A Cultural History, 1855–1940* (Basingstoke: Palgrave Macmillan).
Bradford, Clare (2001) 'The End of the Empire? Colonial and Postcolonial Journeys in Children's Books', *Children's Literature*, 29: 196–220.
Brannigan, John (1998) *New Historicism and Cultural Materialism* (London: Macmillan).
Bratton, J. S. (1986) 'Of England, Home and Duty: The Image of England in Victorian and Edwardian Juvenile Fiction', in John Mackenzie (ed.) *Imperialism and Popular Culture* (Manchester University Press).
Breakwell, I., and Hammond, P. (eds) (1990) *Seeing in the Dark: A Compendium of Cinemagoing* (London: Serpent's Tail).
Bristow, Joseph (1991) *Empire's Boys: Adventures in a Man's World* (London: HarperCollins).
Bryman, Alan (2002) *Biographical Research* (Buckingham: Open University Press).

Buckingham, David (1993) *Cultural Studies Goes to School: Reading and Teaching Popular Media* (London: Falmer Press).
Burnett, John (ed.) (1984) *Destiny Obscure: Autobiographies of Childhood, Education and Family from the 1820s to the 1920s* (London: Routledge).
Butts, D. (ed.) (1992) *Stories and Society: Children's Literature in its Social Context* (Basingstoke: Macmillan).
Cadogan, Mary (1988) *The Chap Behind the Chums* (London: Viking).
Cadogan, M., and Craig, P. (1976) *You're A Brick, Angela! A New Look at Girls' Fiction from 1839–1975* (London: Victor Gollancz).
Cadogan, M., and Craig, P. (1978) *Women and Children First* (London: Victor Gollancz).
Campbell, Joseph (1968) *The Hero with a Thousand Faces* (Princeton University Press).
Cannadine, D. (2001) *Ornamentalism: How the British Saw their Empire* (Oxford University Press).
Cannadine, D., Keating, J., and Sheldon, N. (2011) *The Right Kind of History: Teaching the Past in Twentieth-Century England* (Basingstoke: Palgrave Macmillan).
Carlyle, Thomas (1898) *On Heroes, Hero-Worship and the Heroic in History* (London: Chapman and Hall).
Carpenter, H., and Prichard, M. (1984) *The Oxford Companion to Children's Literature* (Oxford University Press).
Carpenter, Kevin (1983) *Penny Dreadfuls and Comics: English Periodicals for Children from Victorian Times to the Present Day* (London: Victoria and Albert Museum).
Castle, Kathryn (1996) *Britannia's Children: Reading Colonialism through Children's Books and Magazines* (Manchester University Press).
Chambers, A. (1977) 'The Reader in the Book', *Signal*, 23: 64–87.
Chambers, A. (1985) *Booktalk: Occasional Writing on Literature and Children* (London: Bodley Head).
Chatman, Seymour (1978) *Story and Discourse* (Ithaca, NY: Cornell University Press).
Clare, Hilary (2000) 'Lifting the Veil: Researching the Lives of Girls' School Story Writers', *Children's Literature in Education*, 31(3): 159–66.
Clark, Beverly Lyon (1996) *Regendering the School Story* (New York: Routledge).
Cohen, Steven, and Shires, Linda M. (1988) *Telling Tales: A Theoretical Analysis of Narrative Fiction* (London: Routledge).
Constantine, Stephen (1986) 'Bringing the Empire Alive: The Empire Marketing Board and Imperial Propaganda', in John Mackenzie (ed.) *Imperialism and Popular Culture* (Manchester University Press).
Crouch, Marcus (1962) *Treasure Seekers and Borrowers: Children's Books in Britain 1900–1960* (London: The Library Association).
Culler, Jonathan (1981) *The Pursuit of Signs: Semiotics, Literature and Deconstruction* (London: Routledge and Kegan Paul).
Darton, F. J. H. (1982) *Children's Books in England: Five Centuries of Social Life*, 3rd edn, revised by B. Alderson (Cambridge University Press, first published 1932).
Dewey, Peter (1997) *War and Progress: Britain 1914–1945* (Harlow: Longman).
Dixon, Diana (1986) 'From Instruction to Amusement: Attitudes of Authority in Children's Periodicals Before 1914', *Victorian Periodicals Review*, 19(2): 63–7.
Dollimore, J., and Sinfield, A. (1994) *Political Shakespeare: Essays in Cultural Materialism*, 2nd edn (Manchester University Press).

Drotner, Kirsten (1983) 'Schoolgirls, Madcaps, and Air Aces: English Girls and Their Magazine Reading between the Wars', *Feminist Studies*, 9(1): 33–52.
Drotner, Kirsten (1988) *English Children and their Magazines* (New Haven: Yale University Press).
Dunae, Patrick A. (1979) 'Penny Dreadfuls: Late Nineteenth-Century Boys' Literature and Crime', *Victorian Studies*, 22: 133–50.
Dusinberre, J. (1987) *Alice to the Lighthouse* (New York: St Martin's Press).
Eagleton, Terry (1976) *Marxism and Literary Criticism* (London: Methuen).
Eaton, Mick, and Neale, Steve (eds) (1981) *Screen Reader 2: Cinema and Semiotics* (London: The Society for Education in Film and Television, articles reprinted from *Screen*, 1971–73).
Eldridge, John, and Eldridge, Lizzie (1994) *Raymond Williams: Making Connections* (London: Routledge).
Eyre, Frank (1971) *British Children's Books in the Twentieth Century* (London: Longman).
Feather, John (1988) *A History of Publishing* (London: Croom Helm).
Ferrall, Charles, and Jackson, Anna (2010) *'Juvenile' Literature and British Society, 1850–1950: The Age of Adolescence* (Abingdon: Routledge).
Fish, Stanley (1980) *Is There a Text in This Class? The Authority of Interpretive Communities* (Cambridge, MA: Harvard University Press).
Foucault, Michel (1972) *The Archaeology of Knowledge*, trans. A. M. Sheridan Smith (London: Tavistock).
Foucault, Michel (2001) *Power*, trans. Robert Hurley (London: Allen Lane).
Fowler, D. (1996) *The First Teenagers: The Lifestyle of Young Wage-earners in Interwar Britain* (London: Routledge).
Fowler, D. (2008) *Youth Culture in Modern Britain c.1920–1970: A New History* (Basingstoke: Palgrave Macmillan).
Galbraith, Gretchen (1997) *Reading Lives – Reconstructing Childhood, Books and Schools in Britain 1870–1920* (London: Macmillan).
Gallagher, C., and Greenblatt, S. (2000) *Practicing New Historicism* (University of Chicago Press).
Genette, Gérard (1997) *Paratexts: Thresholds of Interpretation*, trans. Jane E. Lewin (Cambridge University Press).
Graves, R., and Hodge, A. (1995) *The Long Weekend: A Social History of Great Britain 1918–1939* (London: Abacus, first published 1940).
Green, M. (1980) *Dreams of Adventure, Deeds of Empire* (London: Routledge and Kegan Paul).
Greenblatt, S. (1989) 'Towards a Poetics of Culture', in H. Aram Veeser (ed.) *The New Historicism* (New York: Routledge).
Grenfell, M., and James, D., with Hodkinson, P., Reay, D., and Robbins, D. (1998) *Bourdieu and Education: Acts of Practical Theory* (London: Falmer Press).
Gunter, Barrie, and Furnham, Adrian (1998) *Children as Consumers: A Psychological Analysis of the Young People's Market* (London: Routledge).
Haas Dyson, Anne (1997) *Writing Superheroes: Contemporary Childhood, Classroom Literacy and Popular Culture* (New York: Teachers' College Press).
Halverson, Cathryn (1999) 'Reading Little Girls' Texts in the 1920s: Searching for the "Spirit of Childhood"', *Children's Literature in Education*, 30(4): 235–48.
Hannabuss, Stuart (1977) 'What We Used to Read: A Survey of Children's Reading in Britain, 1910–1950', *Children's Literature in Education*, 8(3): 127–34.

Hawthorn, Jeremy (1996) *Cunning Passages: New Historicism, Cultural Materialism and Marxism in the Contemporary Debate* (London: Arnold).
Heward, Christine (1988) *Making a Man of Him: Parents and their Sons' Education at an English Public School, 1929–50* (London: Routledge).
Hildick, W. (1970) *Children and Fiction* (London: Evans).
Hilton, Mary, Styles, M., and Watson, V. (eds) (1997) *Opening the Nursery Door: Reading, Writing and Childhood, 1610–1900* (London: Routledge).
Hobsbawm, Eric (1983) 'Introduction: Inventing Traditions', in Eric Hobsbawm and Terence Ranger (eds) *The Invention of Tradition* (Cambridge University Press).
Hobsbawm, Eric, and Ranger, Terence (eds) (1983) *The Invention of Tradition* (Cambridge University Press).
Hoggart, Richard (1957) *The Uses of Literacy* (London: Penguin).
Hollindale, Peter (1988) *Ideology and the Children's Book* (Stroud: Thimble Press).
Holub, Robert C. (1984) *Reception Theory: A Critical Introduction* (London: Methuen).
Hourihan, Margery (1997) *Deconstructing the Hero: Literary Theory and Children's Literature* (London: Routledge).
House of Commons Research Library (1999) Research Paper 99/20, *Inflation: The Value of the Pound 1750–1998* (London: House of Commons).
Hughes, Thomas (1997) *Tom Brown's Schooldays* (London: Penguin, first published 1857).
Humphries, Stephen (1981) *Hooligans or Rebels? An Oral History of Working Class Childhood and Youth* (Oxford: Blackwell).
Hunt, Peter (1991) *Criticism, Theory and Children's Literature* (Oxford: Blackwell).
Hunt, Peter (1994) *An Introduction to Children's Literature* (Oxford University Press).
Hunt, Peter (ed.) (1999) *Understanding Children's Literature* (London: Routledge).
Hyam, Ronald (2006) *Britain's Declining Empire: The Road to Decolonisation, 1918–1968* (Cambridge University Press).
Hyam, Ronald (2010) *Understanding the British Empire* (Cambridge University Press).
Iser, Wolfgang (2000) 'The Reading Process: A Phenomenological Approach', in David Lodge and Nigel Wood (eds) *Modern Criticism and Theory: A Reader*, 2nd edn (Harlow: Pearson).
Jenkinson, A. J. (1940) *What Do Boys and Girls Read?* (London: Methuen).
Johnson, Paul (2005) *The Vanished Landscape: A 1930s Childhood in the Potteries* (London: Orion Books).
Johnson, Randal (1993) 'Introduction', in Pierre Bourdieu, *The Field of Cultural Production* (Oxford: Polity Press/Columbia University Press).
Johnston, I., Bainbridge, J., and Shariff, F. (2007) 'Exploring Issues of National Identity: Ideology and Adversity in Contemporary Canadian Picture Books', *Papers: Explorations into Children's Literature*, 17(2): 75–83.
Jones, Dudley, and Watkins, Tony (eds) (2000) *A Necessary Fantasy? The Heroic Figure in Children's Popular Culture* (New York: Garland).
Kellner, Douglas (ed.) (1994) *Baudrillard: A Critical Reader* (Oxford: Blackwell).
Kingsford, R. J. L. (1970) *The Publishers' Association 1896–1946* (Cambridge University Press).
Kline, Stephen (1993) *Out of the Garden: Toys, TV and Children's Culture in the Age of Marketing* (London: Verso).
Knowles, Murray, and Malmkjaer, Kirsten (1996) *Language and Control in Children's Literature* (London: Routledge).

Kress, Gunter, and Van Leeuwen, Theo (2001) *Multimodal Discourse: The Modes and Media of Contemporary Discourse* (London: Hodder Arnold).
Krips, Valerie (1997) 'Imaginary Childhoods: Memory and Children's Literature', *Critical Quarterly*, 39(3): 42–50.
Kuhn, Annette (2002) *An Everyday Magic: Cinema and Cultural Memory* (London: I. B. Tauris).
Kutzer, M. Daphne (2000) *Empire's Children: Empire and Imperialism in Classic British Children's Books* (New York: Garland).
Leavis, F. R. (1973) *The Great Tradition* (London: Chatto and Windus).
Leavis, F. R. (1979) *Education and the University* (Cambridge University Press).
Leavis, F. R., and Thompson, D. (1964) *Culture and Environment* (London: Chatto & Windus, first published 1933).
Leavis, Q. D. (1990) *Fiction and the Reading Public* (London: Bellew Publishers, first published 1932).
Leeson, Robert (1985) *Reading and Righting* (London: Collins).
Leitch, Vincent B. (1992) *Cultural Criticism, Literary Theory, Poststructuralism* (New York: Columbia University Press).
Lesnik-Oberstein, K. (1994) *Children's Literature: Criticism and the Fictional Child* (Oxford: Clarendon Press).
Lodge, David, and Wood, Nigel (eds) (2000) *Modern Criticism and Theory: A Reader*, 2nd edn (Harlow: Pearson).
Mack, E. C. (1941) *Public Schools and British Opinion Since 1860* (New York: Columbia University Press).
Mackenzie, John (1986a) *Propaganda and Empire* (Manchester University Press).
Mackenzie, John (ed.) (1986b) *Imperialism and Popular Culture* (Manchester University Press).
Mackenzie, John (1986c) 'Introduction', in John Mackenzie (ed.) *Imperialism and Popular Culture* (Manchester University Press).
Magee, Brian (2003) *Clouds of Glory: A Hoxton Childhood* (London: Jonathan Cape).
Mahurter, Sarah (1999) 'Best Loved Books of the 1920s and 1930s', in Pat Pinsent (ed.) *NCRCL Papers 5: Pop Fiction* (London: Roehampton Institute).
Mangan, J. A. (1986) 'The Grit of our Forefathers: Invented Traditions, Propaganda and Imperialism', in John Mackenzie (ed.) *Imperialism and Popular Culture* (Manchester University Press).
Mangan, J. A., and Walvin, James (eds) (1987) *Manliness and Morality: Middle Class Masculinity in Britain and America 1800–1940* (Manchester University Press).
Marchant, James (ed.) (1925) *The Cinema in Education* (London: Allen and Unwin).
Marsden, William (2000) '"Poisoned History": A Comparative Study of Nationalism, Propaganda and the Treatment of War and Peace in the Late Nineteenth- and Early Twentieth-Century School Curriculum', *History of Education*, 29(1): 29–47.
Masterman, Len (1985) *Teaching the Media* (London: Comedia/Routledge).
Mayer, J. P. (1948) *British Cinemas and their Audiences: Sociological Studies* (London: Dennis Dobson).
Mayer, J. P. (1972) *Sociology of Film* (New York: Arno Press and the New York Times, first published 1946).

McAleer, Joseph (1992) *Popular Reading and Publishing in Britain 1914–1950* (Oxford: Clarendon Press).
McCallum, Robin (1999) *Ideologies of Identity in Adolescent Fiction: The Dialogic Construction of Subjectivity* (New York: Palgrave Macmillan).
McGillis, Roderick (1997) 'Self, Other and Other Self: Recognising the Other in Children's Literature', *The Lion and the Unicorn*, 21(2): 215–29.
McGillis, Roderick (ed.) (2000) *Children's Literature and the Postcolonial Context* (New York: Garland).
McKibbin, R. (1998) *Classes and Cultures: England 1918–1951* (Oxford University Press).
Metz, Christian (1974) *Film Language: A Semiotics of the Cinema*, trans. Michael Taylor (Oxford University Press).
Metz, Christian (1981) 'Current Problems of Film Theory: Christian Metz on Jean Mitry's L'Esthetique et Psychologie du Cinéma, Vol II', in Mick Eaton and Steve Neale (eds) *Screen Reader 2: Cinema and Semiotics* (London: The Society for Education in Film and Television, articles reprinted from *Screen*, 1971–73).
Millard, Elaine (2005) 'To Enter the Castle of Fear: Engendering Children's Story Writing from Home to School at KS2', *Gender and Education*, 17(1): 57–73.
Miller, Dean A. (2000) *The Epic Hero* (Baltimore: Johns Hopkins University Press).
Mitchell, Claudia, and Reid-Walsh, Jacqueline (2002) *Researching Children's Popular Culture: The Cultural Spaces of Childhood* (London: Routledge).
Mulhern, Francis (1981) *The Moment of Scrutiny* (London: Verso).
Mulhern, Francis (2000) *Culture/Metaculture* (London: Routledge).
Mulvey, Laura (1989) *Visual and Other Pleasures* (Basingstoke: Macmillan).
Musgrave, P. W. (1985) *From Brown to Bunter* (London: Routledge and Kegan Paul).
Myers, M. (1988) 'Missed Opportunities and Critical Malpractice: New Historicism and Children's Literature', *Children's Literature Association Quarterly*, 13(1): 41–3.
Myers, M. (1992) 'Sociologising Juvenile Ephemera: Periodical Contradictions, Popular Literacy, Transhistorical Readers', *Children's Literature Association Quarterly*, 17(1): 41–5.
Myers, Robin, and Harris, Michael (eds) (1985) *Economics of the British Booktrade 1605–1939* (Cambridge: Chadwyck-Healey).
Nel, Philip (2005) 'Is There a Text in This Marketing Campaign?: Literature, Marketing and Harry Potter', *The Lion and the Unicorn*, 29(2): 236–67.
Nelson, C. (1991) *Boys Will be Girls: The Feminine Ethic and British Children's Fiction 1857–1917* (New Brunswick: Rutgers University Press).
Nelson, C. (1997) 'Authoring and Authority in British Boys' Magazines', *The Lion and the Unicorn*, 21(1): 1–19.
Nodelman, Perry (1992) 'The Other: Orientalism, Colonialism and Children's Literature', *Children's Literature Association Quarterly*, 17: 29–35.
Norrington, A. L. P. (1983) *Blackwell's 1897–1979: The History of a Family Firm* (Oxford: Blackwell).
Orwell, G. (1962) 'Boys' Weeklies', in *Inside the Whale and Other Essays* (London: Penguin, first published 1940).
Pawling, Christopher (1984) *Popular Fiction and Social Change* (London: Macmillan).
Phillips, Jerry, and Wojcik-Andrews, Ian (1996) 'Telling Tales to Children: The Pedagogy of Empire in MGM's *Kim* and Disney's *Aladdin*', *The Lion and the Unicorn*, 20(1): 66–89.

Pinsent, Pat (ed.) (1999) *NCRCL Papers 5: Pop Fiction* (London: Roehampton Institute).
Pollen, Annebella (2013) 'Research Methodology in Mass Observation Past and Present: "Scientifically, about as valuable as a chimpanzee's tea party at the zoo"?', *History Workshop Journal*, 75(1): 213–35.
Porter, Bernard (2004) *The Absent-minded Imperialists* (Oxford University Press).
Protherough, Robert (1983) *Developing a Response to Fiction* (Buckingham: Open University Press).
Pugh, Martin (2009) *We Danced All Night: A Social History of Britain Between the Wars* (London: Vintage).
Purbrick, Louise (2007) *The Wedding Present: Domestic Life Beyond Consumption* (Aldershot: Ashgate).
Quigly, I. (1982) *The Heirs of Tom Brown: The English School Story* (London: Chatto and Windus).
Reynolds, Kimberley (1990) *Girls Only? Gender and Popular Children's Fiction in Britain, 1880–1910* (New York: Harvester Wheatsheaf).
Richards, Frank (1968) 'Frank Richards Replies to George Orwell', in Sonia Orwell and Ian Angus (eds) *The Collected Essays, Journalism and Letters of George Orwell, vol. I: An Age Like This 1920–1940* (London: Secker and Warburg) [available online at www.friardale.co.uk/Ephemera/Newspapers/George%20Orwell_Horizon_Reply.pdf].
Richards, Jeffrey (1984) *The Age of the Dream Palace: Cinema and Society in Britain, 1930–1939* (London: Routledge and Kegan Paul).
Richards, Jeffrey (1988) *Happiest Days: The Public Schools in English Fiction* (Manchester University Press).
Richards, Jeffrey (ed.) (1989) *Imperialism and Juvenile Literature* (Manchester University Press).
Richards, Jeffrey (1997) *Films and British National Identity: From Dickens to Dad's Army* (Manchester University Press).
Richards, Jeffrey, and Sheridan, Dorothy (eds) (1987) *Mass-Observation at the Movies* (London: Routledge and Kegan Paul).
Roberts, Robert (1973) *The Classic Slum: Salford Life in the First Quarter of the Century* (Harmondsworth: Penguin).
Roberts, Robert (1976) *A Ragged Schooling: Growing Up in the Classic Slum* (Manchester University Press).
Rose, J. (1984) *The Case of Peter Pan, or the Impossibility of Children's Fiction* (London: Macmillan).
Rose, Jonathan (2001) *The Intellectual Life of the British Working Classes* (New Haven and London: Yale University Press).
Ross Johnston, Rosemary (2011) 'Reader Response', in Matthew Grenby and Kimberley Reynolds (eds) *Children's Literature Studies: A Research Handbook* (Basingstoke: Palgrave Macmillan).
Ruwe, Donelle (ed.) (2005) *Culturing the Child: 1690–1914* (Lanham, MD: Scarecrow Press).
Ryan, Bill (1991) *Making Capital from Culture: The Corporate Form of Capitalist Cultural Production* (Berlin: De Gruyter).
Samways, George Richmond (1984) *The Road to Greyfriars* (London: Howard Baker Press).
Sarland, Charles (1991) *Young People Reading: Culture and Response* (Milton Keynes: Open University Press).

Sarup, Madan (1993) *An Introductory Guide to Poststructuralist Postmodernism*, 2nd edn (Hemel Hempstead: Harvester Wheatsheaf).
Scannell, Paddy, and Cardiff, David (1991) *A Social History of British Broadcasting*, vol. I: 1922–39 (Oxford: Blackwell).
Scannell, Vernon (1971) *The Tiger and the Rose: An Autobiography* (London: Hamish Hamilton).
Seiter, Ellen (1993) *Sold Separately: Children and Parents in Consumer Society* (New Brunswick: Rutgers University Press).
Sheridan, Dorothy (2000) Reviewing Mass-Observation: The Archive and its Researchers Thirty Years on [9 paragraphs]. *Forum Qualitative Sozialforschung/ Forum: Qualitative Social Research*, 1(3), Art. 26, http://nbn-resolving.de/urn:nbn:de:0114-fqs0003266.
Sheridan, D., Street, B., and Bloome, D. (2000) *Writing Ourselves: Mass Observation and Literacy Practices* (Cresskill, NJ: Hampton Press).
Silverman, Kaja (1983) *The Subject of Semiotics* (Oxford University Press).
Smith, Michelle J. (2011) *Empire in British Girls' Culture: Imperial Girls, 1880–1915* (Basingstoke: Palgrave Macmillan).
Smith, S. (2005) *Children, Cinema and Censorship: From Dracula to the Dead End Kids* (London: I. B. Tauris).
Springhall, John (1987) 'Building Character in the British Boy: The Attempt to Extend Christian Manliness to Working-class Adolescents, 1880–1914', in J. A. Mangan and James Walvin (eds) *Manliness and Morality: Middle Class Masculinity in Britain and America 1800–1940* (Manchester University Press).
Springhall, John (1998) *Youth, Popular Culture and Moral Panics: Penny Gaffs to Gangsta-Rap 1830–1996* (Basingstoke: Macmillan).
Stam, Robert (2000) *Film Theory: An Introduction* (Oxford: Blackwell).
Staples, Terry (1997) *All Pals Together: The Story of Children's Cinema* (Edinburgh University Press).
Stephens, J. (1992) *Language and Ideology in Children's Fiction* (Harlow: Longman).
Stephens, J. (ed.) (2002) *Ways of Being Male* (New York: Routledge).
Storey, John (1993) *An Introductory Guide to Cultural Theory and Popular Culture* (Hemel Hempstead: Harvester Wheatsheaf).
Strinati, Dominic (1995) *An Introduction to Theories of Popular Culture* (London: Routledge).
Styles, Morag, and Arizpe, Evelyn (2001) 'A Gorilla with "Grandpa's Eyes": How Children Interpret Visual Texts – A Case Study of Anthony Browne's "Zoo"', *Children's Literature in Education*, 32(4): 261–81.
Styles, Morag, Bearne, Eve, and Watson, Victor (eds) (1994) *The Prose and the Passion: Children and their Reading* (London: Cassell).
Swartz, David (1997) *Culture and Power: The Sociology of Pierre Bourdieu* (University of Chicago Press).
Tebbutt, Melanie (2012) *Being Boys: Youth, Leisure and Identity in the Inter-war Years* (Manchester University Press).
Thompson, Andrew (2005) *The Empire Strikes Back? The Impact of Imperialism on Britain from the Mid-nineteenth Century* (Harlow: Longman).
Thomson, Jack (1987) *Understanding Teenage Reading: Reading Processes and the Teaching of Literature* (Sydney: Methuen Australia).
Tinkler, Penny (1995) *Constructing Girlhood: Popular Magazines for Girls Growing up in England 1920–1950* (London: Taylor and Francis).

Tinkler, Penny (2000) '"Material Girl"? Adolescent Girls and their Magazines', in Maggie Andrews and Mary M. Talbot (eds) *All the World and her Husband: Women in Twentieth Century Consumer Culture* (London: Cassell).
Todd, Selina (2006) 'Flappers and Factory Lads: Youth and Youth Culture in Interwar Britain', *History Compass*, 4(4): 715–30.
Todorov, Tzvetan (1977) *The Poetics of Prose*, trans. Richard Howard (Ithaca, NY: Cornell University Press).
Townsend, John Rowe (1990) *Written for Children: An Outline of English-language Children's Literature*, 6th edn (London: The Bodley Head).
Trease, G. (1964) *Tales Out of School: A Survey of Children's Fiction*, 2nd edn (London: Heinemann).
Trease, G. (1971) *A Whiff of Burnt Boats* (London: Macmillan).
Tucker, N. (ed.) (1976) *Suitable for Children? Controversies in Children's Literature* (London: Chatto and Windus for Sussex University Press).
Turner, E. S. (1975) *Boys Will be Boys*, 3rd edn (London: Michael Joseph).
Turner, Graeme (1993) *Film as Social Practice*, 2nd edn (London: Routledge).
Vallone, Lynne (1996) 'Introduction: Children's Literature and New Historicism', *Children's Literature Association Quarterly*, 21(3): 102–4.
Veeser, H. Aram (ed.) (1989) *The New Historicism* (New York: Routledge).
Walkerdine, V. (1990) *Schoolgirl Fictions* (London: Verso).
Walkerdine, V. (1997) *Daddy's Girl: Young Girls and Popular Culture* (Basingstoke: Macmillan).
Warner, M. (1994) *From the Beast to the Blonde: On Fairy Tales and their Tellers* (London: Chatto and Windus).
West, Paul (1963) *I, Said the Sparrow* (London: Hutchinson).
Whalley, J. I., and Chester, T. R. (1974) *A History of Children's Book Illustration* (London: John Murray with the Victoria and Albert Museum).
Williams, Raymond (1961) *The Long Revolution* (London: Chatto & Windus).
Williams, Raymond (1977) *Marxism and Literature* (Oxford University Press).
Williams, Raymond (1988) *Keywords: A Vocabulary of Culture and Society* (London: Fontana, first published 1976).
Williams, Raymond (1990) *Culture and Society* (London: Hogarth, first published 1958).
Williams, Raymond (2005) *Culture and Materialism: Selected Essays* (London: Verso, first published 1980).
Wolf, S., and Brice Heath, S. (1992) *The Braid of Literature: Children's Worlds of Reading* (Cambridge, MA: Harvard University Press).
Woodruff, William (2002) *The Road to Nab End: An Extraordinary Northern Childhood* (London: Abacus).
Worton, M., and Still, Judith (eds) (1990) *Intertextuality: Theories and Practices* (Manchester University Press).
Wynne, J. (1997) *Where's Mi Chunks, Mam? The Childhood of a Nobody in Particular. Salford Memories 1930–1939* (Manchester: Neil Richardson).
Zipes, Jack (1983) *Fairy Tales and the Art of Subversion* (London: Heinemann).
Zweiniger-Bargielowska, Ina (2006) 'Building a British Superman: Physical Culture in Interwar Britain', *Journal of Contemporary History*, 41(4): 595–610.

Index

'3rd Form Brains v. 5th Form Beef', 61–2
'6 Yellow Knife Men', 15

advertisements, 12, 24, 146, 157, 158–67
 see also consumerism
Althusser, Louis, 4, 69, 73–4, 76, 90, 184
Amalgamated Press, 6, 7, 33, 35–6, 150, 168, 186, 187
American influences, 106, 118–19, 140, 144
anticipatory spaces, 122, 185
Arizpe, Evelyn, 27
Arnold, Matthew, 18–19

Baden-Powell, Robert, 112–13
Barthes, Roland, 4, 92–5, 123
Baudrillard, Jean, 70–1, 79
Bernstein, Sidney, 121
'big five', 13, 14, 35, 37, 38, 150, 185–7
'The Big Stiff', 13, 89
'Bill Hawkins and his 60 Dunces', 133–5
'Billy Bunter: Film Star!', 139–40
'Billy Bunter's Wembley Party', 109
Birkenhead Vigilance Committee 1931, 117, 118, 119, 120, 131, 132
Birmingham Cinema Enquiry Committee 1931, 117, 120, 130–1, 132
'Black John of the Battles', 104
Blackwell, Basil, 31
'Black Wolf', 15
Bourdieu, Pierre, 4, 27–9, 45, 146–8, 150, 151, 154, 159, 179, 182
Boyd, Kelly, 3, 88, 96–7, 103–4
boys' clubs, 112
boy scouts, 112–13, 131
Boy's Own Paper, 8, 67, 102, 150, 189

Brannigan, John, 23, 24–5
British Film Institute, 5, 116
British Library, 4, 6
'Buffalo Bill's Schooldays', 13, 113
Bull, Johnny, 9, 98, 106, 110
Bunter, Billy, 11, 27, 50, 52–4, 55, 60, 85–6, 98–9, 142–3, 152, 177–9
'Bunter's Body Guard', 10
'Bunter the Crook!', 142–3
'Bunter the Ventriloquist!', 81

Cadogan, Mary, 42–3, 53, 66, 68, 82
Campbell, Joseph, 94–5
Cannadine, D., 31, 79
'The Champ from the Swot Brigade', 15
Cherry, Bob, 9, 81–2, 102, 109–10
cinema, 116–45
 1930s cinema reports, 117
 attendances, 32, 116
 attitudes to, 121, 130–3, 186
 Saturday matinees, 117, 119, 120–1
 serials, 116, 121, 123, 125, 128, 135, 139
 and street play, 118, 128
Cinematograph Film Act 1927, 119
class, 5, 7, 18, 19, 28, 39, 65, 68, 70, 71, 73, 97, 99, 107–8, 113, 118–19, 146, 149, 154, 165, 181
cliffhanger endings, 122, 126–7, 138–9, 185
Cohen, Steven, 123, 125, 127
'Colorado Kid', 13
comics, 2, 33, 36–7, 180, 187
'The Complete Outsider', 9, 82–4
consumerism, juvenile, 3, 96, 152–5, 163–7
 see also advertisements; popular culture
'Contraband!', 49
correspondence, 9, 168–71
cover illustration, 104–5, 156, 172–9
Craig, P., 42–3, 66, 68

206

'The Cruise of the Firefly', 97–9, 102, 106
cultural capital, 147, 149, 165–7, 168, 180, 181–2, 186
cultural materialism, 3, 23, 24, 40

Daily Mail, 43
Daily Mirror, 43
Dale, Dixie, 87–8
Dead-Wide Dick, 13, 15–16, 60–1
'Death in his Guns and Dynamite in his Boots!', 87–8
'Dixon's Dog Academy', 89
dominant social character, 47–8, 51, 66, 68, 90–1, 101, 181, 184
'Douglas Fairbanks Competition', 141
Drotner, Kirsten, 3, 5, 33, 36–7, 38–9, 150, 186

economic capital, 147, 149, 150–1, 152, 179
economics
  of the publishing business, 30, 43, 181–2
Edinburgh Cinema Enquiry, *see* Mackie, John
editors' columns, 9, 14, 34, 140, 146, 155, 158, 159, 167–71
Education Act (1919), 31
Elephant Boy, 134
empire, 58–9, 101, 105, 109–10
Empire Day, 111–12
Empire Exhibition, Wembley 1924–25, 109, 110
Empire Marketing Board, 111–12
'The Eyes They Feared', 89
Eyre, Frank, 2

family, 9, 26, 28, 73, 94, 149
'Famous Five', 9, 52, 83, 105, 142
Feather, John, 2, 30, 32
field, 27–9, 45, 146–8, 149, 150, 152–3, 155, 182–3
  see also Bourdieu, Pierre
film, *see* cinema
film theory, 122–30
'The Finger Points', 120
First World War 1, 66, 68, 93, 107
flashbacks, 124

Flash Gordon's Trip to Mars, 117, 123, 124, 126–7
food, 11, 85–6
  advertising, 164–7
'foreigners', in story papers, 10–11, 105, 106, 114
Foucault, Michel, 23
friendship, 8, 34, 49–50, 56, 60, 62–3, 87, 140

games, school, *see* sport
Gem, 7, 33, 150, 159, 172, 186, 198
gender, 5, 7, 37, 85, 119, 133, 165
  see also masculinity
Genette, Gérard, 4, 146, 155–79
genres, 8, 25, 58, 68, 72, 90, 135–6, 184–8, 190, 193
Girl Guides, 131
girls
  in boys' story papers, 85, 140, 168
  reading, 6, 33, 37–8, 40, 140, 165, 191–4
Graves, Robert, 1
Greenblatt, Stephen, 3, 23
Greyfriars, 7, 8, 11, 15, 49, 51, 54, 57, 60, 80, 82–3, 84, 85, 105, 123, 139, 143
  see also Magnet

habitus, 27–9, 45, 147–8, 149–50, 154, 182
  see also Bourdieu, Pierre
Hamilton, Charles, *see* Richards, Frank
Harmsworth, Alfred, 7, 33–4, 42–4, 53, 68, 95, 149–50, 151, 182
hegemony, 48, 68, 72, 74, 93
heroes
  adult, 52, 89, 97, 103–4
  imperial, 33, 92–116, 184
  on screen, 117, 119, 122, 128, 142, 144
  schoolboy, 49, 52, 79, 96, 98, 99, 115, 165
history
  of children's literature, 1–2, 29, 182, 188
  of publishing, 7, 30
Hobsbawm, Eric, 100–1, 109
Hollindale, Peter, 46–7, 51

Holub, Robert C., 4, 25, 44
horizons of expectation, 25, 26–7
Hotspur
  audience, 37, 189, 191
  characters, 15, 60–2, 86–7, 103, 106, 133, 136
  description, 6, 13–17
  paratexts in, 158–79
  story settings, 89, 113
  see also Red Circle School
houses, school, 8
  in *Hotspur*, 16, 106
humour
  in story papers, 10, 53–4, 60, 99, 105, 176
Hunt, Peter, 1, 2, 18
Hyam, Ronald, 107, 108

Ideological State Apparatus (ISA), 73–4, 90, 184
ideology, 23, 44, 45–7, 48, 51, 53, 64, 69, 73–6, 90, 95, 101, 104, 109, 127, 146, 181, 183
illustration, 30, 61, 128, 146, 156, 172–9
imperialism, Victorian, representation in story papers, 33, 67, 92, 100–15, 184
implied author, 26, 168
'indexes of reality', 129, 130, 135
institutions, 72, 80–2, 86–7, 90, 101, 184
intertextuality, 125, 133–44
Iser, Wolfgang, 4, 25–6, 44, 46, 69, 70, 90, 146
'Is it Goodbye to Red Circle?', 86–7

Jauss, Hans Robert, 25
Jenkinson, A. J., 6, 36–7, 44, 75–8, 89, 119, 150, 153, 154–5, 186, 189–94
Jones, Dudley, 95, 96

kernel events, 123, 135, 137, 139, 177
'The Kids of Caravan College', 15
Kuhn, Annette, 5, 122

'The Last School', 103
Leavis, F. R., 19

Leeson, Robert, 1, 2
leisure, 32–3, 37, 134, 186
lessons, in school, 80–1, 86
libraries, 31–2, 45, 153, 154
Library Association Review, 2, 18
literacy, 124, 131–2, 135, 141–2, 145
lived experience, 21
  see also Williams, Raymond
London County Council Education Committee 1932, 117, 118, 120, 131

Mackenzie, John, 100, 104, 107, 108, 109
Mackie, John (Edinburgh Cinema Enquiry 1933), 117, 119, 132
Magee, Brian, 71, 117, 118–19
Magnet
  characters, 9–11, 50, 53, 79, 82, 96, 102, 142
  circulation, 6, 35, 37, 187, 189, 192
  contents, 7, 11
  origin, 7
  paratexts in, 158–79
  popularity, 38
Mangan, J. A., 101, 107, 111
masculinity, 7, 51, 62–3, 67, 87–8, 93–4, 97, 99–100, 102, 105, 112, 184
mass culture theory, 3, 18, 19, 20–2, 44, 47, 77, 181
Mass-Observation, 4, 39, 57–8, 71, 76
mass production, 33
McAleer, Joseph, 8, 13, 14, 33, 34, 35, 38, 59, 65–6, 150, 184
Merry, Tom, 79, 103
Metz, Christian, 128, 129–30, 135
moral panics, 20, 181, 186
multimodality, 172–3, 180, 187
Mulvey, Laura, 4, 127, 129
muscular Christianity, 100, 102
Myers, Mitzi, 24

narrative poetics, 116, 122–30
narrative style, 6, 13, 25, 49, 52, 60, 90, 94, 99, 133, 138, 144, 158, 171, 175, 177, 180, 181, 185, 187, 188

Nelson, Claudia, 3, 43, 183
new historicism, 3, 4, 23, 24–5, 182
Northcliffe, Lord, *see* Harmsworth, Alfred
Nugent, Frank, 9, 10
Nyman, Kenneth, 121, 122

'Oh Mr Smugg, What a Mug!', 15
Orwell, George, 10, 11, 16, 34, 36, 42, 44, 45, 52, 57, 65, 187

paper costs, 30
paratexts, 146–80
  factual, 157, 167–72
parents, 35, 43, 68, 76, 113, 130, 158, 163–4, 171, 181, 183, 186
penny dreadfuls (penny bloods)
  bad influence of, 33, 39, 43–4, 68, 149, 154, 186
physical description of characters, 11, 49, 54, 59, 61–3, 87, 106
popular culture, 3, 18–29, 135, 153, 159
  criticism of, 29, 155
Porter, Bernard, 107–8, 112
power relations, 4, 19, 23–5, 40, 68, 78, 87, 158, 183
production techniques
  of story papers, 104
'Public Enemies Trained Here', 89
Public Libraries Act (1919), 31
Publishers' Association, 31
Pugh, Martin, 111, 119
punishment
  school, 50–4, 57, 59, 62, 81, 84

Quelch, Mr, 81–4, 109, 110

racism, 105–6, 113–14, 137
radio, 32, 36
reader response theory, 4, 25–7, 29, 65, 70, 146, 148, 182
reading
  approved, 141, 154
  pleasure, 135–6
  spaces and places for, 152–5, 183
'Red Circle in Wartime', 63–4
Red Circle School, 15, 16, 59–60, 63, 80, 86, 106, 123, 139, 173

houses, 16
  see also Hotspur
Reed, Talbot Baines, 8, 67
Richards, Frank, 7, 8, 10, 40, 45, 53, 57, 80, 95, 100, 109, 139, 140, 150, 186
Richards, Jeffrey, 11, 16, 154
Roberts, Robert, 5, 38
Rose, Jonathan, 5, 38, 45–6, 58, 65, 76–7, 78–9, 96, 107, 118, 128
running heads, 14, 158, 167, 171–2, 173

sales, of books, 30, 32
  of story papers, 35, 141, 185
Samways, George, 9, 27
'The School Amid the Snows', 15, 113–14
'The School with a Kick', 89
selective tradition, 22, 100, 148
shared meanings, 126
Sheffield Juvenile Organisations Committee 1932, 117
Shires, Linda, 123, 125, 127
simulation, 70–1, 79–80, 89, 175
Singh, Hurree Jamset Ram, 9, 10, 11, 102, 105–6, 109, 110
Smedley, Mr, 54–7, 81–2, 102–3, 177, 179
smoking, 83
Smugg, Mr, 15, 64, 86, 87, 88, 177
social capital, 147, 165, 168, 180
'The Son of Scarface', 13
sport
  cricket, 53–6, 102–3
  football, 8, 50, 64, 166–7
Staples, Terry, 117, 118, 122, 134–5
Stephens, John, 46–7, 60, 69–70, 75
story papers
  circulation, 35, 43, 187
  definition, 7
  exchange of, 151
  for girls, 33, 37–8
  readership, 6, 13, 70, 97, 140, 153, 164, 167
  response to, 18, 43, 183
structure of feeling, 22, 40, 148, 182
structures of fascination, 127, 143, 144, 185, 186
Styles, Morag, 27

suture theory, 125, 127, 135–6, 138, 139, 185
swapping story papers, 38, 151, 152, 154, 180
'The Swooping Vengeance', 13
symbolic capital, 29, 146–7, 151, 152, 165, 179, 184

'The Teacher from Dartmoor', 15
teachers, 58, 66, 74, 75–80, 90, 130–1, 132, 148, 154, 157, 173
team spirit, 51, 56, 60, 87, 103, 184
Tebbutt, Melanie, 6, 97
Thompson, Andrew, 108, 109, 111
Thomson, D. C., 6, 13, 14–16, 33–4, 36, 59, 63, 65, 95, 108, 135, 150, 151, 160, 182, 186–7
'Tiger Jake's Academy', 15, 89
'The Ting-a-Ling Teacher of Tarza', 113–14
Todorov, Tzvetan, 122–3
Tom Brown's Schooldays (Hughes), 8, 80–1
'Too Tired to Work – Too Lazy to Play!', 61

traditions, 72, 101
invented, 100–1, 109, 115
'The Traitor of the Team', 13

visual pleasure, 121, 125, 135, 139, 145

Watkins, Tony, 95–6
Wharton, Harry, 50, 79, 84, 97, 98, 110, 142
behaviour, 10, 56
character, 9
description, 9
see also Magnet
'When the Fifth Form Went Crazy', 175–7
'Wild Bill Hickok's Schooldays', 136–8
Williams, Raymond, 3, 5, 20–3, 29, 40, 48, 65–6, 72–3, 100, 146, 148, 159, 182
Wolf Dog, 117, 123–4, 127
Woodruff, William, 111, 112, 118–20, 127
'The Worst Master in the School', 55, 56, 103

Printed and bound by CPI Group (UK) Ltd, Croydon, CR0 4YY